BILATERAL LEGACIES

IN EAST AND SOUTHEAST ASIA

The **Institute of Southeast Asian Studies (ISEAS)** was established as an autonomous organization in 1968. It is a regional centre dedicated to the study of socio-political, security and economic trends and developments in Southeast Asia and its wider geostrategic and economic environment. The Institute's research programmes are the Regional Economic Studies (RES, including ASEAN and APEC), Regional Strategic and Political Studies (RSPS), and Regional Social and Cultural Studies (RSCS).

ISEAS Publishing, an established academic press, has issued more than 2,000 books and journals. It is the largest scholarly publisher of research about Southeast Asia from within the region. ISEAS Publishing works with many other academic and trade publishers and distributors to disseminate important research and analyses from and about Southeast Asia to the rest of the world.

BILATERAL LEGACIES

IN EAST AND SOUTHEAST ASIA

EDITED BY **N. GANESAN**

ISEAS

INSTITUTE OF SOUTHEAST ASIAN STUDIES
Singapore

First published in Singapore in 2015 by
ISEAS Publishing
Institute of Southeast Asian Studies
30 Heng Mui Keng Terrace
Pasir Panjang
Singapore 119614

E-mail: publish@iseas.edu.sg
Website: <http://bookshop.iseas.edu.sg>

The responsibility for facts and opinions in this publication rests exclusively with the authors and their interpretations do not necessarily reflect the views or the policy of the publishers or their supporters.

ISEAS Library Cataloguing-in-Publication Data

Bilateral Legacies in East and Southeast Asia / edited by N. Ganesan.
   1. East Asia—Foreign relations.
   2. Southeast Asia—Foreign relations.
   I. Ganesan, N. (Narayanan), 1958–
DS525.8 B59   2015

ISBN 978-981-4620-41-3 (soft cover)
ISBN 978-981-4620-82-6 (e-book, PDF)

Typeset by Superskill Graphics Pte Ltd
Printed in Singapore by Markono Print Media Pte Ltd

CONTENTS

ACKNOWLEDGEMENTS

This edited volume is the outcome of collaborative efforts between a number of institutions and individuals. Funding for the meeting was generously provided by Dr Hari Singh through the Asian Political and International Studies Association (APISA). The funds were in turn provided by a grant from the Swedish International Development Cooperation Agency (SiDA). The Konrad Adenauer Stiftung (KAS) in Seoul provided additional funding for the discussants and the opening and closing dinners. For this generosity I am thankful to the then country representative of KAS, Dr Colin Duerkop. Since then the KAS and Dr Duerkop have gone on to co-fund a number of collaborative projects in Japan, Myanmar, Thailand and Turkey.

The original workshop was hosted by the Jeju Peace Institute in 2008 that provided the venue and administrative support for the meeting. For its efforts I am thankful to Ambassador Han and Dr Tae Ryong Yoon. Since the early conception of the project it has undergone a number of changes that included an expansion of the scope of the project.

Thanks are also due to the two anonymous referees. The time spent on the review process and the revisions arising from it has naturally strengthened the book significantly. Finally, I would also like to thank ISEAS Publishing for seeing the book through in a diligent and expeditious manner.

ABOUT THE CONTRIBUTORS

N. Ganesan is Professor of Southeast Asian Politics at the Hiroshima Peace Institute in Japan where he has been since 2004 and from 2011 to 2013 served concurrently as Visiting Professor at the National Graduate Institute for Policy Studies (GRIPS) in Tokyo. His research and publication interests are in sources of interstate and intrastate tensions. From 1990 to 2003 he was Senior Lecturer in political science and Southeast Asian Studies at the National University of Singapore.

Pavin Chachavalpongpun is Associate Professor at the Centre for Southeast Asian Studies at Kyoto University and was previously a fellow at the Institute of Southeast Asian Studies, Singapore. Earning his PhD from SOAS, University of London, Pavin is the author of *Reinventing Thailand: Thaksin and His Foreign Policy* (2010) and *A Plastic Nation: The Curse of Thainess in Thai–Burmese Relations* (2005). From January to May 2011, Pavin was a visiting lecturer at the Department of Political Science, National University of Singapore.

Tae-Ryong Yoon is HK Research Professor in the Asiatic Research Institute at Korea University, South Korea. He received his PhD in Political Science from Columbia University in 2006. His research interests are international security in general, alliance theory, and Northeast Asian politics (including Korea–Japan–U.S. relations, North–South Korean relations, and the Korean reunification issue).

Ramses Amer is Associate Professor and PhD in Peace and Conflict Research, Associated Fellow with the Institute for Security and Development Policy (ISDP), Sweden. Major areas of his research include (1) security issues and conflict resolution in Southeast Asia and the wider Pacific Asia and (2) the role of the United Nations in the international system. His most recent books are *The Security-Development Nexus: Peace, Conflict and Development* (2012, co-edited with Ashok Swain and Joakim Öjendal); *Conflict Management and Dispute Settlement in East Asia* (2011; co-edited with Keyuan Zou) and *International Relations in Southeast Asia: Between Bilateralism and Multilateralism* (2010; co-edited with N. Ganesan).

Maung Aung Myoe received his BA in International Relations from the University of Mandalay, an MA in the same discipline from the International University of Japan, and a PhD in Political Science and International Relations from the Australian National University. He was a visiting fellow at the Institute of Defence and Strategic Studies (IDSS) and a postdoctoral fellow at the Asia Research Institute, National University of Singapore. His research interests cover Myanmar politics and foreign relations as well as regionalism, security and strategy, and civil–military relations. He is Professor at the Graduate School of International Relations and teaches Southeast Asian Politics and International Relations at the International University of Japan in Niigata.

Lam Peng Er is a Senior Research Fellow at the East Asian Institute, National University of Singapore. He obtained his PhD from Columbia University. His latest single-authored book is *Japan's Peace-building Diplomacy: Seeking a More Active Political Role* (2009).

1

HISTORICAL LEGACIES IN EAST AND SOUTHEAST ASIAN INTERNATIONAL RELATIONS

N. Ganesan

This introductory chapter, and the book in general, deal with the theoretical concept of overhangs or legacies in international relations. An overhang or legacy is a negative perception that derives from historical interactions and subsequently becomes embedded in the psyche of a state, both at the level of the elites and the citizen body. Specifically, the book examines legacies affecting important bilateral relationships in East Asia with a view to understanding the historical origins and how and why they have been utilized and refined for public and policy purposes. The ultimate aim of this chapter and the configurative case studies is to document overhangs or legacies in five sets of East and Southeast Asian bilateral relations and then deal with them on a comparative basis to see if any significant observations can be made. Naturally, such observations are likely to be useful for the political elites and those tasked with discharging policy if they are interested in bringing these bilateral relations to an even keel.

The chapter is divided into three broad sections. The first section briefly surveys international relations and the theoretical contours that have obtained since the conclusion of World War II. Subsequently, the chapter places the discussion within the much more narrow context of Asian international relations and bilateralism. Then the third section identifies and rationalizes the five sets of bilateral relations that have been chosen for this book. Additionally, it lists the common questions that were distributed to all the chapter writers in order to facilitate a comparative treatment in order to document the issues that are similar and dissimilar across the cases. Such an understanding is likely to nuance the findings of the book and assist in setting the agenda for future work on the same or related issues.

INTRODUCTION

The study of international relations has traditionally focused on three levels of analysis.[1] At the highest or global level, the terminology that is normally used is that of a system. This system is meant to be a reference to structural conditions that inform relations between states, providing in turn opportunities as well as constraints for action. Naturally, superpowers and great powers have overwhelming influence in determining the structural characteristics and attendant dynamics at this highest level.[2] The second level or sub-system is the mid-tier level of analysis. This second level obtains at the regional level and displays major characteristic features of the system while taking into account dynamics that are intrinsic or unique to it.[3] Despite a confluence of forces obtaining at this level, it is generally understood that the system provides the basic structural features which are then overlain with a veneer of regional dynamics. At the lowest or unit level of analysis, international relations theorists essentially referred to the study of relations between states.

Within this three-tiered conceptual model, international relations scholars applied different constructs that were in turn underpinned by differing philosophical traditions. The most popular and influential of these was realism that surfaced after World War II and held sway for most of the Cold War and into the 1970s.[4] Classical realism assumed a state of anarchy in international relations. And within this broader reference, states acted out of mutual fear and suspicion regarding the intention of other states. The early versions of this theory focused on the state as the primary unit of analysis and understood international relations as essentially a competitive quest for power between states. It also regarded the political realm as independent and superordinate to all others and the practice of politics as an amoral activity. Systemic structures were thought to bear a disproportionate influence on medium and smaller states in realist theory since they typically had little leverage in the international system. Major criticisms of this school were that it was reductionist in its treatment of states and power as constituting the most important determinant and motivation of countries respectively. The evolution of international relations after 1945 and the ideological and strategic rivalry between the United States on the one hand and the Soviet Union on the other appeared to validate realism, and as a result the theory became intertwined with developments in Europe as well. U.S. hegemony in the social sciences in general and political science in particular was also helpful to the realist interpretation and enterprise.

Later on, however, realism underwent a metamorphosis of sorts and new and more revisionist versions of the theory evolved. Neo-realists, for example, sought to moderate this simplistic view of international relations and conceded the importance of transnational agencies and non-state actors within the broader system. This metamorphosis that realism underwent from the 1970s both accommodated developments in the real world and reflected the fissuring of the dominant school of thought. Structural realism or neo-realism became popular by the 1970s and this sub-school downplayed the centrality of states and their thirst for the acquisition of power in international relations. Kenneth Waltz was one of the foremost theorists from this school.[5] His original contribution was to detail the state of anarchy as one without effective government rather than a state of disarray, and to introduce the three levels of analysis in international relations. Additionally, Waltz argued that the social sciences could not claim predictive ability like the natural sciences since they cannot conduct controlled experiments. Consequently, the best that can be hoped for is a cogent explanation of international relations.[6] In this regard, offshoots of realism had a general tendency to emphasize structural norms or activities that transcended the state. Both neo-realism and structural realism emphasized such norms, although classical realism distanced itself from such looser interpretations. Other well-known proponents of structural realism include Robert Keohane and Joseph Nye.[7] Given the theory's flirtation with international norms and cooperation, a strand of this school branched off into regime theory as well.[8] Notwithstanding these changes to the original school of thought, structural characteristics retained a certain pride of place within the realist and neo-realist traditions.

The earliest intellectual challenge to realism came from liberalism and occurred immediately after World War II. In fact, liberalism competed with realism as the dominant intellectual school of thought informing research in political science. However, it receded into the background by the early 1950s as realism became the dominant and hegemonic school of thought. Liberalism differed from realism in major ways in that it assumed a much more benign international environment and the general willingness of states to cooperate for mutual gain. In this regard, liberalism made fundamentally opposite assumptions from realism regarding the motivations and intentions of international conduct. Liberals tended to emphasize mutual cooperation and mutual gain rather than anarchy and mutual fear. Additionally, liberals tended to focus on political economy or gains arising from mutual economic cooperation rather than conflict arising from the competitive acquisition of power. In international relations theory, liberalism had a strong impact on the study of federalism, communications theory, integration theory, functionalism and systems theory. Some of the most pioneering work in these areas concentrated on the European experience in part because it was the natural landscape for the conduct of such research and also because liberals held out the hope that Europe could be persuaded away from conflict into more regularized and cooperative norms after two world wars.

Owing to realism's hegemony during the course of the Cold War, liberalism and its assumptions were often frowned upon. It was only after *détente* in the 1970s that interest in liberalism revived. There was also a much greater focus on political economy and liberal institutionalism that derived from the study of international cooperation. This variant of liberalism that is sometimes called neo-liberalism also had major differences from neo-realism. David Baldwin identifies six areas where there is general disagreement between the two schools notwithstanding their general agreement of focusing greater attention on international structures and norms.[9] Neo-realists generally believe that international cooperation is the result of states exhibiting self-interest in a state of anarchy whereas neo-liberals emphasize the interdependent nature of international relations. Secondly, although both schools subscribe to international cooperation, neo-realists believe that such an outcome is harder to achieve and sustain and is essentially dependent on state power and resources. Thirdly, neo-realists tend to regard gains arising from mutual cooperation in relative terms. In other words, there is always the lingering question of how the gains deriving from international cooperation will be divided between the states involved. Neo-liberals on the other hand generally subscribe to some notion of absolute gains and emphasize the mutual nature of gains deriving from international cooperation. In other words, neo-liberals regard cooperation as leading to gains compared to a situation where such cooperation and gains deriving from it does not obtain. Fourthly, arising from their core assumptions regarding the centrality of states in the international system and the competitive acquisition of power between states, neo-realists emphasize cooperative norms in security affairs. Neo-liberals on the other hand emphasize cooperation in economic and welfare issues. Fifthly, neo-realists tend to emphasize the capabilities of states as opposed to neo-liberals who emphasize intentions, interests and information. And finally, although both agree on the importance of regimes and international cooperative norms, neo-realists downplay the ability of regimes to seriously mitigate the state of anarchy that is assumed to exist. Neo-liberals on the other hand have a much more optimistic view of international regimes as establishing the template for more collaboration and cooperation in international relations and thereby mitigating the effects of anarchy.

The third and most recent major school of thought in international relations theory is constructivism. This school of thought that became vogue in the 1990s essentially sought to downplay the structural determinism of neo-realism. The school's major contribution to international relations is emphasizing the social nature of political constructions and their impact in turn on international relations. In other words, international relations as we understand it is a socially constructed phenomenon. As a result of this foundational assumption, constructivists argue that reality can be transformed and reshaped by social forces and conditions. Accordingly this approach regards ideas, ideational norms, and cultural practices as being an integral part of the landscape that determines the texture and calibration of international relations. Structural and material conditions are therefore not a given state of affairs like the assumption of anarchy among realists, but rather the conditions deriving from the subjective choices made by elites and society. The most celebrated proponent of this school of thought is Alexander Wendt, and suffice it to say that constructivism has had a significant impact on the study of international relations in the last two decades.[10] Elite preferences, perceptions of identity, cultural values and deliberate choices are often emphasized when this approach is utilized.

Both liberalism and constructivism have had a major impact on the study of foreign policy owing to their focus on identities, interests, cultural norms and strategic choices of elites. For constructivists, foreign policy provides an avenue for social forces that tend in the direction of cooperation and elites who desire certain values and identity and strive to realize that outcome. Well-coordinated foreign policy is for constructivists a function of aggregate identity formation and the conscious appropriation of opportunities to realize structural conditions that sustain and further such a community. Whereas identities may derive from a broad and specific cultural context, elites are important mobilizers of the appropriation of this identity and the formation of regional communities that reflect these norms and values. In this regard both these latter schools of thought are much more sympathetic to the preferences of medium and small states in foreign policy output. Not only do they acknowledge the importance of non-structural conditions in elite decision-making, but more importantly, provide the policymakers of such states with far greater latitude than that assigned by realists. This feature of non-realist thought in international relations theory is especially useful in studying bilateral overhangs or legacies. The reason for this assertion is simply the fact that many of the bilateral overhangs or legacies examined in this book operate quite independently of global structural dynamics. The argument can clearly be made that structural dynamics prohibit overly adventurous policy output for fear of international repercussions. Yet, there is a very real sense in which such dynamics are anchored within the confines of the relationship or the broader regional sub-system at best. There is in fact a growing realization among internal relations scholars that such bilateral relations are deeply informed by contextual attributes rather than general ones of the international system.

One of the most important contributions of the constructivist school is that the process of forming perceptions is fundamentally an inter-subjective one. As noted by Innis Claude, mistrust is often a perception attendant on particular holders of power rather than the power itself.[11] In other words, the intentions or perceived intentions of those affected by such power considerations in turn determine their perceptions and expectations of how such power will be utilized. How well a state tolerates a subservient role then becomes contingent on the expectation that the stronger power will exercise restraint in the use of available power. This is the reason why lesser states often view some more powerful states as benign and others as aggressive. This assessment, that is subjective in turn, conditions how states view the exercise and restraints imposed by a stronger power. Depending then on whether the assessment is positive or negative, the perception settles or unsettles them. The former is an indication of benign intent while the latter is an indication of aggressive intent. This social construction of threats is normally anchored on the basis of a state's historical predispositions and actions. So, for example, Chinese and Korean perceptions of Japanese aggressive intent is deeply informed by the latter's past aggression and the seemingly unrepentant attitude or unwillingness to take responsibility for previous acts.

International relations and order are also deeply informed by perceptions of morality and justice. There must be widespread perception within the international system that some acceptable norms of power and the exercise of it obtain. If such a situation is absent then it is unlikely that structural peace will endure since perceptions of injustice will invite resentment and rebellion.[12] This observation is notwithstanding the fact that structural power and order is also determined on the basis of a rank ordering of power. The perception of whether the distribution of power and the norms attendant on its exercise is therefore interactive with the longevity of an existing arrangement. It is the exercise of such seemingly just power with widespread acceptance that in turn creates what theorists refer to as soft power. Such soft power as opposed to hard power is accumulated on the basis of the regular use of power within predictable and acceptable bounds.[13] In fact, Hedley Bull, a classical realist, makes the point that challenges to an ordered arrangement that is viewed as inherently unjust may well lead to support for a reordered structure that delegitimizes a previous order. And he provides readers with the example of how colonial powers became delegitimized after widespread resistance by subject territories.[14]

Robert Jervis, a realist, for example, argues that there is a restraining role for morality in international relations. Whereas even if a state is not directly concerned with morality in the setting of national goals, morality can influence the policy choices that are available to a state. The choice of a moral means or a lesser evil can inform states even if such a choice is not in the short-term interest of the state.[15] For example, many more enlightened

European states have inhibitions regarding the sale of weapons to countries involved in conflict or the potential for such involvement. Such a policy trades short-term benefits for long-term positive gains for the country in question as well as the international system. Such behaviour leads to an increase in international social capital, to borrow a phrase from Robert Putnam. Jervis identifies three ways that morality can assist in international relations: it serves to inform us of positive criteria to aspire towards as human beings, it assists in deflecting the threats of pseudo-realism or an overwhelming concern with power and narrowly defined self-interest, and ethics can play a guiding role when consequences attendant on a course of action are unclear.[16]

Notwithstanding its overwhelming influence and many sub-schools of thought, international relations theorists have often ignored the overwhelming influence of historically embedded interactions between states that have in turn informed the conduct of international relations. Specifically, such relations are not conducted in abstract, but rather in relation to the needs and priorities of states and statesmen.[17] Such interactions appear to have an overwhelming influence on the relations between geographically proximate states in particular. The confluence of historical interactions and geographical proximity have also led to the creation of structures and practices that have sometimes preceded modern statehood as we currently understand it. In other words, time honoured practices between such states had led in turn to the evolution of certain channels and structures for the conduct of bilateral relations. Specifically, such structures are especially important in the resolution of outstanding issues that periodically crop up between such states or sensitive issues that require immediate resolution in order to prevent a downward spiral in bilateral relations with all the attendant consequences.

BILATERALISM AND OVERHANGS OR LEGACIES

In a recently edited volume on international relations in Southeast Asia, N. Ganesan and Ramses Amer point out that bilateralism is a prevalent form of interaction in Southeast Asia.[18] The case studies analysed in this book document that bilateralism is a well-established foreign policy response in Southeast Asian international relations. Bilateralism is a useful mechanism with substantial historical precedence in the resolution of problems between geographically proximate states. In many instances, bilateralism preceded the onset of multilateralism in Southeast Asia. Nonetheless, no claim is made that such interactions are only useful among geographically proximate states. All states may avail themselves of the usefulness of bilateralism as a policy tool, especially if such interactions are mutually beneficial in problem-solving and mutual gain. Such a platform appears to be popular in the international relations of Northeast Asia as well. Nonetheless, in the Southeast Asian case, it is a truism that bilateralism is significantly enhanced among geographically proximate states.

There appear to be a large number of reasons privileging bilateralism over multilateralism, especially among geographically proximate states. From the findings reported in the book, it is clear that history has privileged bilateralism and provided policy formulators with an established practice and venue in dealing with immediately adjacent states. This historical imperative in turn derived from the geographical necessity of coping with dense transactions and interactions. Consequently, history and geography combine to provide the most forceful evidence in favour of bilateralism. The accumulated interactions and knowledge derived from bilateralism subsequently serve to undergird the practice and establish it as a preferred medium through which international relations may be conducted. Additionally, the case studies also indicate the ready and regular availability of structures permitting bilateral interactions. These may take the form of Joint Border Committee (JBC) meetings as in the case of Malaysia, Myanmar, Thailand and Vietnam or ministerial meetings as in the case of Indonesia, Malaysia and Singapore. Similarly, bilateral fora are equally important in the Northeast Asian context, where delicate issues are often addressed. Such issues have in the past included overlapping territorial claims and boundary demarcations to trade and security-related issues. In light of the growing importance of the ASEAN Plus Three forum and that of the East Asian Summit (EAS) and the East Asian Community (EAC), it may be surmised that such interactions are likely to be significantly enhanced in the future. In fact, the recognition by both China and Japan that they have the historic task of accommodating each other in raising the political and economic profile of the entire region augments such possibilities.

Apart from the convenience of continuing with an established practice, there are many other factors privileging bilateralism. Bilateralism appears to allow for the resolution of problems that are unique to two countries or appear to involve them the most. In this regard it may be argued that levels of compliance in bilateralism are likely to be higher and attendant transactional costs significantly lower than when like issues are negotiated within a multilateral setting.[19] The scope of such agreements also tends to be lesser and the arrangements significantly more flexible, taking into account idiosyncratic considerations that are often extremely important in the region. Additionally, there is the existence of a strongly held normative belief in East Asia that bilateral avenues provide the best forum to resolve conflicts or coordinate policies, as argued by T.J. Pempel.[20]

Bilateralism may involve specific and traditional security discourse markers like overlapping territorial claims as well as non-traditional threats like illegal migration and environmental pollution. The utilization of such fora seems to buffer the issue at hand from excessive publicity that may in turn lead to political posturing. Such posturing is certainly not uncommon in developing countries and Asia where the notion of "face" and propriety often complicate international relations. Posturing often significantly complicates the situation from rational resolution and opens up the possibility of pandering to important domestic political constituencies. When such posturing occurs, a simple issue often becomes conflated with many others. Additionally, it is likely to escalate tensions and often leads to the overall deterioration of bilateral relations. Consequently, quiet and contained bilateral diplomacy is often the forum of choice for neighbouring countries.

The bilateral relationships examined in this volume do tend to suggest that security issues take priority over economic issues at the outset. In other words, there does appear to be sequential logic favouring security matters in the first instance. Conversely, it may be noted that when bilateral security relations are poor between geographically proximate countries, economic activities tend to suffer. This spillover effect is most clearly demonstrated in the case of China–Japan, Japan–Korea, Vietnam–China, Thai–Cambodian and Thai–Myanmar bilateral relations, the case studies chosen for this project. China's trade and investments with Japan are often significantly affected by untoward developments like the case of tainted food products that surfaced in 2008. Similarly, Japan's relations with Korea are often affected when there is disagreement over historical issues and the manner in which narratives are related in Japanese school textbooks. And at the peak of Myanmar's tensions with Thailand, border trading zones are typically closed, much to the chagrin of Thailand. Likewise, when relations between Cambodia and Thailand are strained, both countries often deploy troops along the common border and economic activities slow to a trickle.

On the other hand, when the security environment is favourable, bilateral economic relations tend to be expansive, as is the case between China and Japan, Korea and Japan, China and Vietnam, Vietnam and Thailand and Myanmar and Thailand.

Nonetheless, it should be noted that such fora often privilege larger and more powerful countries as well. In other words, smaller countries with less power and fewer policy instruments may suffer from bilateralism during the negotiation process. In this regard, multilateral fora offer greater protection for smaller states than bilateral ones, as the former are more likely to adhere to rational-legal principles rather than power considerations. The most recent example of such disagreement occurred between Cambodia and Thailand over the land surrounding the UNESCO-designated historical Preah Vihear Temple Complex in 2008. Both countries deployed additional troops along the common border and clashes occurred. Additionally, Thailand was itself in a political crisis with a weak government as well as a military allied with the traditional elite and opposed to the elected government. Prime Minister Hun Sen in Cambodia faced the uncertain prospects of a national election. Further exacerbating the matter was the fact that both countries were involved in a good measure of political posturing. The issue has been dealt with through bilateral contacts and talks, and Thailand in particular stressed its preferences for a purely bilateral approach to dealing with both tensions and disputes. Thus, the Cambodia–Thailand dispute and the heightened tension in 2008 display the pre-eminence of bilateralism in dealing with both border issues and tension between the countries of Southeast Asia. More recently in 2010 when such agreement did not obtain, both countries tentatively agreed to Indonesian mediation through the deployment of unarmed observers at the disputed border. Whereas Thailand was initially reluctant to agree to this arrangement, it eventually relented after some persuasion. As *primus inter pares* in ASEAN and given its recent democratic credentials, Indonesia was fortunately in a position to work out such a mechanism and forestall the situation from worsening. But the fact remains that the Thai military retains a certain independence and latitude with regard to its dealings with immediately adjacent neighbours. Additionally, the political executive, especially those drawn from the military, have little influence in shaping the course of events. Worsening this already complicated internal scenario is the fact that Thailand is home to a number of nationalistic groups that inflame sentiments at the ground level. The

People's Alliance for Democracy (PAD) and the Thai Patriot Network are two such groups that often brought pressure to bear on the Abhisit-led Democrat Party minority coalition government. Yingluck Shinawatra who succeeded Abhisit has been more fortunate, although the 2014 coup against her government by royalist forces leaves open the spectre of much more nationalist foreign policy output. The sudden and sustained departure of Cambodian and Myanmar nationals after the coup was a clear reflection of this problem, and the military only relented to registering and accepting these undocumented migrant workers when pressures from the business lobby groups became pronounced.

It should be noted at this juncture that bilateralism and multilateralism are not mutually exclusive enterprises. In fact, as Etel Solingen points out, states often engage in forum shopping or pick and choose where they deal with a particular issue. Naturally there are many considerations that go into such venue selection. All else held constant, the likelihood of securing the greatest benefit in an issue is likely to be a strong motivation. Alternatively, states may and indeed often do deal with a number of fora simultaneously. Such a practice may involve the bundling of issues on the basis of positive outcomes or for legal or normative reasons. Another way to conceptualize the relationship between bilateralism and multilateralism is to think of them as avenues in a layered process where states retain a core of bilateral transactions that are then supplemented by larger and larger fora as the arena radiates outward not unlike the latticed approach mentioned by Christopher Dent.[21] In such a scenario, states may quite simply reinforce their choices in larger domains to secure preferred outcomes. Whatever the case may be, it is clear that states do not necessarily regard bilateralism and multilateralism as mutually exclusive policy options.

In fact there are quite a few instances where the failure of a bilateral forum to resolve an issue resulted in the issue being brought to a larger multilateral forum. This seems to be the case especially where the issues have legal implications in international law. Overlapping territorial claims provide the best example of just such a development. In 2002 the International Court of Justice (ICJ) ruled on the question of sovereignty over the disputed islands of Ligitan and Sipadan between Indonesia and Malaysia. Similarly, in 2008, the ICJ determined the ownership of Pedra Blanca/Pulau Batu Putih and Middle Rocks between Malaysia and Singapore. Both these cases display the limitations of the regional approach to solving important bilateral issues and the seeming irrelevance of regional mechanisms. On a more positive note, however, disputing countries were able to agree on the utilization of an international dispute settlement mechanism and agree to abide by the terms of its judgement. Conversely, however, China and Vietnam, China and Japan, and Korea and Japan have significant overlapping claims in the South China Sea and East China Sea, respectively, that remain unresolved. There appears to be little will by the parties involved to subject the disputes to any kind of arbitration at the international level, and the issue continues to fester at the bilateral level, periodically straining diplomatic ties. For the time being, territorial occupation appears to constitute the proverbial ownership. Nor have such issues always been peaceful. For example, China and Vietnam were involved in a naval skirmish in 1988 over the disputed Paracel Islands, as mentioned by Ramses Amer in his chapter on China–Vietnam relations. And the allure of fishery and mineral resources in these disputed territories, and by extension their maritime boundaries, make such claims more intractable and potentially dangerous unless there is clear political will to resolve the issue. In the past, China, Japan and Korea have exhibited relative unwillingness to resolve such claims legally compared to their Southeast Asian counterparts, although China has been more willing to negotiate such claims with Vietnam recently. In this regard, Northeast Asian overlapping territorial claims are likely to be significantly more difficult to resolve.

While broad structural imperatives generally shaped bilateral policy output, agency reasons also exerted an important influence in bilateral relationships. In other words, political elites in the countries involved were often responsible for setting the general tone and temper for bilateral relations with neighbouring countries. Similarly, political personalities were as important as historical episodes like the outbreak of conflict or previous hostilities in the shaping of bilateral relations. These historical overhangs are still clearly evident in the case of China–Japan, China–Vietnam, Japan–Korea, Cambodia–Thailand and Thailand–Myanmar relations. In this regard it may be surmised that history has a powerful impact on formative perceptions in bilateral relations. This formative impact may then be reinforced or altered by elites.

Elites in Asian countries often exercise power that is disproportionate to their office. Rational-legal power is often buttressed by powerful constituencies, clientelism and tremendous access to public and natural resources. Consequently, their imprint on policy output is significantly enhanced. Since many of these countries have political systems with little diffusion of power, decisions made by elites are strictly top-down. As a result, good and bad relations are amplified many times over. Another clear demonstration of the impact of elites in the state of bilateral relations is their impact on the periodization of the relationship. This impact is very clear in many of the relationships, especially if regimes had remained in power for a long period of time. Hence, the idiosyncratic imprint of the likes of Mao Zedong and Deng Xiaoping in China, Park Chung Hee in Korea, Ho Chi Minh in Vietnam, Ne Win in Burma and Hun Sen in Cambodia are clearly visible. If two such elites disliked each other, the impact on bilateral relations would have been profound. For example, it was common knowledge in diplomatic circles that Chinese political elites intensely disliked the former Vietnamese foreign minister, Nguyen Co Thach. This bad chemistry in turn had a very negative impact on China–Vietnam bilateral relations. Similarly, Thaksin's nationalistic rhetoric significantly deteriorated Thailand's bilateral relations with Malaysia and Cambodia, while his business interests led to an even-keeled relationship with Myanmar. Perhaps the sobering and positive outcome of frayed bilateral relations is this: rational structural imperatives blunt the potentially damaging impact of agency factors.

Structural imperatives have had a definitive impact on East Asian international relations. Until 1991 the dynamics associated with the Second and Third Indochinese Conflicts had a formative impact on regional international relations. The Second Indochina Conflict spilled over from the dynamics of the Cold War wherein the United States sought to contain the spread of communism in Southeast Asia as well as the policies of China and the Soviet Union. In turn, China and the Soviet Union were opposed to U.S. military intervention in the Indochinese countries. After the conclusion of the Second Indochina Conflict in 1975, the Sino–Soviet rivalry in the Asia-Pacific came to the forefront. Ironically, the emergence of the Third Indochina Conflict was characterized by rivalry among the communist-ruled Asian countries of Cambodia–Vietnam and China–Vietnam, respectively. The collapse and subsequent implosion of the Soviet Union in 1991 had a profound impact on regional structures that modelled themselves on either the communist or non-communist side of the Cold War divide. The broader developments led in turn to the resolution of the Cambodia Conflict, the full normalization of relations between China and Vietnam as well as Vietnam and ASEAN. These developments allowed ASEAN to shed its Cold War origins and interests and expand to incorporate the three Indochinese states and Myanmar. Hence, structural imperatives have a great deal of impact on regional developments. They have informed and conditioned regional international relations as well as the form and agenda of multilateral institutions in Southeast Asia. In this regard, idiosyncratic policy output was often restrained by structural conditions.

The looser structural conditions of the post–Cold War period have in turn allowed for far more discretion in the evolution of regional organizations and the regional agenda. In fact, this structural loosening led to the dispersion of the previously convergent foreign and defence policies of the ASEAN states. The new environment brought about new challenges, and with it, new problems and new perceptions of threat. Hence, it is no coincidence that bilateral relations between geographically proximate states deteriorated substantially in the 1990s. Not only did the new environment bring about new challenges, it also allowed for much more idiosyncratic foreign policy output. This was not necessarily a negative development because regional states acquired far more independence and latitude in policy output than before; however, it marked the start of a new learning curve. This curve challenged and tested the limits of the informal arrangements and accommodation that multilateralism had brought to regional relations. It also tested the limits to which state sovereignty became an issue in the regional management of regional problems.

The political violence that followed in Cambodia, Myanmar and Timor Leste during this period all became issues that tested ASEAN's mettle. The absence of procedural protocol in dealing with internal problems within ASEAN was a liability that attracted much negative attention. Yet, this informality and the absence of enforcement mechanisms for compliance spelled the loss of significant gains that had accrued from before. Moreover, there is precious little regional multilateral organizations can do when the situation within a country or between countries deteriorates. ASEAN's deeply cherished non-intervention principle also returned the members to basic principles of power and influence in dealing with each other. There were attempts to remedy this problem through the formation of an ASEAN Troika in the 1990s, but it has proved to be of little use thus far. It is to be hoped that ASEAN members and their major dialogue partners accede to the Treaty of Amity and Cooperation (TAC) lodged with the United Nations. Hopefully, TAC will provide sufficient deterrence against the outbreak of conflict between member states. TAC requires that signatories agree to resolve differences between states without resorting to violence. Nonetheless, when relations were frayed between Myanmar and Thailand, and more recently between Cambodia and Thailand, there was no mention of TAC or the promise to avoid conflict. States involved in those situations merely attended to domestic constituencies and concerns.

Importantly, looser structural arrangements have also led to a much closer and more cooperative relationship between Northeast Asia and Southeast Asia. Although the Asian financial crisis of 1997 severely tested and deteriorated the economies of many Asian countries like Indonesia, Korea and Thailand, it also provided major opportunities for a recalibration of regional networks and architecture. Were it not for the crisis, ASEAN would not have initiated a currency swap arrangement with external partners and worked towards a meeting of the Finance Ministers of China, Japan and Korea with those of ASEAN. In fact it was this embryonic idea that in turn snowballed and led to the convening of the EAS in Kuala Lumpur in 2005. The location of the meeting was also no coincidence since it was Malaysia under Prime Minister Mahathir that had previously lobbied hard for the realization of an East Asian Economic Grouping (EAEG) — that was subsequently downgraded to an East Asian Economic Caucus (EAEC) — in ASEAN deliberations. The resistance of the United States and Australia to the idea made the EAEG impossible in the 1990s. In addition, the United States promoted its own idea of the Asia-Pacific Economic Cooperation (APEC) forum with its regional allies in tow. And Indonesia, as *primus inter pares* in ASEAN, was simply unwilling to go along with a Malaysian prescription for regional order. Naturally, the poor chemistry between Malaysia's Mahathir and Indonesia's Suharto simply made the idea stillborn.

This book draws on the concept of historical overhangs or legacies among important bilateral relationships in East Asia. Significant bilateral relations are those that have traditionally been problematic with the potential to deteriorate into armed conflict. The concept of overhang or legacy, as utilized in international relations, essentially refers to negative historical memories that both inform and influence public perceptions as well as those of policymakers. To borrow a phrase from political scientist Giovanni Sartori, the concept has negative connotative value. Whereas the perception is derived from important historical episodes, it is the manner in which they are interpreted and the way that they linger on perceptions that make them enduring. Consequently, an overhang or legacy essentially establishes an initial frame of reference on which an observer tags on other developments. In this regard, an overhang or legacy provides the broad landscape against which subsequent interactions are interpreted and gauged.

Preliminary evidence indicates that overhangs or legacies have not only been kept alive but consciously cultivated and embellished in order to make them more durable and invoke emotional responses. There is a sense in which such negative and stereotypical images are constructed or have a constructivist angle. Over time, however, such constructions invariably acquire a life of their own and become deeply embedded in the psyche of the countries involved. Quite apart from such independent volition, such overhangs or legacies also have the potential to become condensation symbols that charge public opinion and negatively influence a situation.[22] In other words, although the overhang or legacy exists independently, it can be stoked or transformed to serve a specific purpose. Naturally, such negative images are best and often deployed during times of adversity when pre-existing strained relations with geographically proximate countries are easily invoked. Given this dynamic, an added concern is whether the overhangs or legacies serve the function of a causal factor for poor bilateral relations or merely undergird them and are utilized when appropriate. In order to isolate the nature of the overhang or legacy and its significance on the bilateral relationships examined, it therefore becomes necessary to identify the issues that have contributed to the overhang or legacy and whether they are independent variables or merely intervening ones in the process of policy formulation. In order to test this hypothesis, the chapter writers have briefly examined two recent examples of deteriorated relations and the contribution or impact of the overhang or legacy on the situation that existed. It is also important to identify the major sources of this narrative and how they may be blunted to enable more cooperative bilateral relations to obtain in the future.

KEY RESEARCH QUESTIONS

This book addresses a number of core and common questions. These questions are central to the concept of critical historical junctures and overhangs or legacies, and also help provide the basis for a comparative treatment of the different configurative case studies. The comparative treatment of the cases will allow for nuancing differences between them and lead to much richer observations and conclusions. The core questions addressed by all chapter writers are as follows:

(1) When and how did the critical historical juncture that led to the formation and crystallization of the overhangs or legacies occur? Chapter writers were asked to identify whether the episode arose as a result of external stimuli, domestic ones, or an admixture of the two.

(2) How long did the said important juncture last? There may well be differences between a clearly identifiable symbolic moment, like the collapse of the Berlin Wall in Germany that signified the collapse of communism in Eastern Europe. Alternatively, the juncture may extend over a period of time across a policy domain or may crystallize in the course of a few successor administrations.

(3) Were there clearly discernible cleavages or internal crises that constituted the antecedent conditions for the strained relations? The importance of such cleavages should be clearly demonstrated within the sociopolitical environment of the country in question. Such contextualization will assist in establishing the specificity of critical variables in a particular country. Locating the context is also likely to identify the communities that were involved in the creation of the overhang or legacy and the constituencies that are likely to be affected by it or, conversely, sustain it.

(4) Under what conditions do bilateral overhangs or legacies become invoked? Are certain personalities, pressures, interest or occupational groups or regime types more likely to stoke tensions through the utilization of overhangs or legacies? So, for example, in the case of Thailand there is a strong correlation between Democrat-led governments and bilateral tensions with Burma/Myanmar. Alternatively, is nationalism sometimes expressed in terms of the virtuous self and the stereotypical other, where the bilateral partner is characterized as being fundamentally bad and worthy of punishment and/or retribution?

(5) How are historical overhangs or legacies kept alive and replicated or refined? Is there general recognition of the overhang or legacy at the elite and societal levels? Are there any previous, current or ongoing attempts to ameliorate the impact of historical overhangs or legacies? So for example, in a number of countries in Northeast Asia, the recording

of history in official textbooks is seen as one of the ways of dealing with negative historical legacies. Are there such past or ongoing efforts, and if not, why not? Chapter writers were also asked, where possible, to identify recent examples of the flare-up of an overhang or legacy and explain it.

On the basis of the description of important overhangs or legacies and core questions to be addressed, the following countries and bilateral relationships were judged to be worthy of further research and discussion: China–Japan, Japan–Korea, China–Vietnam, Myanmar–Thailand and Thailand–Cambodia. The chapters that follow discuss these bilateral relationships and narrate their importance both in history and the present, paying special attention to the questions raised. The chapters are then compared for commonalities and differences in the types of issues that are typically involved, how these issues became embedded in the bilateral discourse, what are the constituencies that invoke them and under what circumstances, and finally, what are the possibilities of such issues eventually fading into the background. A summary of the findings appears in the concluding chapter.

There are a number of other peripheral questions that are important for comparative and policy purposes that pertain to the applicability of the findings across domains. In other words, the results obtained from these findings may well yield further hypotheses to be tested or refined in the field. Of special interest is the applicability of measures that have reined in overhangs or significantly ameliorated their impact. Whatever findings may obtain from this book, one thing is certain — it is incumbent upon political elite to muster sufficient political will and resources to overcome overhangs or legacies. Additionally, since such overhangs or legacies obtain within the context of a bilateral relationship, such efforts must be pursued by both countries in the relationship simultaneously to achieve progress.

Notes

1. See, for example, Kenneth Waltz, *Theory of International Politics* (Reading, MA: Addison-Wesley, 1979), p. 4; Barry Buzan, *People, States and Fear*, 2nd ed. (New York: Harvester-Wheatsheaf, 1991), pp. 153–81; and K.J. Holsti, *International Politics: A Framework for Analysis*, 5th ed. (New Jersey: Prentice-Hall, 1988), pp. 13–16.

2. A superpower is described as one that is able to change the texture of international relations unilaterally and during the period of the Cold War typically referred to the United States and the Soviet Union. Great powers are able to achieve a similar outcome except that they have to act in concert to do so. For a sampling of the literature on the problems confronting lesser states in the international system, see Robert O. Keohane, "Liliputian's Dilemmas: Small States in International Politics", *International Organization* 23, no. 2 (1969): 291–310 and David Vital, *The Inequality of States* (Clarendon: Oxford University Press, 1967).

3. See J. David Singer, "The Levels-of-Analysis Problem in International Relations", *World Politics* 14, no. 1 (October 1961): 77–92 and William R. Thompson, "The Regional Subsystem: A Conceptual Explication and a Propositional Inventory", *International Studies Quarterly* 17, no. 1 (March 1973): 89–117.

4. The most prominent discourse on classical realism in the post–World War II period was Hans J. Morgenthau, *Politics among Nations*, 6th ed. (New York: Knopf, 1976). Realists often trace their lineage to the Greek philosopher Thucydides and the Italian statesman Niccolo Machiavelli, among others.

5. See Kenneth Waltz, *Man, the State and War* (New York: Columbia University Press, 1954).

6. Kenneth Waltz, *Theory of International Politics* (Reading, MA: Addison-Wesley, 1979).

7. See, for example, Joseph Nye and Robert O. Keohane, *Power and Interdependence: World Politics in Transition* (Boston: Little Brown, 1977) and Robert O. Keohane, ed., *Neorealism and its Critics* (New York: Columbia University Press, 1986).

8. Stephen D. Krasner, ed., *International Regimes* (Ithaca, NY: Cornell University Press, 1983).

9. See David A. Baldwin, "Neorealism, Neoliberalism and World Politics", in *Neorealism and Neoliberalism: The Contemporary Debate*, edited by David A. Baldwin (New York: Columbia University Press, 1993).

10. The pioneering article was Alexander Wendt, "Anarchy is What States Make of It: The Social Construction of Power Politics", *International Organization* 46, no. 2 (1992): 391–425. The later and more detailed work is *Social Theory of International Politics* (Cambridge: Cambridge University Press, 1999). Much of the work on ASEAN by Amitav Acharya, for example, is well within the constructivist tradition. See his *The Quest for Identity: International Relations of Southeast Asia* (Singapore: Oxford University Press, 2000) and *Whose Ideas Matter? Agency and Power in Asian Regionalism* (Singapore: Institute of Southeast Asian Studies, 2010).

11. Inis L. Claude, *Power and International Relations* (New York: Random House, 1962), pp. 64–55.

12. See, for example, Gregory T. Russell, "(Review on) Order and Justice in

International Relations", *Ethics and International Affairs* 18, no. 1 (2004): 107–9. I am indebted to Tae Ryong Yoon for bringing this article to my attention.

13. The classic reference on soft power is Joseph S. Nye Jr., *Soft Power: The Means to Success in World Politics* (New York: Public Affairs, 2004).

14. Hedley Bull, *The Anarchical Society: A Study of Order in World Politics* (New York: Columbia University Press, 1977), p. 98. Again, I am indebted to Tae Ryong Yoon for alerting me to this source.

15. Robert Jervis, "Morality and International Strategy", in *The Meaning of the Nuclear Revolution: Statecraft and the Prospects of Armageddon* (Ithaca, NY: Cornell University Press, 1989), pp. 107–35.

16. Ibid., pp. 133–35.

17. The early exception to this rule was James Rosenau, who understood the domestic inputs into foreign policy. See his *Domestic Sources of Foreign Policy* (Glencoe: Free Press, 1967) and *Linkage Politics* (Glencoe: Free Press, 1969).

18. See, for example, N. Ganesan and Ramses Amer, eds., *International Relations in Southeast Asia: Between Bilateralism and Multilateralism* (Singapore: Institute of Southeast Asian Studies, 2010). The discussion on bilateral relations in this chapter draws on the conclusion from that book.

19. On this point, see Etel Solingen, "Multilateralism, Regionalism, and Bilateralism: Conceptual Overview from International Relations Theory", in *International Relations in Southeast Asia*, edited by N. Ganesan and Ramses Amer (Singapore: Institute of Southeast Asian Studies, 2010).

20. T.J. Pempel, "Challenges to Bilateralism: Changing Foes, Capital Flows, and Complex Forums", in *Beyond Bilateralism: U.S.–Japan Relations in the New Asia Pacific*, edited by Ellis Krauss and T.J. Pempel (Stanford: Stanford University Press, 2004).

21. Christopher Dent, "The New Economic Bilateralism in Southeast Asia: Region-Convergent or Region-Divergent?" *International Relations of the Asia-Pacific* 6, no. 1 (2006): 81–111.

22. On the concept of condensation symbols, see Murray Edelman, *The Symbolic Uses of Politics* (Urbana: University of Illinois Press, 1964).

2

HISTORICAL OVERHANG OR LEGACY IS WHAT STATES MAKE OF IT:
The Role of Realism and Morality in Korea–Japan Relations

Tae-Ryong Yoon

"Historical overhang or legacy", the key concept for this book, is defined by N. Ganesan as "negative *perception* that derives from historical interactions and subsequently becomes embedded in the *psyche* of a state, both at the level of the elites and the citizen body."

We have another similar concept, "historical animosity", which is traditionally employed for describing or explaining the fluctuations in Korea–Japan relations. The term "animosity" is defined as "a feeling of strong dislike, ill will, or enmity that tends to display itself in action", and "feeling" is defined as "an emotion or emotional perception or attitude".[1] Accordingly, we may define historical animosity as "an emotion or emotional perception or attitude of strong dislike, ill will, or enmity that has historically developed between states and that tends to display itself in the states' actions or behaviors." Thus, the word animosity itself indicates it is a type of *emotion* and *perception* at the same time. However, the usual identification of emotion with irrationalism by most experts on Korea–Japan relations is somewhat misleading in that scholars on emotion do not regard it as always irrational, but they consider emotion as rational at least sometimes.[2]

Both definitions have *cognitive* and *psychological* aspects. Moreover, perception and emotion are not necessarily separate phenomena. Rather, they reinforce each other in affecting Korea–Japan relations negatively. With this interaction in mind, this chapter analyses the nature of the historical overhang or legacy in Korea–Japan relations from a theoretical perspective that regards historical overhang or legacy as being inseparably intertwined with both a state's *realpolitik* calculation of its national interest and its moral consideration of *justice* in bilateral encounters.

Here I will discuss, first, the historical background of Korea–Japan relations; second, the realist nature of historical overhang or legacy in Korea–Japan relations; third, the history-perception gap, historical injustices, and historical overhang or legacy in Korea–Japan relations. I conclude that the persistent historical overhang or legacy in Korea–Japan relations is not just the effect of emotionalism and irrationality alleged to be characterized by the behaviour of the two states; rather, the persistence is the result of both states' *realpolitik* considerations and Korea's resentment towards Japan regarding unresolved historical injustices.

HISTORICAL BACKGROUND OF KOREA–JAPAN RELATIONS

Critical Historical Junctures

Ancient and Medieval History: Geography Making Interactions Inevitable

From ancient times, geographical proximity between the Korean peninsula and Japan has made their bilateral interactions inevitable. Throughout Japanese history, relations with Korea have been of special importance. It was mainly by way of Korea that later Neolithic culture reached Japan, carried by migrants whose ancestral home was in northeastern Asia. There was a series of immigrations on a small scale by families and groups not satisfied with their life in Korea. There was some degree of fusion between the aboriginal and the later arrivals.[3]

With the passage of time the migrants during their sojourn in Korea came under the influence of a culture superior to their own — the early metal culture of China. The bronze culture of northern China spread to southern Manchuria and thence to Korea by about 300 BC, and in the course of time affected the Neolithic culture of Korea. Migrants passing from Korea to the western shores of Japan began to introduce things and processes belonging to a metal culture.[4]

The effect of Chinese culture upon Korea, and consequently upon Japan, was intensified by a great expansion of Chinese power under the Han emperors. This power was extended by conquest in 108 BC to the northern half of the Korean peninsula. Chinese colonies were established in that region and thereafter certain tribal rulers in western Japan began to send missions to the colonial government established near the present Pyongyang. During the flourishing period of the Wei dynasty from 220 to 265, embassies were sent from Japan to the Chinese governor in Korea, who resided near present-day Seoul. When the Wei dynasty fell in AD 265, Chinese power in Korea diminished. But Japanese leaders continued their intercourse with Korea and they began to take part in struggles among Korean Kingdoms. Japan's participation was hastened by fear of the aggressive kingdom of Koguryo in northern Korea which began to threaten its southern neighbours and thus to cause anxiety to Japan.[5] So, from an ancient period, Japan started to get involved in power struggles in the Korean Peninsula.

In order to gain the fullest access to the advantages of association with the paramount regional state, Japan was not averse to acknowledging publicly its superior international status. Thus, according to John Welfield, in AD 239, Himiko, Queen of Yamatai, the first recognizable Japanese state, concluded an alliance with the powerful Chinese kingdom of Wei. During the Yamato period the Japanese allied themselves, first, with the Korean kingdom of Paekche, then, when Paekche's influence declined, with the mighty northern state of Koguryo, which had established a virtual hegemony of Northeast Asia and had thrice brought the Chinese Empire to its knees. When, in the mid-seventh century, Koguryo was defeated by the combined armies of the T'ang dynasty and its Silla allies, Japan shifted to a policy of close cooperation with China.[6] As such Japan has preferred bandwagoning to balancing, in its struggle for power in Northeast Asian international relations.

This indicates that there is no reason to believe that today's historical overhang or legacy between Korea and Japan dates back to ancient times.

Korea itself did not form a unified state but was divided into several ancient kingdoms. The Korean Peninsula was a bridge between mainland Asia and Japan that conveyed advanced civilization to Japan. At points in time Japan had formed alliances with different Korean kingdoms: Paekche, Koguryo, and Silla. This means that Japan–Korea relations were partially amicable.

In medieval times there were two historical events that negatively affected Korea–Japan relations: the invasion of Japan by a united force of Mongols and Koreans (the united kingdom of Koryo) and Japan's invasion of Korea.

By 1259, Khubilai, the Great Khan of the Mongols, had become Emperor of China, and in 1264 he established his capital in Beijing. The kingdom of Korea lost its independence, submitting to Mongol suzerainty. Korea's weakness was dangerous, since any great power that established itself in China tended to expand into Manchuria and Korea and thus threaten Japan. The Mongols, ignorant of seafaring matters, could invade Japan only by utilizing Korean ships and sailors. The Koreans were not willing collaborators. Yet they could scarcely withstand Mongol demands.[7]

The Mongol army was put to sea in November 1274. It was composed of 15,000 Mongol and Chinese troops and 8,000 Korean troops. About 7,000 Korean sailors together with Chinese seamen formed the crews of the invasion fleet composed of about three hundred large vessels and four or five hundred small craft. The islands of Tsushima and Iki were captured easily. The fleet then made a southeasternly turn towards Kyushu. In the end, however, luckily for the Kyushu men, at night on 19 November a great storm threatened and the weather-wise Korean pilots pressed the Mongol generals to re-embark their army, lest they should find themselves isolated on shore, their ships on the rocks and all possibility of retreat cut off. However, when daylight came many vessels sank in the open sea during the tempest — according to some accounts two hundred vessels were lost. Korean records say that 13,000 men of the invading force lost their lives, most of them by drowning. The invasion had failed, and the remnants of the Mongol force made their way back to Korea in disorder and distress.[8]

The second Mongol invasion in 1281 failed again for the same reason. The order to attack was given by Khubilai on the fourth day of the New Year. The Korean fleet was ready to put to sea in the spring, but the unwieldy Chinese armada was delayed. The fighting was started when the Korean commanders under Mongol pressure tested their strength by an attack upon Tsushima. But an epidemic of sickness prevented a further attempt. The ships did not put to sea until early summer. On 10 June the Korean fleet reduced Iki and then steered for the Chikuzen coast where they landed on 23 June. The month of August usually brings typhoon weather to the waters surrounding Japan. A great hurricane arose and beat with violence upon the shores of Kyushu for two days. It came to be known in Japanese annals as the *Kamikaze* (神風)[9] or Divine Wind, for it blew the enemy fleet to perdition. This was on the fifteenth and sixteenth days of August. The victory for Japan was complete. Khubilai wished to make a third attempt, but by 1286 he was so deeply committed on the mainland that Japan was no longer in immediate danger.[10]

More devastatingly negative effects on the historical legacy between Korea and Japan were made by Japan's invasion of Korea in 1592.

Oda Nobunaga, Toyotomi Hideyoshi, and Tokugawa Ieyasu unified Japan and created the lasting pattern of centralized feudalism. By 1590 Japan had once again been reunited politically. Hideyoshi dreamed of more worlds to conquer, which meant China. He may also have been motivated by the practical objective of giving outlet abroad to the excess military spirit and power those centuries of incessant warfare had built up in Japan. When Korea — Chosun ruled by the Yi dynasty — refused his armies free passage, he dispatched to the peninsula in 1592 an invading force of 160,000 men. The Japanese, with their firearms, quickly overran Korea but then withdrew southward in the face of massive Chinese armies. After long but unsuccessful negotiations, Hideyoshi renewed the war in 1597, but upon his death the next year, the Japanese armies withdrew precipitously. The invasion had a devastating effect on Korea, and Korean porcelain makers and printers were brought back to Japan by the retreating army.[11]

The Japanese invasion was an unmitigated disaster for Korea. Many cultural treasures and monuments were destroyed, the central government was further weakened, agriculture declined seriously, land registers were lost, and the whole tax system disrupted. Korea never fully recovered from Japan's invasion.[12]

As Reischauer notes, "this Japanese invasion has been emphasized in the historic memories of the Koreans and still contributes to the bitterness between them and the Japanese."[13] For instance, on 11 August 2010 a memorial service for the war dead during Hideyoshi's invasion was hosted by a Korean private foundation at *mimisuka* (耳塚, ear tomb) in Kyoto.

According to a record at that time, the Japanese returned with 214,000 noses as spoils of war cut from 185,000 Koreans and 29,000 Chinese. Originally *mimisuka* was called *hanasuka* (卑塚, nose tomb); however, Hayashi Razan, a Confucian scholar at the time of Tokugawa Ieyasu, proposed to call it ear tomb as a euphemism, because nose tomb sounded too barbaric. About 20,000 noses are inside the tomb now.[14] History may never die. However, the memory of war atrocities is probably reinforced all the more by Japan's invasion and colonization of Korea in modern history.

Modern History: Japan's Invasion and Colonization of Korea

Naturally, the most recent history is remembered more vividly than the older history. Thus the more modern history has a more profound effect on the present historical overhang or legacy in Korea–Japan relations.

After Commodore Perry forced Japan to give American ships access to their ports in 1853, the treaty for opening Japan's door was signed in 1854 and a full trade treaty was subsequently signed in 1858. The new Japanese leaders replaced the old feudal system with more effective centralized rule and started Japan on technological modernization. The whole transformation came to be known as the Meiji Restoration, launched in 1868. Efforts were made to modernize the economy.[15]

Japan had from the outset of the Meiji era harboured imperialistic designs towards Korea. In August 1875, Japanese men-of-war ventured into Korean waters at Kanghwa Bay, where they were fired upon by coastal defence forces. Japan used this incident as an excuse to force Korea to agree to establish diplomatic relations. In February 1876, Korea unwillingly opened three ports and accepted an unequal treaty, like the ones that the West had imposed on China and Japan. The treaty held Korea to be an independent nation, but China still regarded Korea as a tributary state. The struggle for power between China and Japan led to a naval clash off the coast of Inchon on 25 July 1894; Japan dispatched troops against China on 29 July and declared war three days later. In March 1895, Li Hung-chang arrived in Shimonoseki to work out a peace treaty. The two parties agreed to the Treaty of Shimonoseki. The terms provided for China to recognize the independence of Korea; cede the Liaotung Peninsula, Formosa, and the Pescadores to Japan; pay indemnity of 360 million yen; and open four additional ports. This Sino–Japanese War successfully launched Japan as an imperialistic power.[16]

After the Sino–Japanese War, rivalry between Russia and Japan developed in Korea. Japan favoured a policy of persuading Russia to recognize Japan's special interest in Korea in return for Japanese recognition of Russian interests in Manchuria. Russia, however, was unwilling to relinquish its influence in Korea. This rivalry in the end led the Japanese main fleet to proceed to Port Arthur and attack the Russians there on 9 February 1904. On the next day, Japan declared war. As a result of the war, by agreeing to conclude the Portsmouth Treaty, Russia recognized Japan's paramount interests in Korea and ceded the southern half of Sakhalin Island. The Russo–Japanese War established Japan as a major military and political power in the world.[17]

Japan signed a secret agreement with Russia in 1907, which in effect divided Manchuria into Japanese (south) and Russian (north) spheres of interest. Korea was another arena into which Japan moved swiftly. Japan, in extending its influence, received the sanction of the United States by means of the Taft–Katsura memorandum of July 1905. In this agreement, the United States consented to Japanese control of Korea in return for Japan's assurance that Japan would not extend its influence into the Philippines. In the following month, when the Anglo–Japanese alliance was renewed, England also recognized Japan's paramount interest in Korea.[18]

Japan then proceeded to turn Korea into a protectorate and, finally, a colony. In November 1905, Ito Hirobumi established a Residency General, whose primary task was the management of Korea's foreign affairs. This arrangement was put into effect in February 1906, and Ito became the first Resident General. After Ito was assassinated by a Korean patriot, the annexation moved swiftly and, in August 1910, Korea was absorbed by Japan and "the hardest and most relentless form of Imperial administration" was imposed upon Korea.[19]

REALIST NATURE OF HISTORICAL OVERHANG OR LEGACY IN KOREA–JAPAN RELATIONS[20]

There is a tendency for most experts on Korea–Japan relations to regard the historical overhang or legacy as a phenomenon related to irrationality. Is this really well founded? Here I will repudiate the notion that frictions arising from historical overhang or legacy are peculiar, irrational, emotionalist, and inconsistent with realist logic.

Geopolitics and Cognitive Tendencies

First of all, close geography does not necessarily bring about an amicable relationship in international politics. The geographical closeness between Korea and Japan is often expressed by a set phrase: "Japan and Korea are close but distant neighbours"; close in geography but distant in mind. This cliché is often used to underline the abnormal nature of Korea–Japan relations. However, it is the prevalent phenomenon that geographical contiguity intensifies the security dilemma among neighbouring states. Considering the water between Japan and Korea as a buffer zone, it is no wonder that the proximity of the two distrusting states in the modern world should make them feel insecure and make it difficult to develop an amicable relationship, because technological advancement (including weapons technology) will further shorten the "psychological geography" and exacerbate the security dilemma.[21]

Moreover, it is not easy to eliminate historical overhang or legacy and to change the established way of thinking, because "decision-makers tend to fit incoming information into their existing theories and images"[22] and "scholars and decision-makers are apt to err by being too wedded to the established view and too closed to new information, as opposed to being too willing to alter their theories".[23] We should also recognize that "there is an overall tendency for decision-makers to see other states as more hostile than they are"[24] and that "actors tend to see the behavior of others as more centralized, disciplined, and coordinated than it is".[25] The Korea–Japan relationship is no exception to these biased cognitive tendencies, which still obstruct hearty reconciliation of the two states. All this suggests that the continuity of the historical overhang or legacy and bilateral frictions can be due to other factors than just irrational emotionalism.

Those who employ a "descriptive-historical" or "psycho-historical" approach emphasize the overshadowing influence of a historical overhang or legacy on Korea–Japan relations. This "traditional" approach, though, has one thing in common with the most recent and sophisticated version of the realist analysis of Korea–Japan relations:[26] both regard historical animosity not only as an irrational emotion but also as unrelated to realpolitik thinking. The former emphasizes the continuity, and the latter underlines the change in Korea–Japan relations, but neither focuses on *change and continuity* at the same time.

Persistence of a historical overhang or legacy in Korea–Japan relations is not necessarily contradictory to the realist logic. For instance, when we have in mind neorealism's usual assumption of "worst case scenario" in state relations, we may infer that the historical overhang or legacy lasting in Korea–Japan relations is a reflection on (or a warning against) the possibility of Japan's re-emergence as a hegemonic power in Northeast Asia. Then, unlike the usual emphasis on the negative role of historical overhang or legacy, *too much realism* may be the main obstacle rather than too little realism (or too much emotionalism).

Conflict of Interests on Grand Strategy, Lack of Apology, and Confusing Identity

Most realists have a hard time explaining the Korea–Japan relationship because they pay exclusive attention to the existence of common threats while overlooking the intrinsic "conflict of interest" the two states have. Cooperating against these common threats is in Korea–Japan's interest, but having friction over conflicting interests is also consistent with the realist logic.

There were warning words spreading in the form of a Korean rhyme towards the middle of 1946, when the U.S.–Soviet talks on a unified Korea were nearing a stalemate:

> *Ssoryôn saram ege sokji malgo* [Don't be deceived by the Soviets],
> *Miguk saram mitchi malla* [Don't count on the Americans],
> *Ilbon saram irônani* [The Japanese will soon rise again],
> *Chosôn saram choshim hara* [So, Koreans, look out for yourselves]!

This atmosphere was natural to Koreans who had suffered from foreign invasions. Japan was the most recent external power that deprived Korea of its national sovereignty and forcefully abolished the Choson dynasty, the symbol of a long tradition. The rhyme is an expression of realpolitik concern by the Korean people, who do not want to see their country dominated by external powers again.

Official state-to-state relations between Korea and Japan were delayed until Japan regained its national sovereignty in 1952. Korea's independence was also delayed until 1948. It was not until the American Occupation of the ROK (Republic of Korea, or South Korea) was over that its official policy towards Japan began to form. The truth of the matter is, however, that many artefacts of Japanese colonization continued into South Korea's post-independence period.[27] This was especially true of older bureaucrats who were educated, trained and served under the Japanese. They had an influence as they were recruited to assist in the building of the new state. Not only did they serve as bureaucrats, but they were also actively recruited into the police force and the military. Since the country was poverty stricken in the wake of Japanese colonial extraction, these bureaucrats were the only ones available to build the new state. Ironically, those who participated in the Korea–Japan normalization talks from 1951 to 1965 were graduates of nine Japanese Imperial Universities or old civil servants during the colonial period. Fortunately, given their familiarity with Japanese ways, they were able to deal with their interlocutors effectively.

It should be noted that this same irony attended on the Japanese system as well. Japan also continued to maintain its old bureaucracy after the war and the American protection of the previous legacy was true of both Japan and Korea. The conservative trend of class formation is attributable to the emergence of the Cold War. The Americans suppressed left-wing elements and communists in the process of state building. Following Russian occupation of northern Japan and American occupation of southern Japan, there were disagreements on how to deal with a liberated Korea. Each of the occupying powers therefore supported affiliated and sympathetic forces in the already divided Korean society. And this state of affairs preceded the formal division of the country in 1948 when competing governments were established in Seoul and Pyongyang. Compared to the land reforms and nationalization undertaken in the North, South Korea remained very much within the previous conservative mould.

Whereas the colonization of Korea by Japan did not directly impinge on the country's post-independence economic development, there were similar cultural and intellectual traits and currents.[28] This in turn led to the Korean introduction of Japanese technology and the push for rapid economic development and modernization. The Korea–Japan normalization process also served as a boon to South Korea when the Korean military government under Park Chung Hee utilized hundreds of millions of dollars in grants and loans for industrialization of the country. Similar to Japan, emphasis was placed on the development of heavy and chemical industries.

The first president of South Korea, Syngman Rhee, with his long-time career as a fighter for independence, is notorious for his anti-Japanese policy and was often blamed either for having ignored national interests or for having utilized nationalistic (anti-Japanese) emotionalism for domestic political purposes. However, the friction between Korea and Japan in the early formative period was not just the results of the historical overhang or legacy itself. Especially after the Korean War broke out on 25 June 1950, the common threats from the communist neighbours were clearly perceived both by Korea and Japan. Also, as a response to heightened common threats, the United States re-engaged in the Korean Peninsula and assumed an influential position that could play both *positive* and *negative* roles in the process of reconciliation between Korea and Japan.

The U.S. role could be seen as positive in that American officials pressured Korea and Japan to meet each other for talks on normalization and provided good offices despite repeated failures. However, the U.S. role also had negative aspects regarding Korea–Japan relations. For instance, in September 1951 during the Korean War, the United States and forty-seven other nations signed a non-restrictive and relatively brief treaty of peace with Japan in San Francisco. Simultaneously, as the essential quid pro quo for this "generous" peace treaty on the part of the United States, a bilateral U.S.–Japan Mutual Security Agreement was signed at the same time. In April 1952 the Occupation of Japan formally ended and Japan re-entered the global arena as the key U.S. ally in Asia.[29]

The Korea–Japan bilateral conflicts in this formative period are usually attributed to historical overhang or legacy and emotionalism between the two states, and especially to Korean President Syngman Rhee's anti-Japanese sentiments. However, there is evidence that President Rhee did want to overcome the historical overhang or legacy and was well aware of the necessity of a strategic partnership with Japan. However, Rhee had a different grand strategy in mind in dealing with the communist threats in Northeast Asia, and Washington did not share his views. He wanted to see America keep the earlier policy towards Japan, summarized as democratization and demilitarization, or as building Japan as "a Switzerland in East Asia". But after America's decision to "reverse course", his strategic views could no longer be shared by the United States.

The United States changed the earlier policy of weakening Japan into that of strengthening Japan. As John Dower commented, if the peace treaty was really "generous" to Japan, it must have been at least partly at the cost of South Korea's national interests.[30] At least from the perspective of the Korean people recently liberated from harsh Japanese imperialism, Japan was overprotected by Washington's scheme of grand strategy against the communist threats.

The Impact of the Korean War on the Historical Overhang or Legacy in Korea–Japan Relations

At this juncture I will look further into the effect of the heightened common threat on Korea–Japan relations during the Korean War. It is interesting to know that such a rare case of politicians tapping the possibility of a Korea–Japan military alliance existed.

The Korean War heightened the level of threat perception. It especially increased Korea's incentives for cooperation with Japan. It also heightened the level of U.S. engagement. This engagement resulted from the strategic beliefs of U.S. leaders that Korea could be a chain of falling dominoes.[31] The increased level of threats and U.S. pressure led the country to anticipate more Korea–Japan cooperation. Simultaneously, the U.S. intervention meant that Korea and Japan could afford not to cooperate too much because they could count on the United States.

In this light it is remarkable that President Syngman Rhee even tapped the possibility of a military *alliance with Japan*, though it was privately sought and destined to fail due to Japan's fear of entrapment. As long as the United States was strongly supporting the South Korean military to expel immediate North Korean threats, Japan had an incentive to avoid direct military involvement. Moreover, Japan's concern was more about relations with other powerful neighbours.[32]

Selig Harrison's comment in 1980 may have been much more valid in the 1950s. According to him, most Japanese appeared less fearful of an eventual Communist triumph in Korea than of two other possible outcomes. One would be a conflict entailing U.S. intervention that could in turn embroil Japan militarily, complicating relations with other powers. The other fear involves a precipitate U.S. disengagement from South Korea that would not allow Japan time to reshape its approach to the peninsula. Similarly, Kei Wakaizumi also emphasized the "profound apprehension that such a conflict may draw Japan into a conflict with China or the Soviet Union, or that it may damage its relations with the United States".[33]

At any event, it is also noticeable that the normalization talks started during the Korean War in October 1951. The very fact that the talks started at all indicates an effect of perceived common threat (and U.S. pressure).

In the meantime, despite the continuation of President Rhee's concern for possible future domination of Japan over Korea even during the Korean War, there was much evidence that Korea–Japan cooperation increased rapidly under an unprecedented level of external threats. Despite Japan's indirect and secretly direct participation in the Korean War, however, the deep U.S. engagement relieved Japan's abandonment fear and heightened its entrapment fear instead. The conservative Japanese government resisted American pressure for rapid remilitarization and continued to do so over the ensuing decades. To avoid a situation where an increase of Japanese military forces leads to irresistible American pressure, Prime Minister Yoshida, as well as his aides and successors in their secret conversations with the Americans, frequently referred to popular support for the constitutional restraints on rearmament. The "spirit of Article Nine" was one of their most effective bargaining cards.[34]

In other words, Japan was playing a delicate game of maintaining an appropriate level of cooperation with Korea. Although perceived threats compelled Japan to do something for American war efforts, deep U.S. engagement allowed Japan not to cooperate too much for fear of over-entrapment in the Korean War.

These dynamic Korea–Japan relations indicate that the historical overhang or legacy is inseparably related to the two states' realpolitik concerns.

The Enemy of My Enemy is My Friend

In the case of Korea–U.S. relations, the logic of "the enemy of my enemy is my friend" worked. The U.S. decision to be a "friend in need" for Korea made the dormant historical overhang or legacy in the South Korean people's minds less salient.

Compared with Korea–U.S relations, Korea–Japan relations improved very slowly, and there were a series of confrontational incidents before their final achievement of diplomatic normalization in 1965. The major reason for the retardation of the good relationship was neither due to the lack of vision of a desirable goal, nor the lingering historical overhang or legacy alone. There were and are many political disputes between the two states due to conflicting self-interests and confusing self-identities. For its own domestic and international political reasons, Japan neither firmly committed itself to the defence of South Korea, nor did it close the possibility of normalizing relations with North Korea, by maintaining its principle of *seikei bunri* (separation of politics and economy).

In other words, Japan's political decision to be neither a "clear friend" of South Korea nor a "clear enemy" of North Korea created a problem of identity confusion. Therefore, in the case of Korea–Japan relations, the logic of "the enemy of my enemy is my friend" did not work. The North–South Korean confrontation has put Japan in an awkward situation, hindering the development of positive relations with all its neighbours.

In light of the discussion above, to see historical overhang or legacy as the immediate cause of Korea–Japan friction is to put the cart before the horse. However, neither is it appropriate to regard the historical overhang or legacy as insignificant in explaining Korea–Japan relations. When political disputes occur between the two based on different conceptions of self-interest, the historical overhang or legacy intervenes as an inflaming factor. Perception can be changed if it is misperception. If politicians have the will and intellectual ability to persuade themselves and the people, they have an opportunity to also change perceptions.

HISTORY PERCEPTION GAP, HISTORICAL INJUSTICES, AND HISTORICAL OVERHANG OR LEGACY IN KOREA–JAPAN RELATIONS

A majority of the experts analyse Korea–Japan relations in terms of historical overhang or legacy, focusing on the *constantly* conflictual side of the relationship. They have usually provided a detailed diplomatic history of Korea–Japan relations full of conflictual incidents. They have also produced extensive literature on Korean nationalism or the history of the Korean independence movement against Japanese imperialism.[35]

The persistent historical overhang or legacy indeed has affected Korea–Japan relations even since their diplomatic normalization in 1965,[36] twenty years after the end of Japan's colonial rule over Korea (1910–45). Therefore, it is no wonder that analysts argue that Korea and Japan have a "special" historical relationship that cannot be understood without considering the two states' history perception gap. They usually stress the idiosyncratic nature of the relationship, which without the "burden of history" should have been much more cooperative during the Cold War.

According to one version[37] of this approach, the Korea–Japan relationship is characterized by a series of "quasi-crises". These crises result from history perception gaps.[38] However, while this approach can describe the unstable baseline of or the continuity in Korea–Japan relations, it cannot explain the *change* — a series of ups-and-downs, especially the cases of "ups" — in their relations. The psycho-historical approach regards bridging the perception gap as the most important factor for amicable relations. This approach is usually pessimistic about the prospects for the relationship as long as the perception gap between the two remains unchanged.

Against this approach, Victor Cha criticizes the fact that "scholars and practitioners have grown accustomed to throwing up their hands in frustration and blaming historical animosity". He argues that "this has become a stale and over-utilized argument".[39] Instead, Cha's quasi-alliance model,[40] by employing Glenn Snyder's theory of alliance politics and the concept of "alliance security dilemma"[41] — that is, the inverse structure of abandonment/entrapment fears — seeks to explain Korea–Japan cooperation/friction as a function of U.S. engagement in or disengagement from the Northeast Asian region: When the United States disengages from Northeast Asia there is Korea–Japan cooperation because of their multilateral symmetric abandonment fears regarding the United States; when the United States engages in the region, there is Korea–Japan friction because of their bilateral asymmetric abandonment/entrapment fears.

This version of the realist approach pays exclusive attention to the indirect or unintended consequences of the U.S. policy on Korea–Japan relations, while ignoring other multiple or contradictory aspects of U.S. policy.[42] In other words, in analysing Korea–Japan relations, Cha, not unlike those who employ historical overhang or legacy alone, makes the same mistake of "putting all his eggs in one basket" in the sense that he is trying to explain too much with a single variable: the U.S. policies. An oversimplified analysis runs the risk of not only distorting the reality but also providing irrelevant policy prescriptions.

I do not deny the significance of the U.S. role in Korea–Japan relations. However, Korea and Japan themselves do have their own roles to play. The long history of Korea–Japan relations tells us the simple fact that the two states are themselves the most important actors in Korea–Japan relations. This sounds too unintuitive and too obvious to be true to most pundits. However, no matter how important the roles the United States and other countries — including enemy states — may play, they are all outsiders that have only secondary influence.

In this light, one of the most important tasks for both Korean and Japanese intellectuals and experts is to figure out why the historical overhang or legacy is so persistent and how to overcome it. As some scholars point out, "the argument for a coalition among the three liberal markets still hinged on a traditional strategy of balancing against the socialist bloc and did not actually address the next key question: *How can Koreans and Japanese actually resolve historical questions* and facilitate their growing need for mutual security cooperation?"[43]

At the end of World War II the South Korean leadership preferred early settlement of the disputes with Japan. President Rhee was aware of the benefits that good relations with Japan would bring about under the international political situation of increasing communist threats. He set a clear goal of diplomatic normalization. The real problem was never the lack of a vision of a desirable common goal — alignment with Japan against communist threats — but the obstacles Korea and Japan faced in the process of achieving that goal, especially the "perception gap" on the issue of the colonial past between Japanese and South Korean leaders. Japan's refusal to apologize for the past colonial rule intensified the impression that the Japanese were arrogant and unrepentant about past wrongdoings under an advantageous international situation in which Japan's strategic role as a bulwark against communist threats was highly appreciated by the United States.

In this context, different views between Korea and SCAP (Supreme Commander for the Allied Powers) authorities in Japan on Korea-related issues, such as the legal status and properties of Korean residents in Japan,[44] reinforced the impression that the U.S. mediation was neither fair nor balanced and that the United States sided with *"morally* wrong" Japan. Therefore, the U.S. pressure or sometimes "intended silence" was not so effective in narrowing the perception gaps between the two states.

What would have happened if Japan had apologized at that time as Emperor Akihito did in October 1998? During the state visit by South Korean President Kim Dae Jung, Emperor Akihito said, "The history of close exchange had a reverse side at one period when Japan brought great suffering on the people of the Korean Peninsula. The deep sorrow that I feel over this never leaves my memory."[45] Prime Minister Obuchi Keizo also expressed "poignant remorse" and "sincere apology" for Japan's conduct during its colonial rule of the Korean Peninsula and President Kim accepted the apology.[46]

One Korean proverb says, "One piece of word can pay for debts of a thousand-*yang*."[47] Korea–Japan relations may have progressed much faster if the same thing had occurred in the early formative period. This kind of apology would have relieved Korea of the confusion about Japan's identity and have had a positive effect on their relations. However, at that time no Japanese high official was "courageous" enough to express such an apology openly; no Korean high official was "generous" enough to forgive Japan by considering that Japan was at that time going through a very hectic and humiliating period after the defeat.

After the first preliminary talks for normalization failed in October 1951, there were a series of negotiations. After the first two conferences failed, the third conference resumed from 6 to 26 October 1953 after the Korean War. The chief Korean delegate, Minister Kim Yong-Sik, requested the withdrawal of the Japanese property claims in Korea left in the wake of Japan's defeat, which was obviously made as a bargaining chip to neutralize any property claims in Japan by South Korea. He pointed out that the ROK was making no claim for compensation for "losses sustained by the Korean people under the thirty-six years of rule by the Japanese government". At least to the Korean people, Japan's property claims seemed absurd and outrageous because they felt unbearably exploited under Japan's rule. This led to an exchange of mutual recrimination between Kim and the chief Japanese delegate, Kubota Kanichiro.

Japanese Foreign Minister Okazaki made a remark that supported Kubota on 22 October 1953, although later he said Kubota expressed only his personal view and not the Japanese government's view.[48] Kubota's remark offended the ROK government and people, and the conference broke off as a result. It was not resumed until Japan publicly withdrew Kubota's statement four years later in 1957.

Bruce Cumings also noted, "Many Japanese leaders cling to the idea that they did wonders for Korea during the colonial period."[49] I quote Olson and Cumings, just to make a point that in international relations, moral questions are ceaselessly raised. Without narrowing the perception gaps on issues related to moral or normative problems first, it is not only hard to start a cooperative relationship, but also difficult to expand the hard-won cooperation.[50] These kinds of complicated issues in Korea–Japan relations include property claims, problems in regard to fisheries, the legal status and treatment of Koreans in Japan, and the issue of title to the Dokdo/Takeshima islets, which are usually and mistakenly attributed to the historical overhang or legacy alone, just because they have developed against a long historical backdrop.[51]

For instance, Dokdo/Takeshima is to the Koreans a symbol of national interest and national prestige. Any part of a state's territory is strategically important to its own people for the maintenance of its territorial integrity

— which is a realist priority in pursuing national interest. More than that, however, Japan's claim on Dokdo gives an impression to Koreans that the Japanese hold a callous attitude to the historical *injustices* they inflicted; Koreans believe that Japan's claim to the island is based on the fact that it was forcefully incorporated into Japanese territory in 1905 when Korea was deprived of its diplomatic sovereignty by Japan. The colonial experience was such a physical and moral humiliation for Koreans that the "never again" syndrome is strong towards Japan.

Although Kubota's statements left deep scars, in the long run it was also a part of the "learning" experience for Japan that such remarks would set back relations an enormous extent.[52] After the break-off of the conference due to Kubota's remarks, the ripple effect was felt throughout the relations in general. The ROK National Parliament issued a resolution criticizing Japanese Foreign Minister Okazaki as well as Kubota, urging the ROK government to seize the Japanese ships violating the Rhee Line (Peace Line). On 23 October 1953, two days after the break-off, Japan decided to forcibly close the Korean Mission to Japan unless the ROK agreed to reciprocally allow Japan to open the Japanese Mission to Korea in Seoul. Japan also announced it would stop offering subsidies to Korean residents in Japan and that it would repatriate illegal Korean residents to the homeland.[53] In the vortex of these political disputes involving the "perception of history", fisheries and territory, total trade between the two states decreased 43 per cent from US$21.27 million to US$12.16 million.

In December 1955 during this volatile situation there was an exchange of open letters between Kagawa Toyohiko[54] and President Rhee. This exchange suggests not only that Korea's realpolitik fears of losing autonomy with regards to Japan impeded Korea–Japan cooperation, but also that moral/normative aspects are very important in promoting cooperative relations and that the two are inseparable.

Ironically, the demands of a notoriously anti-communist politician, Syngman Rhee, on Japanese repentance and apology, could only be satisfied by the JCP (Japan Communist Party). Kanzaki Yoshio, one of the JCP's three councilmen, said in August 1957, "Before the Tokyo government starts blaming Korea, it should improve its treatment of Korean residents and *repent more* Japan's oppression of Korea", adding that Japan should stop looking down on Koreans.[55] This suggests that if progressive (or moderate) political forces had taken power both in Japan and South Korea — which would not have been impossible without intervention by the United States or Soviet Union — ROK–Japan (or a unified Korea–Japan) relations might have improved much earlier and faster. Although the assumption of non-intervention by the two emerging superpowers itself is a big *if*,[56] and at that stage in history no official American agency could have put itself in the position of supporting socialism, early opinion surveys by the American Military Government established that a majority of the Korean people favoured a socialist economy.[57] Similarly, in Japan the first lower house election held in April 1947 gave the JSP (Japan Socialist Party) a plurality of seats and resulted in the establishment of Japan's only Socialist-led government, with Katayama Tetsu, leader of the JSP's right wing, as prime minister, although he ruled a coalition government that was dominated by conservatives.[58] Therefore, the possibility of a moderate or neutral regime did exist, although the actual probability was low.

Another reason for the lingering historical overhang or legacy in Korea–Japan relations is that the Korean leadership commonly held the view that in Korea–Japan relations, the *norm* of reciprocity or sovereignty[59] was not properly observed, because, as Welfield points out, "Korea, despite repeated Japanese attacks on its territory between the fourth and the seventh centuries, and again in the sixteenth century, never attempted to invade its eastern neighbor, although it certainly possessed the means to do so."[60] Korea's indignation at Japan's violation of the norm of reciprocity (or sovereignty) is also related to realist concerns.

When the South Korean government invited experts on Japanese history, politics and economy to Ch'ôngwadae (the Blue House) presidential office for numerous study meetings in preparation for a state visit in October 1998, President Kim Dae Jung asked Choe Sang-Yong, who heads Korea University's Asiatic Research Center, why Japan and South Korea cannot settle their past the way Germany and France did. "Japan and Germany are different", Choe answered. "Germany basically had the Nazis take war responsibility but Japan could not and did not blame the emperor. Furthermore, Germany and France fought three wars in the past with both sides winning and losing them. But Japan colonized South Korea."[61] It is not known whether President Kim accepted or agreed with Choe's views, but we can infer that the ROK's leadership and Korean intellectuals generally share similar views that the norm of reciprocity was violated in that Korea was unilaterally victimized by Japan.

It is interesting to note that after President Park Chung Hee was elected as civilian president in 1963, he expressed similar views, reminding Japan of the reciprocity norm. During a state visit to West Germany in December 1964, German Chancellor Erhard recommended to President Park to hasten Korea–Japan normalization following the example of German-French relations. President Park responded as follows,

> Of course, Korea–Japan relations should be normalized as soon as possible. There will be good news soon. But Korea–Japan relations are different from German–French relations. *You [German and French people] fought each other fairly with might and main.* Thus it is also easy to apologize and correct the past wrongdoings. However, *we were stabbed behind the back [by the Japanese] even without having a chance to fight a war with Japan.* When we extended our hands to the Japanese as a sign of suggestion for amicable relationship, they aimed guns at us. That's why our people have bad feelings towards them.[62] [emphasis mine]

The discussion above indicates that Korea–Japan's perceived common threats, the U.S. role in Korea–Japan cooperation/conflict, unresolved Korean resentment over historical injustices, historical overhang or legacy and the norm of reciprocity are interacting in a complicated manner to result in the present state of Korea–Japan relations.

Indeed, realist theory more broadly understood is not necessarily diametrically opposed to the traditional "psycho-historical" approach. A realist theory, especially Stephen Walt's balance-of-threat theory,[63] emphasizes the importance of perceived threats in alliance formation, one of whose components is the aggressive intentions of the other states.[64] Although Walt clearly announces himself as a realist, he departs from the neo-realist emphasis on states' capabilities in the absence of crystal-clear criteria of judging the *intentions* of states. As Wendt points out, in an important revision of Walt's theory, Stephen Walt implies that threats are socially constructed.[65] In Walt's balance-of-threat theory, perceived threat is mainly determined by whether perceived intentions of other states are aggressive or not. In this process of defining a state's perceptions on other states' threats and intentions, historical experience or the history of reciprocity could play a significant role.

A prominent Japanese scholar once related Japan's wartime atrocities with the Japanese sense of superiority and transfer psychology. This issue of Japan's wartime atrocities was dormant for a long time during the Cold War because the emergence of normative or ethical issues was blocked in a life-and-death struggle between the two ideological blocs. Therefore, it was not until the end of the Cold War that the issues of Japan's atrocities were openly raised in Korea–Japan relations.

Sex Slavery ("Comfort Women")

The "comfort women" tragedy is perhaps the most internationally sensationalized issue among multiple unsettling legacies of Korea's colonial history. The term is a translation of the Japanese euphemistic officialese *ianfu* and refers to young females of various ethnic and national backgrounds who were forced to offer sexual services to the Japanese troops before and during World War II. Estimates of their total number range between fifty thousand and two hundred thousand. It is believed that a great majority were Korean. The ordeals suffered by comfort women are not only *historical injustices* but also a contemporary issue.[66]

The problem never received serious consideration by political leaders of the post-colonial Korean government. It was only after Korean women leaders and victim-survivors brought the comfort women issue to the attention of the United Nations in 1992 that the international community redefined the issue as that of "military sexual slavery". With the help of international human rights activists and the active participation of several victim-survivors, the Korean activists helped to elevate the comfort women issue from a post-colonial bilateral dispute between Korea and Japan into a universal issue of violations of women's human rights in armed conflict.[67]

The 1990s witnessed numerous civil lawsuits filed by Asian survivors of sexual slavery and forced labour against the Japanese government and major Japanese corporations. However, the government of Japan has repeatedly stated that the issue had already been resolved, and that reparations had been made in the form of compensation for the losses suffered by the states fighting Japan, as stipulated by multinational (San Francisco) and bilateral (various state-to-state) treaties in the early post-war period.[68] The survivors of sexual slavery asked for the Japanese government's *official* apology and reparations, but no progress has yet been made. Therefore, international pressure on Japan for it is mounting.

For instance, in 2007 the U.S. House of Representatives passed a resolution urging Japan to apologize for coercing thousands of women to work as sex slaves for its military during World War II. Though largely symbolic, the nonbinding resolution has caused unease in Japan and added tension to an otherwise strong alliance. Officials in Tokyo say their country's leaders, including Prime Minister Abe Shinzo, have apologized repeatedly for the Imperial Japanese Army's policy of forcing women to work in military brothels in the 1930s and 1940s. The supporters of the resolution, however, say Japan has never assumed full responsibility for the treatment of the women. Tom Lantos, chairman of the House Foreign Affairs Committee, labelled as "nauseating" what he said were efforts by some in Japan "to distort and deny history and play a game of blame the victim". He also said, "Inhumane deeds should be fully acknowledged.... The world awaits a full reckoning of history from the Japanese government."[69]

However, Abe told reporters in Tokyo, "The resolution is regrettable. I explained my views and the government's response on this matter during my visit to the U.S." The House resolution urges Japan to "formally acknowledge, apologize and accept historical responsibility in a clear and unequivocal manner" for the suffering of so-called "comfort women".[70]

Abe caused anger throughout Asia, and among even supporters in Washington, in March 2007, when he said there was no evidence that the women had been coerced into working as prostitutes. After decades of denial, the Japanese government acknowledged its role in wartime prostitution after a historian discovered documents showing government involvement. In 1993 the government issued a carefully worded official apology, but it was never approved by parliament. Japan has rejected most compensation claims, saying post-war treaties settled them.[71]

Forced Labour

Roughly seven million Koreans were mobilized for labour during wartime efforts in 1939–45. Five million of them, including student labourers and female labourers, were mobilized in worksites within Korea. Roughly two million were sent overseas. They were mobilized without justifiable employment for the war effort. The majority of forced labourers were sent to three major destinations in Japan: coal mines, construction sites, and industrial plants. By 1945 roughly one-third of the total coal miners and construction workers in Japan were Korean forced labourers. Others were sent to metallurgical mines and industrial sites such as iron and steel plants, shipyards, and other factories in the Japanese empire. Under brutal police control, management surveillance, and debilitating working conditions, the Korean labourers suffered from hunger, fear, torture, and murder.[72]

It was in the post–Cold War 1990s that a renewed effort to redress the injustices of the past began to redefine these victims. Democratization in South Korea gained momentum under presidents Kim Young-Sam, Kim Dae-Jung, and Roh Moo-Hyun, and the political leadership and growing civil society of this era paid renewed attention to World War II atrocities, reparations, and broader themes of coming to terms with the past. Since the first lawsuit was filed in Tokyo District Court against the Japanese government on 6 December 1991, a series of them has followed. Through these suits, both countries have learned the lesson that the political will of the leadership is essential to reconciliation, because in the end remembrance is a political act. In the lawsuits of the 1990s the reasons behind Japan's reluctance to embrace responsibility were re-examined and narrowed down to three salient points: the lack of a collective memory within Japanese society; the conservative leadership's lack of political will to reconcile; and Japan's ambivalent identification as both victim and aggressor in World War II. The *changes* in Japanese court rulings and the out-of-court settlements in recent years strongly suggest that *Japan is slowly moving towards accepting responsibility* for compensation and admitting that it violated the human rights of the victims of forced labour.[73]

Biological Warfare Experiment

In 1925 the Geneva Convention prohibited the use of chemical and bacteriological weapons. However, Unit 731 — the secret biological warfare unit — was set up by the Japanese military in the northeast of China following the Japanese invasion. The headquarters were on the outskirts of Harbin in Manchukuo. As part of its research programme, it experimented on humans and animals. Unit 731 used large numbers of Chinese people for experiments. Many Chinese who rebelled against the Japanese occupation were arrested and sent to Pingfan where they became guinea pigs for Unit 731. Some Russian prisoners were also victims. The prisoners subjected to experiments were called *maruta* (literally "logs") by the Japanese. Every year the military police and the Manchukuo civilian police rounded up approximately 600 *maruta* to send to Pingfan. They were infected with particular pathogens by such means as injections or being given contaminated food or water. They would then be observed and their symptoms meticulously recorded. After succumbing to disease, the prisoners were usually dissected, and their bodies were then cremated within the compound.[74]

Unit 731 also conducted frostbite experiments on the *maruta*. The prisoners were tied up outdoors in temperatures as cold as –20 degrees Celsius and parts of their bodies were sprayed with salt water in order to induce frostbite. Their arms were hit with hammers to determine whether they were frostbitten. They were then immersed in hot water of various temperatures in order to determine how recovery from frostbite could best be facilitated. *Maruta* also were subjected to poisonous gas experiments.[75] Although these kinds of experiments themselves are appalling, it is more surprising to know that no one, not even Shiro Ishii who was in charge of the unit, was indicted.

Undoubtedly, the United States unduly allowed Japanese misbehaviour to go unpunished. A newspaper article epitomizes the nature of U.S.–Japan "cooperation" right after the war, which was achieved at the expense of "justice" and demonstrates how devastating the distortion effects the Cold War situation created on East Asian international politics.

Sheldon Harris, a U.S. historian, gives us a dismal picture of the reality. The ultimate disclosures in the mid- to late-1940s of Japanese biological warfare human experimentation did not appal those individuals who were apprised of these criminal acts. Instead, the disclosures whetted the appetites of scientists and military planners among both the victors and the vanquished. Rather than being motivated to abandon such actions, research using involuntary or uninformed subjects instead proliferated. Scientists in the United States alone conducted at least several hundred tests with human subjects who were not informed of the nature of the experiments, or of the danger to their health. In 1993 and 1994 the Clinton administration began to lift the veil of secrecy concerning United States' experiments with human subjects in hundreds of studies. We now know that American scientists tested humans with mustard gas and other chemical agents, exposed others to radiation tests, and still others to a variety of pathogens without the subjects' knowledge or consent.[76]

In Japan, scientists who participated in involuntary human experiments during World War II dominated the administration and controlled the areas of research of the country's National Institute of Health (NIH) for half a century after the end of the war. At least seven of the NIH's directors and five of the institute's vice directors during the 1930s and 1940s engaged in biological warfare experiments that employed human test subjects.

But these known war criminals were employed by this institution, were given great powers within the organization, and continued to use humans without their consent during the course of more than forty years. The NIH's Vice Director Masami Kitaoka authorized experiments on prisoners, babies and patients in psychiatric hospitals in 1947 and from 1952 until 1955. Another researcher conducted bacteriological experiments on infants hospitalized in Tokyo's National First Hospital in 1952. Similar experiments continued thereafter.[77]

According to Harris, it was scientists who initiated the movement to create biological, chemical and nuclear weapons. Neither the military nor the politicians in those countries who supported research in these areas sponsored such projects until their nation's leading scientists approached them. In Japan, Shiro Ishii and his fellow researchers promoted the development of biological weapons, not the fanatical militarists who dominated government in the decades before World War II.[78]

Reflecting on this reality, it is not insignificant that in August 2002 in a court ruling on the case of the vivisection and biological warfare victims of Unit 731 v. the Japanese government, the Tokyo District Court ruled that the Japanese government should pass a special act on this issue in the Diet,[79] though the Japanese government has not taken action yet.

On 6 December 1991 a renewed historical controversy erupted between Korea and Japan when three Korean former "comfort women", with support from feminists in Korea and Japan, and other male victims of the war among the resident Koreans in Japan, brought a suit against the Japanese government. Simultaneously, the Society for Pacific War Victims and Surviving Family Members filed in Tokyo District Court the first lawsuit demanding compensation from the Japanese government. The thirty-five plaintiffs in this case included former soldiers, civilian employees of the military, forced labourers, and the three surviving comfort women. Since this case was filed, war victims of various nationalities have brought around sixty more lawsuits in Japanese courts and around forty in U.S. courts. These lawsuits represent the range of victims of wartime atrocities: forced labourers, military and civilian employees, comfort women, atomic bomb victims, and the vivisection and biological warfare victims of Unit 731. The defendants were the Japanese government, private corporations, and sometimes both.[80]

The victims groups developed inter-group exchanges and bonding in terms of spirit, tactics, and political, legal, and international networking.

For instance, the forced labour group, which was the most vocal and active among resident Koreans in Japan, was inspired and influenced by the successful tactics of the comfort women activism centred in the Council for Countermeasures of the Labour Volunteer Corps (Chongdaehyop). The council's proactive publicity tactics successfully politicized the issue under President Roh Tae-Woo and it was further internationalized under the UN-led global feminism movement. The council's adoption of the tactic of litigation in 1991 along with other victims also inspired legal activism among various victims groups in the following decade. This tactic challenged the conventional concept of interstate compensation for historical injustices and stressed individual rights to compensation from government and private corporations for past injustices. The leadership of the UN in the human rights and women's rights movements played an important role in establishing the idea that individuals have standing in international law and a right to claim enforcement of fundamental human rights and freedom, as well as restitution. The internationalization of the comfort women issue was a good example of the proactive role of the UN.[81]

Rulings for the lawsuits filed in 1991 started to be announced in 1997. Most of the cases were dismissed, with the courts citing either the validity of the compensation waiver agreement in the 1965 Basic Treaty or the expiration of the statute of limitations. However, some jurists and private corporations are moving towards accepting the concept of Japan's responsibility for compensation after 1945. Whether or not the plaintiffs won their cases, the litigation had several profound effects on the reconciliation between the two countries. First, it provided a grand educational opportunity for Japan and Korea. Second, victimhood was redefined in the process and a more comprehensive approach to psychological and cultural healing, through restoring universal human rights of the victims, was adopted. Third, the litigation illuminated the divided nature of Japan's memories of World War II and underscored the lack of political will for reconciliation within the LDP leadership. Japanese jurists and even private corporations are now increasingly pressuring Japanese conservative political elites to accept Japan's responsibility and come up with a political solution for the redress movement. Fourth, an empowering transnational civic activism developed. The court battles provided rallying points for victims, civil society activists, research groups, human rights lawyers, and journalists in both societies.[82]

There have been good signs at the government level too. For instance, in 2007 and 2008 the two governments made meaningful progress in resolving historical issues caused by Japanese colonial rule. As a part of the three-year plan to accept all ethnic Koreans in Sakhalin who were forcefully relocated by Japan, the Korean government brought home 305 ethnic Koreans from October to December of 2008 with Japanese financial support. In addition, the remains of 160 Koreans — who were forced to move and were buried in Japan — were returned home in January and November of 2008. The return was made possible by the agreement of the two heads at the ASEAN Plus Three meeting in 2007. One hundred and thirty Hansen's disease patients who were quarantined at a hospital in Sorok-do during the Japanese colonial period received monetary compensation from the Japanese government in 2008. The Act on Relief for Atomic Bomb Survivors of Japan was revised in June 2008, entitling Korean survivors to receive Atomic Bomb Survivor's Certificates and be paid relief allowances through the Japanese embassy and consulate in Korea. The Korea–Japan Joint History Research, which began in 2002 in order to establish an accurate perception of Korea and Japan's shared history, commenced its second-term activities in 2007 and held a joint symposium in Tokyo on 19 December 2008.[83]

CONCLUSION: HISTORICAL OVERHANG OR LEGACY IS WHAT STATES MAKE OF IT

Analysing the historical overhang or legacy in Korea–Japan relations, I argue that the historical overhang or legacy is not just a matter of irrationality and emotionalism; rather, it is complicatedly intertwined with the two states' realpolitik considerations of their national interests, and Korea's normative resentment of historical injustices that still await rectification. The historical overhang or legacy is what Korea and Japan themselves have made of it throughout their bilateral interactions. Its persistently negative effects on the bilateral relations substantiate the fact that an unjust order imposed by the strong in the Cold War context has been unstable. As long as the historical injustices go unrectified, this situation will continue.

Until now, the studies on Korea–Japan relations have focused on either the psycho-historical, or realpolitik nature of the relationship. I argue that both the normative and realpolitik nature of the historical overhang or legacy should be addressed with the same weight.

Fortunately, in the post–Cold War era some positive changes are occurring in the baseline of Korea–Japan relations, although the changes are very slow, and thus have not resulted in conspicuously friendly Korea–Japan relations. These delicate changes in the long run coexist with the repeated ups-and-downs due to realpolitik calculations of the two states. For instance, as the research shows, the recent changes in Japanese court rulings and the out-of-court settlements suggest that Japan is slowly moving towards accepting responsibility for compensation after 1945 and admitting that it violated the human rights of the victims of forced labour. In August 2002 in a court ruling on the case of the vivisection and biological warfare victims of Unit 731 v. the Japanese government, the Tokyo District Court ruled that the Japanese government should pass a special act on this issue in the Diet. Also, some jurists and private corporations are moving towards accepting the concept of Japan's responsibility for compensation after 1945, increasingly pressuring Japanese conservative political elites to accept Japan's responsibility and come up with a political solution for the redress movement.[84]

The U.S. role in Korea–Japan relations showed meaningful change too. For instance, in 2007 the U.S. House of Representatives passed a resolution urging Japan to apologize for coercing thousands of women to work as sex slaves for its military during World War II. Though largely symbolic, it indicates that the United States has started to address historical injustices.

Despite these positive changes, the territorial dispute on Dokdo/Takeshima is really a thorny issue, having the potential to disrupt the whole relationship. In July 2008 the Japanese government newly included reference to Dokdo in the teacher's guidebook for Japan's middle schools. This kind of incident and the resultant dispute over the territorial issue remains a stumbling block towards an amicable relationship between the two countries. The territorial dispute is all the more difficult to resolve because it is not only a realpolitik issue, but also one of an historical injustice, at least to Koreans, who resentfully regard Japan's claim as dating back to its unjust colonial rule of Korea. Unfortunately, therefore, if the Japanese government does not voluntarily decide to recognize Korea's ownership of Dokdo as a means of rectifying historical injustices undertaken during Japan's colonial rule, truly amicable Korea–Japan relations would be almost impossible.

Notes

1. *Webster's Encyclopedic Unabridged Dictionary of the English Language* (New York: Gramercy Books, 1996).
2. See Neta C. Crawford, "The Passion of World Politics: Propositions on Emotion and Emotional Relationships", *International Security* 24, no. 4 (Spring 2000): 116; Jon Elster, *Alchemies of the Mind: Rationality and the Emotions* (Cambridge University Press, 1999); "Rationality and Emotions", *Economic Journal* 106, no. 438 (September 1996): 1386; Klaus Scherer, "Emotions Can Be Rational", *Social Science Information* 24, no. 2 (1985): 331–35.
3. George Sansom, *A History of Japan to 1334* (Stanford, CA: Stanford University Press, 1958), pp. 12–13.
4. Ibid., p. 13.
5. Ibid., pp. 14–17.
6. John Welfield, *An Empire in Eclipse: Japan in the Postwar American Alliance System: A Study in the Interaction of Domestic Politics and Foreign Policy* (London and Atlantic Highlands, NJ: Athlone Press, 1988), p. 2.
7. Sansom, *A History of Japan to 1334*, p. 439.
8. Ibid., pp. 442–44.
9. Japanese Prime Minister Yoshida once referred to the Korean War as kamikaze: "a gift from the gods". See John K. Fairbank, Edwin O. Reischauer, and Albert M. Craig, *East Asia: Traditions and Transformation*, rev. ed. (Boston: Houghton Mifflin, 1989), p. 5.
10. Sansom, *A History of Japan to 1334*, pp. 445–50.
11. Fairbank, Reischauer, and Craig, *East Asia*, pp. 395–97.
12. Ibid., p. 316.
13. Edwin O. Reischauer, *The Japanese Today: Change and Continuity* (Cambridge, MA: Belknap, 1977, 1988), p. 65.
14. Gilho Kim, "Mimisuka wiryongje/미미쓰카 위령제" [Memorial service at Mimisuka], *Jeju Today*, 20 August 2001 <http://www.ijejutoday.com/news/articleView.html?idxno=110119>.
15. Reischauer, *The Japanese Today*, pp. 80–83.
16. Mikiso Hane, *Modern Japan: A Historical Survey*, 2nd ed. (Boulder, CO: Westview, 1992), pp. 157–62.
17. Ibid., pp. 171–79.
18. Ibid., p. 179.
19. Ibid., pp. 179–80.
20. This part is a summary version of my previous work: Tae-Ryong Yoon, "Searching for a New Paradigm for Korea–Japan Relations", *IRI Review* 12, no. 2 (*Kukje kwan'gye y n'gu*) (Ilmin International Relations Institute, Korea University, Fall 2007).
21. For a discussion of the relationship of technology, geography, and security

dilemma, see Robert Jervis, "Cooperation under the Security Dilemma", *World Politics* 30, no. 2 (January 1978): 194–99.

22. Robert Jervis, "Hypotheses on Misperception", *World Politics* 20, no. 3 (April 1968): 455.

23. Ibid., p. 459.

24. Ibid., p. 475.

25. Ibid.

26. Victor D. Cha, *Alignment Despite Antagonism: The United States–Korea–Japan Security Triangle* (Stanford, CA: Stanford University Press, 1999).

27. I am indebted to Sung Chull Kim for this observation. For a treatment of the impact of Japan's colonization of Korea, see Wonik Kim, "Rethinking Colonialism and the Origins of the Developmental State in East Asia", *Journal of Contemporary Asia* 39, no. 3 (August 2009): 382–99.

28. See Jonghoe Yang, "Colonial Legacy and Modern Economic Growth in Korea: A Critical Examination of Their Relationships", *Development and Society* 33, no. 1 (June 2004): 1–24.

29. John W. Dower, *Japan in War and Peace: Selected Essays* (New York: New Press, 1993), p. 156.

30. For instance, President Rhee complained that the United States was not concerned about the ROK but only cared about strengthening Japan, and that the United States forced the ROK to buy Japanese products without building factories in Korea. See Sil Pak, *Han'guk oegyo pisa* [A hidden history of Korean diplomacy] (Seoul: Kirinwôn, 1980), p. 382.

31. See Robert Jervis and Jack Snyder, eds., *Dominoes and Bandwagons: Strategic Beliefs and Great Power Competition in the Eurasian Rimland* (New York: Oxford University Press, 1991).

32. Sung-Hwa Cheong, *The Politics of Anti-Japanese Sentiment in Korea: Japanese–South Korean Relations under American Occupation, 1945–1952* (New York: Greenwood, 1991), p. 83.

33. Franklin B. Weinstein and Fuji Kamiya, eds., *The Security of Korea: U.S. and Japanese Perspectives on the 1980s* (Boulder, CO: Westview, 1980), p. 44.

34. Ibid., p. 231.

35. For a study on Korean nationalism, see Man-Gil Kang, "The Nature and Process of the Korean National Liberation Movement during the Japanese Colonial Period", *Korea Journal* 36, no. 1 (1996): 5–19.

36. For my analysis of the 1965 Korea–Japan diplomatic normalization process, see Tae-Ryong Yoon, "Learning to Cooperate Not to Cooperate: Bargaining for the 1965 Korea–Japan Normalization", *Asian Perspective* 32, no. 2 (2008): 59–91.

37. Chung-In Moon, "International Quasi-Crisis: Theory and a Case of Japan–South Korean Bilateral Friction", *Asian Perspective* 15, no. 2 (1991): 99–123.

38. For a Japanese historian's urge to bridge the perception gap by first correcting the Japanese people's distorted view of Korea, see Takashi Hatada, "Han-Il kwan'gye wa yôksahak" [Japanese–Korean relations and historiography], *Han-Il kwan'gyesa ûi chaejomyông* [Refocusing on history of Korea–Japan relations] (Seoul: Yôksa yôn'guhoe, 1992).

39. Victor D. Cha, *Alignment Despite Antagonism: The United States–Korea–Japan Security Triangle* (Stanford, CA: Stanford University Press, 1999), p. 5.

40. Cha defines quasi-alliance as "the relationship between two states that remain unallied despite sharing a common ally". See Ibid., p. 36.

41. Glenn H. Snyder, *Alliance Politics* (Ithaca, NY: Cornell University Press, 1997); "The Security Dilemma in Alliance Politics", *World Politics* 36, no. 4 (1984): 461–95.

42. Korea–Japan relations are affected by the United States in a significant way. We could consider at least six causal lines of Korea–Japan relations where the role of the United States looms large but is contradictory in its effects on Korea–Japan cooperation. For details, see Tae-Ryong Yoon, "Searching for a New Paradigm for Korea–Japan Relations", *IRI Review* 12, no. 2 (*Kukje kwan'gye y n'gu*) (Ilmin International Relations Institute, Korea University, Fall 2007), pp. 189–94.

43. Tae-Hyo Kim and Brad Glosserman, eds., *The Future of U.S.–Korea–Japan Relations: Balancing Values and Interests* (Washington, DC: CSIS Press, 2004), p. x.

44. The Korean residents in Japan were not allowed to take all their property when they wanted to return to Korea after the end of the war.

45. Nicholas D. Kristof, "Korean Leader, in Japan, Urges Healing of Old Wounds", *New York Times*, 8 October 1998.

46. *Asahi Shimbun*, 9 October 1998.

47. The yang was Korea's unit of currency prior to adopting the won.

48. Yong-Sik Kim, *Saebyôk ûi yaksok: Kim Yong-Sik oegyo 33-nyôn* [Promise at the dawn: Thirty three-year diplomacy of Kim Yong-Sik], pp. 208–9.

49. Bruce Cumings, *Korea's Place in the Sun: A Modern History* (New York: Norton, 1997), pp. 318–19.

50. For a discussion of the moral aspect of international politics, see Mervyn Frost, *Ethics in International Relations: A Constitutive Theory* (Cambridge University Press, 1996).

51. For detailed discussions of the pending bilateral issues, see Kwang Bong Kim, *The Korea–Japan Treaty Crisis and the Instability of the Korean Political System* (New York: Praeger, 1971), pp. 40–77; Soon-Won Lee, "Korean–Japanese Discord, 1945–1965: A Case Study of International Conflict" (PhD dissertation, Rutgers, the State University of New Jersey), pp. 41–126.

52. For a discussion of the importance of learning in promoting cooperation among

states, see George W. Breslauer and Philip E. Tetlock, eds., *Learning in U.S. and Soviet Foreign Policy* (Boulder, CO: Westview, 1991); Joseph S. Nye, Jr., "Nuclear Learning and U.S.–Soviet Security Regimes", *International Organization* 41, no. 3 (1987): 371–402.

53. Sil Pak, *Han'guk oegyo pisa*, pp. 309–10.

54. Toyohiko Kagawa is a well-known Christian leader. He had written an open letter, "Appeal to President Syngman Rhee", in the Japanese daily *Mainichi Shimbun* on 13 December 1955.

55. Douglas H. Mendel, Jr., *The Japanese People and Foreign Policy: A Study of Public Opinion in Post-Treaty Japan* (Westport, CT: Greenwood, 1961), p. 181.

56. See Philip E. Tetlock and Aaron Belkin, eds., *Counterfactual Thoughts Experiments in World Politics: Logical, Methodological, and Psychological Perspectives* (Princeton, NJ: Princeton University Press, 1996); James D. Fearon, "Counterfactuals and Hypothesis Testing in Political Science", *World Politics* 43, no. 2 (1991): 169–95.

57. Donald Stone Macdonald, *U.S.–Korean Relations from Liberation to Self-Reliance: The Twenty-Year Record: An Interpretative Summary of the Archives of the U.S. Department of State for the period of 1945–1965* (Boulder, CO: Westview, 1992), p. 230.

58. Gerald L. Curtis, *The Japanese Way of Politics* (New York: Columbia University Press, 1988), pp. 10–11.

59. The norm of reciprocity is implied by that of sovereignty. See Robert O. Keohane, "International Institutions: Two Approaches", in *International Institutions and State Power: Essays in International Relations Theory* (Boulder, CO: Westview, 1989), p. 165.

60. John Welfield, *An Empire in Eclipse: Japan in the Postwar American Alliance System: A Study in the Interaction of Domestic Politics and Foreign Policy* (London and Atlantic Highlands, NJ: Athlone, 1988), p. 2.

61. "Kim Took a Realistic Approach; Now It's Japan's Turn", *Asahi Shimbun*, 12 October 1998.

62. Tong-Wôn Yi, *Taet'ongryông ûl kûrimyô* [I miss President Park], pp. 98–100.

63. Stephen M. Walt, *The Origins of Alliances* (Ithaca, NY: Cornell University Press, 1987); see also Stephen M. Walt, "Alliance Formation in Southwest Asia: Balancing and Bandwagoning in Cold War competition", in *Dominoes and Bandwagons: Strategic Beliefs and Great Power Competition in the Eurasian Rimland*, edited by Robert Jervis and Jack Snyder (New York: Oxford University Press, 1991).

64. According to Walt, "The degree to which a state threatens others is the product of its aggregate power, its geographical proximity, its offensive capabilities, and the aggressiveness of its intentions." Walt, *The Origins of Alliances* (Ithaca, NY: Cornell University Press, 1987), pp. 22, 265.

65. Alexander Wendt, "Anarchy Is What States Make of It", *International Organization* 46, no. 2 (1992): 396.
66. Chunghee Sarah Soh, "The Korean 'Comfort Women' Tragedy as Structural Violence", in *Rethinking Historical Injustice and Reconciliation in Northeast Asia: The Korean Experience*, edited by Gi-Wook Shin, Soon-won Park, and Daqing Yang (Routledge, 2008), pp. 17, 20.
67. Ibid., pp. 21–22.
68. Hideko Mitsui, "The Resignification of the 'Comfort Women' through NGO Trials", in *Rethinking Historical Injustice and Reconciliation in Northeast Asia: The Korean Experience*, edited by Gi-Wook Shin, Soon-won Park, and Daqing Yang (Routledge, 2008), p. 36.
69. "House Wants Japan Apology on Sex Slaves", *New York Times*, 31 July 2007.
70. Ibid.
71. Ibid.
72. Soon-Won Park, "The Politics of Remembrance: The Case of Korean Forced Laborers in the Second World War", in *Rethinking Historical Injustice and Reconciliation in Northeast Asia: The Korean Experience*, edited by Gi-Wook Shin, Soon-won Park, and Daqing Yang (Routledge, 2008), pp. 56–57.
73. Ibid., pp. 60, 71–72.
74. Yuki Tanaka, *Hidden Horrors: Japanese War Crimes in World War II* (Boulder, CO: Westview, 1998), pp. 135–39.
75. Ibid., pp. 138–39.
76. Sheldon H. Harris, *Factories of Death: Japanese Biological Warfare, 1932–45, and the American Cover-Up* (London, Routledge, 1994), pp. x–xi.
77. Ibid., p. xi.
78. Ibid., p. x.
79. Park, "The Politics of Remembrance", p. 62.
80. Ibid., p. 60.
81. Ibid., pp. 60–61.
82. Ibid., pp. 61–63.
83. Ministry of Foreign Affairs and Trade (MOFAT – Republic of Korea), *2009 Diplomatic White Paper*, p. 53.
84. Gi-Wook Shin, Soon-won Park, and Daqing Yang, eds. *Rethinking Historical Injustice and Reconciliation in Northeast Asia: The Korean Experience* (Routledge, 2008).

3

THE HISTORY CONUNDRUM IN JAPAN'S RELATIONS WITH CHINA

Lam Peng Er

Bedevilling Sino–Japanese relations into the twenty-first century, the history issue raises many questions, but no simple solution is in sight.[1] Why have China and Japan not buried the hatchet like France and Germany, but continue to carry their burden of history even though the two Northeast Asian powers are emerging as among each other's best trading partners? Why are the many "apologies" Japan has made over its invasion of China between 1931 and 1945 deemed insufficiently "sincere" by many Chinese? Why did Prime Ministers Koizumi Junichiro and Abe Shinzo insist on visiting the Yasukuni Shrine (the symbol of Japanese militarism to many Chinese and Koreans) even though such visits were repugnant to his Northeast Asian neighbours and plunged bilateral relations to its nadir?

Undoubtedly, antagonism over competing interpretations of history between the two neighbours continues to dampen their bilateral ties. But one must not take a reductionist view of Sino–Japanese relations and perceive them through the prism of historical contention. Indeed, why were historical disputes not a constant irritant or catalyst to a permanent crisis in Sino–Japanese relations throughout much of the post-war period?[2] Why did the history issue surface only sporadically to ruffle post-war bilateral ties before the advent of the Koizumi administration? And why is history a matter of bilateral dispute during the second and not the first Abe administration?[3] Why was the history issue between Beijing and Tokyo swept under the carpet for the most part of the Cold War era? Are there other issues which supersede the history problem in bilateral relations?

For analytical purposes, we can focus on the history issue, but Sino–Japanese ties are complex and multifaceted and in reality this is just one among many problems, and not necessarily always the most significant one to dog bilateral ties. Other challenges for China and Japan include territorial disputes in the East China Sea, especially over the Japanese-administered Senkaku (Diaoyu) islands; the structural shift in East Asia (the rise of China coupled with the relative decline of Japan) and its implications for international relations; and Tokyo's alliance with Washington, which obliges the former to provide logistical support to its U.S. ally in the event of a crisis in the Taiwan Straits or Korean Peninsula — much to the chagrin of Beijing. Tokyo and Washington deepened their alliance in 2015 by revising the 1997 U.S.–Japan Defence Guidelines. Not surprisingly, Beijing views with great concern the bolstering of the U.S.–Japan Alliance and the Abe administration's push for Tokyo's participation in collective security by reinterpreting Article 9 of the pacifist Japanese Constitution in 2014.

While the history issue occasionally looms large in bilateral ties, China and Japan are economic partners and strategic competitors, but not adversaries yet.[4] The history issue has neither condemned nor transformed the Asian neighbours into enemies engaging in a vicious arms race to destabilizes East Asia. Even in the worst of times when Koizumi's and Abe's Yasukuni Shrine visits sent bilateral relations into a tailspin, there were no ruptures in diplomatic relations, although top bilateral summits in each other's capital were suspended. The trilateral summits along with South Korea have also been a casualty of Japan's historical and territorial dispute with its two Northeast Asian neighbours.

This chapter first examines the critical historical junctures in post-war Sino–Japanese relations. Controversies over revisions to Japanese history textbooks and prime ministers' visits to the Yasukuni Shrine already surfaced during the Cold War era, but common geopolitical interest to forge a united front among China, Japan and the United States against the Soviet Union meant that the history issue was not allowed to deteriorate ties between the two Asian neighbours. Indeed, the Cold War years after the normalization of diplomatic relations in 1972 were considered the halcyon days of bilateral ties while the history issue remained relatively dormant.[5] Ironically, bilateral ties took a turn for the worse over the history issue in the twenty-first century rather than a decade or two after the end of World War II.

I argue that there were four critical junctures which very negatively coloured Japanese elite and public opinion towards China: (1) The 1989 Tiananmen Massacre (which has nothing to do with the history question between the two neighbours). (2) President Jiang Zemin's disastrous 1998 state visit to Japan, where he berated his hosts at every turn for not making an appropriate apology.[6] The 2010 incident that saw Sino–Japanese relations plunge when a Chinese fishing boat collided with two Japanese coastguard vessels in the vicinity of the disputed Senkaku (Diaoyu) islands. The Kan Administration initially considered charging the Chinese captain under Japanese law. This was utterly unacceptable to Beijing, which does not recognize Tokyo's sovereign jurisdiction over the disputed islands. (4) The Noda Administration's decision in 2012 to nationalize three Senkaku (Diaoyu) islands, causing bilateral relations to hit a new low. It can be noted that only one of these four cases touched on the history conundrum, one on China's domestic political violence (the Tiananmen Massacre), and the other two on territorial disputes. Simply put, the burden of history, while undoubtedly a highly emotional issue, is one among many problems confronting Sino–Japanese relations in the twenty-first century.

The next section is an analysis of Koizumi's wilful disregard for Chinese objections to his Yasukuni Shrine visits. In this section, I will examine Koizumi's own credo about his visits to the shrine and the right-wing interest groups which supported his bid to become LDP president and prime minister of Japan. Next is a brief discussion of Koizumi's successors — Abe Shinzo, Fukuda Yasuo and Aso Taro — and how they sought to defuse tensions in Sino–Japanese relations, especially over historical matters.

The last section is a discussion of regime change in Japan and its implications for Sino–Japanese relations and a resolution of the history issue. Unfortunately, bilateral ties between a new Japanese ruling party and Beijing did not improve significantly after fifty-four years of conservative LDP rule.[7] Although the advent of the new reformist Democratic Party of Japan (DPJ) led by Prime Minister Hatoyama Yukio initially improved bilateral ties, relations nose-dived again during the tenure of the next two DPJ prime ministers, Kan Naoto and Noda Yoshihiko, even though the three DPJ prime ministers did not visit the Yasukuni Shrine. Moreover, the manifesto of the DPJ was to build better ties with China and to anchor the bilateral relationship within a broader East Asian Community. But territorial disputes marred bilateral relations despite a new ruling party in Tokyo which initially had high hopes to forge better relations with Beijing.

CRITICAL HISTORICAL JUNCTURES

As stated earlier, the puzzle is why have China and Japan not reconciled like France and Germany and jointly built a regional community?[8] Indeed, France and Prussia/Germany fought each other in 1870, 1914–18 and 1939–45. Perhaps it is easier to answer why France and Germany have reconciled. First, the utter destructiveness of the two world wars and the elimination of the Nazis in Germany made reconciliation possible and more desirable. While the Nazis committed genocide against the Jews and gypsies, they did not slaughter French civilians on a massive scale.[9] To be sure, there is the case of the French village of Oradour-Sur-Glane which was destroyed and 642 of its inhabitants massacred by a column of German Waffen-SS troops in June 1944, and the village remains a ruin to this day as a memorial to the cruelty of the Nazi occupation of France.[10] Moreover, thousands of Jews in France were sent to Nazi concentration camps during the occupation. Conceivably, Franco-German reconciliation would have been more difficult if there had been the equivalent in scale and deeds of the Nanjing Massacre (including rapes and pillage) in France. Chinese historiography alleges that around three hundred thousand (mostly civilians) were massacred by the Japanese military in Nanjing alone. Moreover, Chinese estimates of the death toll (military and civilian) in China from the Japanese invasion range from ten to twenty million. And Unit 371, a covert biological and chemical warfare R&D unit of the Imperial Japanese army conducted lethal human experiments on men, women and children during the Second Sino–Japanese War (1937–45). Arguably, it would be a lamentable ignorance of Chinese history if one were to say that the scale, scope and devastation of Imperial Japan's invasion of China was the same as Nazi Germany's invasion of France.

Second, France and Germany were democracies and NATO allies who shared a common Soviet threat during the Cold War era, and they were no longer troubled by territorial disputes. However, China and Japan have different regime types and values, no longer share a common threat today, and have unresolved territorial disputes in the East China Sea. Beijing and Tokyo had an opportunity to address their historical problems when they normalized relations in 1972, but they did not in their eagerness to forge an alignment in the context of the Cold War.

Third, the United States played a different role as an occupational force in Germany and Japan. In the case of Germany, Hitler committed suicide and there was the wholesale dismantling of the Nazi regime. However, the United States kept Hirohito as emperor instead of putting him on trial or forcing him to abdicate, kept the bureaucracy intact, and conducted only a limited purge of the militarists. The United States apparently felt that retaining Hirohito as emperor would facilitate the U.S. occupation of Japan by gaining the cooperation of the Japanese, who might have resisted had their emperor been removed. But since World War II (the Pacific War to Japan) was fought in the name of the emperor, the following argument can be made: why should the Japanese feel guilty or genuinely apologetic when the United States, China and the rest of the world did not condemn Hirohito as a war criminal, and even accorded him due respect in state visits or when their ambassadors were accredited in Tokyo?[11] If Emperor Hirohito did not take personal responsibility for a war fought in his name, why should the Japanese feel a sense of personal guilt about the war?[12]

Conceivably, if the United States had forced Emperor Hirohito to abdicate or indicted him as a war criminal, the Japanese people would have been forced to confront their past sooner. And if the post-war Japanese leadership had shown remorse and contrition sooner after a clear break with the pre-war regime centred on a "divine" emperor, it would have been easier to reconcile with their neighbours. Simply put, the historical conundrum between Japan and its neighbours was, in part, due to the fault of the United States for failing to make a clean break between the pre- and post-war regimes during its occupation of Japan between 1945 and 1952.

Moreover, the price Japan had to pay to end the U.S. occupation and embrace the San Francisco peace treaty in the context of the Cold War, was to recognize Taiwan as the Republic of China and a legitimate government and not the Maoist People's Republic of China. If then prime minister Yoshida Shigeru had been given a free hand to forge diplomatic relations with Beijing, the Japanese would have been forced to confront and to resolve the history issue sooner. As stated earlier, diplomatic relations between Tokyo and Beijing were only established in 1972.

Normalization of Relations: An Opportunity Missed

Then prime minister Tanaka Kakuei established diplomatic ties with China in 1972, after President Nixon and NSC (National Security Council) Adviser Henry Kissinger visited Beijing to forge an alignment against Moscow in the context of the Cold War. China was apparently more interested in isolating Taiwan by securing official recognition from Japan and obtaining Japanese friendship against the "expansionist" Soviet hegemon than achieving closure of the history problem. Beijing did not press Tokyo for war reparations or explicit apologies for its invasion of China and the Nanjing Massacre. However, Tokyo extended ODA (official development assistance) to Beijing in lieu of reparations. Simply put, China's geopolitical interests trumped the history issue at the time.

Enshrinement of the Class A War Criminals

The subsequent critical juncture which was unknown to the Chinese and Japanese public at the time was when the chief priest of the Yasukuni Shrine secretly reposed the spirits of the fourteen class A war criminals in 1978. Under the new post-war secular constitution which stipulates a separation between state and religion, the government cannot order the chief priest to repose or transfer spirits from one shrine to another (until Japan's defeat in World War II, Yasukuni Shrine was a state-run institution to promote Emperor worship and patriotism).

Hitherto, the visits by various Japanese prime ministers to Yasukuni were not controversial to the Chinese and Koreans because the spirits of the class A war criminals were not reposed at that shrine. With hindsight, reposing the spirits of the class A war criminals was a historical juncture which would eventually cause considerable trouble to bilateral ties.

A counterfactual argument is that Koizumi's annual visits to Yasukuni between 2001 and 2006 and Abe's visit to the same shrine in 2013 would not have rocked Sino–Japanese relations if the spirits of the class A war criminals were not reposed at Yasukuni or if their spirits had been exorcised and moved to another shrine earlier.

The Nakasone Era

The history issue in Sino–Japanese relations became prominent only during the stint of then prime minister Nakasone. The first furore occurred in 1982 over Japanese history textbooks, which euphemistically stated that Japanese troops "advanced" instead of "invaded" China.[13] The second was when Nakasone visited Yasukuni Shrine in 1985, not in his "personal capacity", but as prime minister. By then it was public knowledge that the spirits of the fourteen class A war criminals were reposed at that shrine. The tension was defused when Nakasone did not visit Yasukuni Shrine in person again during his premiership. Apparently, Nakasone realized that visiting the shrine again would pose a serious problem for his friend, Chinese leader Hu Yaobang, who came under domestic political attack for being pro-Japanese. During this period the history issue did not rupture bilateral ties, which were generally good especially when both countries along with the United States forged a united front against the Soviet Union.

1989 Tiananmen Incident

The turning point in Japanese mass opinion towards China was the 1989 Tiananmen incident when the CCP (Chinese Communist Party) and its PLA (People's Liberation Army) forcibly put down a social movement for political reform. As stated earlier, this was a critical juncture in Sino–Japanese relations that has nothing to do with historical disputes. Until the Tiananmen incident, the Japanese tended to view Japan–China relations through a rosy "friendship" paradigm underpinned by guilt over Imperial Japan's invasion of the mainland and a lack of information about man-made disasters by the CCP such as the Great Leap Forward and the Cultural Revolution.[14] Shocked by the vivid images of Tiananmen, the Japanese woke up to the reality that, when push comes to shove, the CCP is prepared to shoot its own people to stay in power. Can the CCP lecture Japan on human rights when it is guilty of human rights abuses itself? Japanese public opinion towards the mainland plunged and has never quite recovered. The subsequent history disputes only aggravated the negative outlook towards China caused by the Tiananmen incident.

Since the Tiananmen incident, the CCP has sought to bolster its legitimacy by promoting patriotism and projecting itself as the nationalistic champion of China against the Japanese invaders in Chinese history textbooks. Not surprising, instead of wartime memories fading away with a new generation, the socialization process of the Chinese educational if not propaganda system has raised a new generation of students, many of whom harbour hatred against Japan. Chinese television programmes today also perpetuate a hatred of the Japanese invaders, with war serials running in different channels. Even though World War II ended seventy years ago (at time of writing), anti-Japanese movies and serials on TV are simultaneously broadcast into Chinese living rooms day and night.[15]

Even though the West initially ostracized China for its crackdown on the protesters and dissidents during and in the aftermath of the Tiananmen incident, Japan was the first major power to end China's diplomatic isolation when Emperor Akihito visited Beijing in 1992. Against the backdrop of China's international isolation after the Tiananmen incident, China did not pick a fight with Japan over historical issues. In the following year, the conservative LDP fell from power. Then prime minister Hosokawa Morihiro, leading a non-conservative ruling coalition, declared: "I would like to take this opportunity to offer anew our deep remorse and apologies for our nation's past acts of aggression." Hosokawa apologized on his own accord without any duress from China.

Fiftieth Anniversary of the End of World War II

The fiftieth anniversary of the end of World War II was a golden opportunity for Japan and China to seek closure to their historical dispute. Then prime minister Maruyama Tomiichi led the pacifist Japan Socialist Party (JSP) in a ruling coalition with the conservative LDP. He tried but failed to obtain a unanimous resolution from the Lower House to apologize for Japanese imperial aggression against the Asian countries. Not surprising, the right-wing elements within the LDP opposed an explicit apology for Imperial Japan's invasion of Asia. Instead, he issued an apology in his capacity as prime minister based on a cabinet decision on 15 August 1995:

During a certain period in the not-too-distant past, Japan, through its colonial rule and aggression, caused tremendous damage and suffering to the people of many countries, particularly those of Asia. In the hope that no such mistake will be made in the future, I regard, in a spirit of humanity, these irrefutable facts of history, and express here once again my feelings of deep remorse and state my heartfelt apology.

We should note that this apology was not extended specifically to China and there was no explicit description of what Imperial Japan actually did to the Chinese.

Subsequently, all succeeding Japanese prime ministers, including Koizumi Junichiro and Abe Shinzo, have accepted the "Maruyama statement" as Tokyo's official position on the history issue towards its Asian neighbours. If the ruling coalition had not been led by a pacifist and socialist prime minister at the time of the fiftieth anniversary of the war's end, it would have been unlikely for Japan to issue an official apology to its neighbours. In the same year, the ruling coalition also agreed to establish an Asian Women's Fund to compensate the "comfort women" — a euphemistic term for sex slaves who serviced the Imperial army.

The controversy in Japan over the Maruyama apology was a catalyst for a group of revisionist historians who subsequently launched their own textbook which whitewashed Japanese imperialism in Asia, sought to instil Japanese pride in its traditions and past, and avoid a "masochistic view of history" that emphasized that Japan was bad.[16] Not surprisingly, this nationalistic textbook would lead to much criticism from China and Korea. In actuality, less than one per cent of schools in Japan have adopted this right-wing textbook, but damage was done to Sino–Japanese relations because of the negative fallout from this controversy.

Presumably, grudging apologies from Japan to its neighbours are considered by many to be insincere because actions speak louder than words — the circulation of right-wing history textbooks vetted by the Ministry of Education and prime ministers' visits to Yasukuni Shrine suggest inconsistency if not duplicity in Japanese attitudes towards the history issue. To be sure, Japan is a democracy with a spectrum of views towards the history problem. There are also views from the mainstream centre and left which criticize the right-wing within and outside the LDP for its lack of remorse towards Japanese imperialism.[17]

It is also useful to note that the Cold War structure, which placed China and Japan on the same side against the Soviet Union after the early

1970s, had collapsed by 1991. In this regard, both sides no longer share a common strategic interest against a common enemy, which would have given an added incentive for them to mitigate or downplay their historical differences. By the fiftieth anniversary of the war's end, China had become a rising power and is increasingly assertive in world affairs. During the mid-1990s, Beijing conducted nuclear tests, engaged in missile tests in the Taiwan Straits to coerce Taipei, and staked its claim over the Spratlys in the South China Sea. In the case of Japan, its bubble economy burst in 1991 and it was unable to shake off a stubborn recession. By then, a popular view was that China was emerging as a "threat" to Japan.[18]

Jiang Zemin's 1998 visit to Japan

President Jiang Zemin was China's first head of state to make an official visit to Japan to mark a new era of warmer bilateral ties, but the trip turned out to be an utter public relations disaster. Earlier, Tokyo extended a written apology to Seoul and Jiang expected an apology in a similar format.[19] However, then prime minister Obuchi Keizo rebuffed Jiang for at least three reasons. First, the written apology was offered for Imperial Japan's colonization of Korea; Japan invaded but did not colonize China. Second, then president Kim Dae Jung extended an olive branch to Tokyo and declared that henceforth South Korea would seek a "future-oriented" relationship with Japan instead of harping on the past. There was no assurance from the Chinese that they would cease playing the history card against Japan once a written apology was given. Third, Jiang Zemin's behaviour in Japan was extremely boorish to many observers. He raised the issue of an apology at the official dinner hosted by Emperor Akihito and then demanded an apology at every stop during his trip. While Jiang's incessant insistence on an apology might have won him kudos from Chinese nationalists, it went down very badly, even among Japanese who were friendly to China, for a simple reason. In East Asia and other regions too, it is considered poor manners for a guest to constantly berate his host in his own house. Instead of both countries marking a new era of better ties, Jiang Zemin and Obuchi failed to sign their prepared communiqué.

As stated earlier, Jiang's official trip, clouded by the history issue, turned out to be a flop. But one wonders whether there were more serious reasons then underpinning the tensions between the two Asian neighbours.

Earlier, the Chinese were already unhappy with the decision by the United States to dispatch two carrier fleets to the Taiwan Straits when Beijing conducted its missile tests to coerce Taiwan. Subsequently, President Bill Clinton and Prime Minister Hashimoto Ryutaro made a joint declaration in 1996 that obliged Japan to provide logistical support to the United States in the event of a crisis in "areas surrounding Japan". This can be interpreted as Tokyo's commitment to support Washington should the latter choose to intervene in the Taiwan Straits. The Clinton–Hashimoto Joint Declaration was then codified as the 1997 U.S.–Japan Defence Guidelines. To Beijing, Taiwan is a part of China and therefore a core interest. It cannot brook any "interference" from the United States or Japan, whose support may encourage Taiwan to flirt with *de jure* independence. A year after the 1997 U.S.–Japan Defence Guidelines, an unhappy Jiang visited Japan and made things worse.

Knowing that Jiang's bellicose behaviour towards Japan had backfired, Beijing subsequently dispatched Prime Minister Zhu Ronji to Tokyo in 2000 to patch things up. To soften China's image, Zhu had a "townhouse" style meeting with selected Japanese from different walks of life and tried to charm his audience by playing the erhu, a stringed instrument. Zhu also carefully sidestepped the history issue to avoid exacerbating tensions in Sino–Japanese relations. In this regard, while Beijing and Tokyo had differences over their burden of history, both sides were not prepared to play hardball over the issue to the extent that important ties were jeopardized. However, Prime Minister Koizumi turned out to be the exception to the rule.

Koizumi's Visits to Yasukuni Shrine

As mentioned earlier, then prime minister Nakasone visited Yasukuni Shrine, but he desisted from subsequent visits to avoid damaging Sino–Japanese relations. Between Nakasone's and Koizumi's tenures as prime minister, the only other prime minister to have visited Yasukuni Shrine was Hashimoto Ryutaro. Hashimoto visited Yasukuni in 1996 and was vociferously criticized by China. To avoid deterioration in bilateral ties, Hashimoto did not visit Yasukuni Shrine again as prime minister, even though he was the honorary adviser to the Japan War–bereaved Families Association, a conservative interest group which supports the LDP and Yasukuni Shrine visits to honour the memories of their loved ones.

Unlike Nakasone and Hashimoto, Koizumi stubbornly insisted on annual visits to Yasukuni and succeeded in dragging Sino–Japanese relations to rock bottom.[20] Koizumi was an iconoclast and an *enfant terrible* in Japanese politics. In the 2001 LDP presidential election, Koizumi ran as a reformer who pledged to revitalize a stagnant Japan.[21] Although he was a dark horse not supported by the LDP parliamentary factions, the LDP prefectural chapters and rank and file voted for Koizumi out of a sense of crisis. To outbid his LDP rival Hashimoto Ryutaro in the party presidential election, Koizumi promised to visit the Yasukuni Shrine if he were to become party president and prime minister. Presumably, this electoral strategy would secure support from the LDP right-wing and the War–bereaved Families Association, an important vote gatherer for the conservative party.

However, Koizumi's approach to the Yasukuni Shrine cannot be attributed solely to his cynical use of it to secure the LDP presidency. Apparently, his family background influenced his personal credo towards the shrine and the victims of war. His father, Koizumi Junya, sought to revitalize the Kagoshima region by building a civilian airport there.[22] Towards the end of the war, the military converted the airport into a base for kamikaze pilots. More than a hundred young men flew from the base on a one-way mission for emperor and country. Even though it was not the original intention of the Koizumi family to build a kamikaze base, it felt a moral burden because many kamikaze pilots perished. Koizumi has grieved and cried at the Chiran Peace Museum for kamikaze pilots in Kagoshima prefecture. To Koizumi, his visits to the Yasukuni Shrine were not to glorify war but to pay his respects to the victims of war, which include kamikaze pilots too. But to Koizumi's critics, Yasukuni hosts the spirits of the class A war criminals and foreign relations should not be the extension of the personal predilection of the prime minister, but the national interest of Japan. And that interest necessitates the keeping of relations with China on an even keel.

Koizumi's approach to international relations also appears to be simplistic. He assumed that if relations with the U.S. superpower and ally were excellent, then Japan's place in the world would be secure. Koizumi was quick to dispatch the SDF (Self-Defense Forces) to Iraq for "humanitarian assistance" under special legislation to support the United States. Again, he was quick to dispatch the Maritime SDF to the Indian Ocean to provide logistical support and refuelling to U.S. vessels engaged in the Afghanistan war theatre in another piece of special legislation. But Koizumi was slow to patch things up with China, even though the expanding Chinese market helped to lift Japan from its decade-old recession. To be sure, Koizumi has reiterated that China is not a threat but an opportunity to Japan. But his stubborn refusal to abstain from visiting Yasukuni Shrine again as prime minister sent Sino–Japanese relations spiralling into a deep freeze between 2001 and 2006.

Ironically, there was some good that emerged from the political storm over the Yasukuni Shrine. The Japanese media devoted much space to the meaning of Yasukuni and Koizumi unwittingly created the circumstances which led to the post-war generation of Japanese learning more about their past, the role of Yasukuni in Japan's national narrative and why the Chinese and Koreans were furious with Koizumi.[23]

Hawks and Doves: Abe, Fukuda and Aso

Even before the new DPJ government held the reins of power in 2009, relations with China were already on the mend under LDP prime ministers Abe Shinzo, Fukuda Yasuo and Aso Taro. Despite Abe's reputation as a nationalistic hawk (who came to power by gaining national prominence over his steadfast critique of North Korea for its past abduction of Japanese citizens), he sought a thaw in Sino–Japanese relations. Abe opted for ambiguity on the question of Yasukuni Shrine visits by declaring that he would neither confirm nor deny whether he would make a trip there after becoming prime minister in 2006. Because Abe already had strong nationalist credentials, he did not need to visit Yasukuni to secure support from the political right. China was pragmatic and flexible enough to accept Abe's position, even though he did not unequivocally say that he would not go to the shrine. Moreover, China did not officially lambast Abe when he opined that the "comfort women" were not forced into sexual slavery. Ironically, it was Senator Mike Honda who initiated a resolution by the U.S. House of Representatives to condemn this view.[24]

However, Abe's right-wing populism was not enough to keep him in office. He lost the 2007 Upper House Election due to his lackadaisical attitude towards millions of missing pension records, the poor selection of ministers caught up in scandals, and repudiating the domestic reforms of Koizumi by readmitting many "postal rebels" back to the LDP.[25] Abe resigned in 2007 due to poor health exacerbated by these problems and was succeeded by the dovish Fukuda Yasuo. Fukuda continued his family tradition of maintaining friendly ties with China. His father Takeo was the prime minister who forged a friendship treaty with China in 1978. Unlike Abe, Fukuda Yasuo categorically said that he would not visit Yasukuni Shrine because "there is no need to do things that others hate".[26] Earlier, when Fukuda was the cabinet secretary during the Koizumi administration, he commissioned an advisory council, which recommended that Japan should establish a secular memorial to honour its war dead. If Japan were to adopt this proposal in the future, it would obviate the need for prime ministers to honour the war dead at Yasukuni.

Given the friendly disposition of Fukuda to China, Beijing gave him a splendid and warm welcome, the style of which was usually extended only to a visiting head of state (the emperor and not the prime minister is the symbol of state in Japan). Fukuda also made a trip to the Temple of Confucius in Qufu, Shandong in 2007 to emphasize the common cultural heritage of both Asian neighbours. In the following year, President Hu Jintao reciprocated by visiting Nara, the ancient capital of Japan which was modelled after Changan (present day Xian), the capital city of Tang China to reiterate the common civilization between them. Historical issues were not a problem with the Fukuda administration and relations were cordial between the top Japanese and Chinese political elites. However, according to public opinion polls, a majority of the Japanese public remained unfriendly towards China. This was cumulatively due to the legacy of Tiananmen, Koizumi's Yasukuni Shrine visits, and the crackdown on Tibetan dissidents just a month before Hu visited Japan.

Worn out by the immense difficulty of governing now that the Upper House was controlled by the opposition parties, Fukuda resigned as prime minister after barely a year in office and was succeeded by Aso Taro. To avoid rocking Sino–Japanese relations once again, Aso did not visit the Yasukuni Shrine and therefore did not trigger any negative reaction from China. During the controversy over Yasukuni, Aso actually proposed that the spirits of the class A war criminals should be reposed at another shrine. This is known as *bunshi* or "de-enshrinement" in Japanese. The logic was that if the spirits of these criminals are no longer at Yasukuni Shrine, then not only the prime minister but the emperor too can pay their respects to the war dead there. Aso was prime minister for a year until he lost the Lower House Election in 2009, which ushered in a new ruling party after fifty-four years of perennial LDP rule.[27]

Regime Shift and the Hatoyama Administration

The collapse of conservative LDP one-party-dominance and the advent of the reformist DPJ government in 2009 represented another critical juncture and a turning point in Sino–Japanese relations. While the Hatoyama administration reaffirms that the U.S.–Japan Alliance remains the cornerstone of Tokyo's foreign policy, it seeks a more balanced and equal relationship with its ally and also better relations with China. A centrepiece of Hatoyama's foreign policy vision is an East Asian Community in which China and Japan are pivotal members.

Given the fact that Prime Minister Hatoyama had no desire to visit Yasukuni and has a friendly disposition towards China, the history issue was ostensibly no longer a thorn in the flesh of bilateral relations then. Shortly after the DPJ captured the national government, Ozawa Ichiro, the party's secretary general and power behind the political throne, led 143 DPJ members of parliament and a delegation of more than six hundred to meet President Hu Jintao. In a departure from protocol, the new government also pressured the Imperial Household Agency to allow then Chinese Vice President Xi Jinping to meet Emperor Akihito, even though the request was not submitted a month in advance — as is the accepted practice. To the Japanese right wing, the Ozawa-led delegation falling head over heels to take individual photographs with President Hu and breaching protocol to make it an exception for Xi to meet the emperor were too obsequious to Beijing. Notwithstanding the territorial dispute in the East China Sea, relations seemed to have improved considerably. Reflecting the better atmosphere between the two national governments, Japanese public opinion also improved a little towards the mainland, although it was still marked by lingering suspicion.

Hatoyama's DPJ Successors: Kan Naoto and Noda Yoshihiko

Kan Naoto and Noda Yoshihiko were short-lived prime ministers (a year each). Kan was mostly interested in domestic reforms and did not have any foreign policy vision that included an East Asian Community with China. The Kan administration mishandled relations with China when the latter's fishing boat collided with two Japanese coastguard vessels in the vicinity of the Senkaku (Diaoyu) islands in 2010. Hitherto, the LDP government would simply catch and release Chinese "trespassers" in the surroundings of the Senkaku (Diaoyu) Islands. But the new and inexperienced DPJ government sought to "catch, detain and charge" the Chinese captain under Japanese law. Beijing could not accept this because acquiescence to the Japanese judicial process would mean that it had accepted Tokyo's sovereignty over the Diaoyu (Senkau) Islands. Under duress from China, the Kan administration released the Chinese captain from detention. This incident was very damaging to Sino–Japanese relations.

In 2012 the Noda administration nationalized three Senkaku (Diaoyu) Islands to pre-empt the Tokyo metropolitan government led by the right-wing Governor Ishihara Shintaro from purchasing them from a private owner. This action infuriated Beijing and led to massive anti-Japanese demonstrations in at least eighty-five Chinese cities. Indeed, the nationalization of the Senkaku islands brought bilateral relations to a new low.

The LDP and Abe Are Back

Abe Shinzo became prime minister after decisively winning the December 2012 Lower House Election. The electorate was generally disgusted by the incompetence of the DPJ government and was concerned about the moribund Japanese economy rather than being a show of support for Abe's right-wing nationalism. With the attraction of Abenomics to resuscitate the Japanese economy (which has been in the doldrums since the burst of its bubble economy in 1991), Prime Minister Abe again decisively won the July 2013 Upper House Election. Earlier, Abe regretted not visiting the Yasukuni Shrine as prime minister. In the same year, Abe visited the Yasukuni Shrine and both China and South Korea reacted with fury.

Abe's right-wing agenda is to nurture a new identity for Japan as a "normal" state not hamstrung by a pacifist constitution and supine to its neighbours over historical issues. Unable to command a two-thirds majority in both houses of parliament and to win a national referendum on removing Article 9 (the famous no-war clause) from the constitution, Abe succeeded in making a cabinet decision in June 2014 for Japan to engage in collective security. The crossing of the Rubicon by engaging in collective security is of course very worrisome to China and South Korea.

CONCLUSION

The prognosis for better Sino–Japanese relations is rather bleak for the foreseeable future because the historical problem has become intertwined with intractable territorial disputes and geostrategic competition. China is rising and Japan is seeking to both rebound from its economic malaise and become a "normal state" engaging in collective security. Moreover, Tokyo is strengthening its alliance with the United States, which views Beijing as a competitor to its hegemony. Not surprisingly, Beijing is sensitive to the two allies "ganging up" against its rise.

There is however an imponderable which may impact on the history issue and Sino–Japanese relations in the future. China today is chalking up rapid growth like Japan and the newly industrializing economies of South Korea, Taiwan, Singapore and Hong Kong in the past. But there is no guarantee that the ruling CCP, state institutions and avenues for mass political participation and consultation can adapt fast enough to keep up with the rapid socio-economic changes on the Chinese mainland. If there is a severe and sustained economic downturn in China within the next decade or two amidst rising expectations among the Chinese masses, there may be the temptation for the CCP to harness nationalism to bolster its legitimacy. Historically, Chinese nationalism is often synonymous with anti-Japanese sentiments. This may trigger a vicious cycle of confrontational nationalism between China and Japan.

Beijing is chalking up double-digit growth in its military spending. In contrast, the Japanese military budget has remained flat over the past decade, in part due to financial austerity. Tokyo's defence spending only rose a little under the Abe administration. Perhaps it is inevitable that as China emerges as a great power, it will continuously upgrade its military hardware and software, and will build a blue-water navy within the next two decades to project its power and protect its interests globally. This will be of grave concern for Japan. Even if issues like Yasukuni Shrine visits by Japanese prime ministers or revisionist history textbooks do not flare up again, tension will arise if China becomes much more heavily armed. But insofar as Tokyo keeps its alliance with Washington, the former should not overreact to China's military modernization because its American ally is still the undisputed military power in the world. The reality of East Asia's geopolitical arithmetic is: one (United States) plus three (Japan) is still greater than two (China).

Another worrying feature in Sino–Japanese relations is that a large majority of Chinese and Japanese view each other's country negatively. Will such negativity be transmitted to the next generation or will the historical dust eventually settle after another half century? Perhaps a facilitator to better relations is for both countries to address the problems of their own history textbooks. The Japanese side should get rid of the vetting system of history textbooks by the conservative (if not reactionary) Ministry of Education, while the CCP should not poison the minds of its young against post-war Japan in its patriotic education to bolster regime legitimacy. But given the domestic politics of both countries, such proposals are unlikely to be adopted.

Notes

1. From the Chinese perspective, the bilateral history conundrum has four clusters: denial of Imperial Japan's invasion of China and its atrocities, especially the Nanjing Massacre; the lack of a "sincere" apology and contrition; Japanese revision of history textbooks to whitewash its invasion of China; and the "comfort women" issue — a euphemism for the procurement of Korean, Chinese and even Dutch women as sex slaves for the Japanese Imperial army.

2. See, for example, Michael Heazle and Nick Knight, eds., *China–Japan Relations in the Twenty-First Century: Creating a Future Past?* (Cheltenham, Gloucestershire: 2007). The editors of this volume argue that history casts a shadow on Sino–Japanese relations in the twenty-first century. For a nuanced argument that geopolitics can sometimes trump the history issue in Sino–Japanese relations, see Yinan He, "National Mythmaking and the Problems of History in Sino–Japanese Relations", in *Japan's Relations with China: Facing a Rising Power*, edited by Lam Peng Er (London: Routledge, 2006), pp. 68–91. Indeed, the puzzle in Sino–Japanese relations is why does history matter sometimes but not so much in other times?

3. Abe Shinzo was Japanese prime minister between 2006 and 2007 and again from 2012.

4. China is Japan's number one trading partner. In 2013 Japan's total trade with China was valued at US$311.995 billion. Exports to China totalled US$129.883 billion, while imports from China amounted to US$182.112 billion. See Japan External Trade Organization, "Analysis of Japan-China trade in 2013 and outlook for 2014", 28 February 2014 <http://www.jetro.go.jp/en/news/releases/20140228009-news> (accessed 2 July 2014).

5. Ezra Vogel, Yuan Ming, and Tanaka Akihiko called these halcyon days the "golden age" of Sino–Japanese relations. See Ezra F. Vogel, Yuan Ming, and

Tanaka Akihiko eds., *The Golden Age of the U.S.-China-Japan Triangle: 1972–1989* (Cambridge: Harvard University Asia Center, 2002).

6. According to the authoritative annual survey by Japan's cabinet office, 68.5 per cent of Japanese public opinion was friendly to China in 1988, but this figure plunged to 51.6 per cent the following year because of aversion to the Tiananmen incident. It continued to decline after that. By 2009 only 38.5 per cent of Japanese public opinion was friendly towards China. See Naikakufu daijin kanbo seifu hokoku shitsu, *Gaiko ni kansuru yoron chosa* [Public opinion survey on International Relations], October 2009.

7. The LDP was out of power at the national level for only ten months, between 1993 and 1994.

8. Arguably, the European Union would have been impossible if not for Franco–German reconciliation. Indeed, a key reason why an East Asian Community is unfeasible is because of a lack of historical reconciliation between China and Japan.

9. To be sure, Nazi Germany bombed French towns and cities and thousands of civilians died in that carnage. Arguably, Nazi Germany's attitudes and treatment of Russians in its invasion of Russia were considerably worse than its invasion of France.

10. I would like to thank my anonymous referee for highlighting this.

11. On the failure of Japan to offer a "genuine" apology to the satisfaction of its neighbours, see Jennifer Lind, *Sorry States: Apologies in International Politics* (Cornell: Cornell University Press, 2008) and Alexis Dudden, *Troubled Apologies and Japan, Korea and the United States* (New York: Columbia University Press, 2008).

12. Hebert Bix argues that Emperor Hirohito, while by no means a one-man dictator, was an active participant who had complicity in Japan's war of aggression against its neighbours. See Herbert P. Bix, *Hirohito and the Making of Modern Japan* (New York: Harper Collins, 2000). Hirohito as the Showa Emperor lived until 1989. If he had passed away much earlier, the Japanese would probably have grappled with the historical issue sooner.

13. On the history textbook disputes in 1982, 1986 and 2001, see Daiki Shibuichi, "Japan's History Textbook Controversy: Social Movements and Governments", *Electronic Journal of Contemporary Japanese Studies*, 4 March 2008 <http://www.japanesestudies.org.uk/discussionpapers/2008/Shibuichi.html>.

14. On the rosy "friendship" paradigm adopted by the Japanese before the rude awakening of the Tiananmen incident, see the chapters by Kokubun Ryosei, "The Shifting Nature of Japan–China Relations after the Cold War" and Kamachi Noriko, "Japanese Writings on Post-1945 Japan–China Relations", in *Japan's Relations with China: Facing a Rising Power*, edited by Lam Peng Er (London: Routledge, 2006), pp. 21–36; 50–68.

15. The Chinese TV viewer has many choices besides anti-Japanese war serials, but if one were to surf the Chinese TV channels today, one would see ubiquitous anti-Japanese war programmes broadcast every day and night. Between May and June 2014, when the author stayed in Beijing for a month, there was one night when Chinese television simultaneously broadcasted five different anti-Japanese serials and movies. In a sense, the patriotic war against Imperial Japan continues on TV in the Chinese living room today.

16. Right-wing revisionists organized the Japanese Society for History Textbook Reform, popularly known as Tsukurukai in Japanese.

17. There is the case of a liberal historian, Ienaga Saburo, whose textbook was censored by the Ministry of Education for factual errors and matters of opinion regarding Imperial Japan's war. Ienaga fought a long-running legal battle with the ministry for violating his freedom of speech.

18. See Amako Satoshi, ed., *Chukoku wa kyoi ka* [Is China a threat?] (Tokyo: Keiso shoten, 1997).

19. Lam Peng Er, "Japan's Differing Approaches on the Apology Issue to China and South Korea", *American Asian Review* (US) 20, no. 3 (2002): 31–54.

20. Lam Peng Er, "Japan's Deteriorating Ties with China: The Koizumi Factor", *China: An International Journal* 3, no. 2 (2005): 275–91. See also "Koizumi's visits to the Yasukuni Shrine" in Ming Wan, *Sino–Japanese Relations: Interaction, Logic and Transformation*, edited by Ming Wan (Stanford: Stanford University Press, 2006), pp. 235–61.

21. Lam Peng Er, "Koizumi Junichiro: The Iconoclast who Remade Japanese Politics", in *Dissident Democrats in Asia*, edited by Haig Patapan, John Kane, and Benjamin Wong (New York: Palgrave, 2008), pp. 129–46.

22. The following account is from "Ties That Tempt Fate: Koizumi and Yasukuni Shrine", *Mainichi Shimbun*, 13 August 2001.

23. Wakamiya Yoshibumi, editor of the liberal *Asahi Shimbun*, and Watanabe Tsuneo, editor of the centrist and arguably conservative *Yomiuri Shimbun*, engaged in a lively debate and came to the conclusion that Japan should build a secular national memorial to replace Yasukuni. See Wakamiya Yoshibumi and Watanake Tsuneo, "Yomiuri and Asahi editors call for a national memorial to replace Yasukuni", *Japan Focus*, 14 February 2006. This is an abridged version of the original article which appeared in *Ronza*, 9 February 2006.

24. The U.S. House of Representatives passed the following resolution that Japan:
    (1) should formally acknowledge, apologize, and accept historical responsibility in a clear and unequivocal manner for its Imperial Armed Forces' coercion of young women into sexual slavery, known to the world as "comfort women", during its colonial and wartime occupation of Asia and the Pacific Islands from the 1930s through the duration of World War II;

(2) would help to resolve recurring questions about the sincerity and status of prior statements if the Prime Minister of Japan were to make such an apology as a public statement in his official capacity;

(3) should clearly and publicly refute any claims that the sexual enslavement and trafficking of the "comfort women" for the Japanese Imperial Armed Forces never occurred; and

(4) should educate current and future generations about this horrible crime while following the recommendations of the international community with respect to the "comfort women".

25. Earlier, Prime Minister Koizumi purged LDP MPs who opposed his postal reforms by denying them the party label in the 2005 Lower House Election and also dispatching a number of young and attractive female "assassins" to run as candidates against the "postal rebels" in their electoral constituencies. Koizumi won a strong mandate from the electorate for his postal reforms. Many critics felt that Abe betrayed the electorate who supported the Koizumi-led LDP by readmitting the postal rebels back to the party and therefore losing his credentials as a reformer.

26. "Fukuda Leads Japan PM Race, Won't Visit Yasukuni", *China Daily*, 16 September 2007.

27. The LDP was in power between 1955 and 2009 except for ten months between 1993 and 1994. Due to the arrogance and miscalculation of Ozawa Ichiro (the brains behind a eight-party ruling coalition nominally led by then prime minister Hosokawa), the Japan Socialist Party (the largest component of the coalition) was humiliated after it was left out of the ruling parliamentary grouping (*kaiha* in Japanese). Smarting from the humiliation, the socialists did the unthinkable by forging an unholy alliance with their erstwhile enemy, the LDP, and obtaining a parliamentary majority. For another lick at power, the socialists sold their soul by abandoning the hallmark of unarmed neutrality and accepted the U.S.–Japan alliance. If the LDP had been out of power for a few more years, it would probably have suffered from more defections in its ranks. And if the Hosokawa-led government had lasted for a few more years, a more stable non-LDP government would probably have been more conciliatory with China and Korea over the history issue, because there are fewer right-wing nationalists in that coalition.

4

CHINA–VIETNAM BILATERAL OVERHANG OR LEGACY

Ramses Amer

The main aim of this chapter is to analyse and assess China–Vietnam relations and the legacy of history. The study outlines the development of bilateral relations between China and Vietnam both historically and contemporarily with a focus on the latter period. Existing and potential issues of dispute are identified and assessed. The legacy of the long historical interaction is discussed in the context of the contemporary relationship.

The chapter is structured as follows: First, the China–Vietnam relationship is outlined both historically and contemporarily. Second, the existing and potential issues of dispute in the current relationship are identified and assessed. Third, the legacy of historical interaction is discussed. Fourth, the study is concluded by a summary of the development of the China–Vietnam relationship together with a broader discussion.

HISTORICAL RELATIONS[1]

Two parallel processes marked the period of direct Chinese rule over Vietnam from 111 BC to AD 939. One was the colonization of Vietnam by Chinese migrants and the other was the Vietnamese drive to regain political independence from the Chinese Empire. Apart from a steady migration from China to Vietnam of people such as administrators, farmers and landlords, there were also persons seeking refuge from political upheavals in other parts of the Chinese Empire.[2]

During the more than one thousand years of direct Chinese rule over Vietnam, a number of rebellions occurred. From the Trung rebellion, in the first century AD (40–43) — a genuinely Vietnamese one — to the Ly rebellion, in the sixth century, periods of dependence and semi-independence alternated, with the latter gradually becoming more predominant.[3] The Chinese migration that aimed at colonizing Vietnam gradually led to the emergence of a new Sino–Vietnamese ruling class, a social and economic decolonization of Vietnam, and efforts to establish political independence from the Chinese Empire. This led to new rebellions, but they all failed due to the strength of the Chinese Empire. After the fall of the Tang dynasty, in AD 907, the prospects for Vietnamese independence increased and, in AD 939, Vietnam regained complete independence.[4]

Relations between China and Vietnam remained strong even after Vietnam had regained independence. Vietnamese emperors paid tribute to the Chinese emperors in exchange for receiving blessings and protection from the Chinese side. Chinese culture and thinking continued to have a great influence on Vietnam. This can be seen from the prominent role that Confucianism played in Vietnamese society. Chinese influence was also evident in the fields of art and literature.[5]

However, relations between China and Vietnam were not always harmonious. In times of internal strife in Vietnam, Chinese emperors took advantage of the opportunity to interfere militarily in order to gain direct control, as the Ming emperor did from 1407 to 1428, or in order to assist a threatened or deposed monarch, as in the case of the last Vietnamese emperor of the Le dynasty in 1788. On both occasions the Vietnamese eventually defeated the Chinese. Another period of militarized conflicts occurred in the late thirteenth century when the Mongols ruled China and tried to expand their political control into Vietnam. Eventually Vietnam won a decisive battle in 1288.

Vietnam also served as a safe haven for Chinese who were fleeing from political upheavals in China. One wave of migrants came after the fall of the Song dynasty in the later part of the thirteenth century. Another wave came in connection with the demise of the Ming dynasty during the seventeenth century when the Manchus ousted this dynasty. Beginning in the eighteenth century a more steady process of Chinese immigration started, which, at the outset, was not explicitly connected to political events in China. The Ming refugees and later Chinese migrants played an important role in expanding Vietnamese control in the Mekong River Delta area.[6]

During the period of French colonial rule over Indochina — gradually established during the second half of the nineteenth century — Chinese migration increased, and authorities in China became increasingly active in attempts to influence French policies towards the Chinese migrants. During the period of French colonial rule over Vietnam, Vietnamese nationalists looked at developments in China as a source of inspiration in their anti-colonial struggle.

During the War with France — also known as the First Indochina War (1946–54) — the support provided by the People's Republic of China (PRC) after it was established in 1949 was of crucial importance to the armed struggle of the Vietminh in the war against the French. Eventually the war ended in 1954 with the decisive victory of the Vietminh at the Battle of Dien Bien Phu and with the Geneva Conference held shortly thereafter. China's role at that conference was important, and the outcome agreed upon was a compromise, with Vietnam being divided into two parts.[7]

CHINA–VIETNAM RELATIONS 1954–75[8]

Relations between the countries were very close in the 1950s, and for two decades China provided the Democratic Republic of Vietnam (DRV) with extensive economic and military assistance. China sent thousands of advisers to assist in various fields. China also provided considerable assistance during the Vietnam War. In fact, relations between China and Vietnam were described as close as "lips and teeth" in the 1950s. However, irritants developed during the 1960s and into the first half of the 1970s due to different perceptions of the Soviet Union and divergent views on relations with the United States. After the 1973 Paris Agreement, which led to the withdrawal of American troops from Vietnam and established a ceasefire in the Vietnam War, the Vietnamese claimed that Chinese leaders had advised them to diminish the level of the fighting in the south for a few years. This advice was perceived by the Vietnamese as aimed at keeping Vietnam divided. China rejected this claim.[9]

CHINA–VIETNAM RELATIONS 1975–91[10]

Following the end of the war in Vietnam in late April 1975, relations between China and Vietnam went through dramatic changes, from seemingly good and normal relations to war in early 1979. Relations deteriorated over a number of issues.[11] First, there were differences in opinions concerning the Soviet Union[12] and China was uneasy about Vietnam's relations with that country. As relations with China deteriorated in 1978 Vietnam gradually moved closer to the Soviet Union, and eventually an alliance between the two countries was formalized through the Treaty of Friendship and Cooperation signed on 3 November 1978. Second, there were conflicting interests in Cambodia.[13] China's gradually increased support for Cambodia in the conflict between Vietnam and Cambodia in 1978 also caused tension between China and Vietnam. The Vietnamese military intervention in Cambodia in late December 1978 led to a further deterioration in Vietnam's relations with China. Third, the territorial disputes between the two countries along the land border, in the Gulf of Tonkin and in the South China Sea caused tension. The maritime disputes contributed to the deterioration of bilateral relations by adding two more issues to the deepening differences between the two sides; however, it is difficult to discern their specific impact. The clashes that occurred along the land border were indications of the divergences with regard to other issues and of the overall deterioration of bilateral relations rather than important disputed issues in their own right. Fourth, the situation of the ethnic Chinese in Vietnam and the way in which this minority was treated emerged as a disputed issue. It was the mass migration of ethnic Chinese from Vietnam in the spring of 1978 that officially led to the open and public deterioration of bilateral relations between the two countries. Talks on the issue of "repatriation" to China of the ethnic Chinese in Vietnam were held from mid-June to mid-July and from early August to late September 1978, but no agreement was reached.[14]

The overall deterioration of relations led to a militarized conflict that escalated into China's attack on Vietnam in February and March 1979. China declared that the attack was a response to Vietnamese attacks on China. China claimed to have captured three of six provincial capitals in the bordering provinces of Cao Bang, Lang Son, and Lao Cai as well as seventeen cities and counties before announcing a withdrawal on 5 March. China announced that the withdrawal was completed by 16 March.[15]

Attempts at negotiations between the two states were made from April 1979 to March 1980, but the points of discussion were too far from each other to enable any agreement. Vietnam wanted to discuss problems solely related to the armed conflict between the two states and ways of reducing tension around the common border. China agreed to discuss these issues but also wanted to discuss the presence of Vietnamese troops in Cambodia and Laos, the situation of the ethnic Chinese in Vietnam as well as territorial problems between the two states.

The relations remained tense during and after these talks, especially so along the common border, where both sides had many troops stationed. There were mutual accusations about military incursions and enemy shelling became part of everyday life in certain areas of the bordering provinces. There seems to have been a link between Vietnamese offensives in Cambodia and increased Chinese military activity on the Sino-Vietnamese border. There were increased activities from late June to early July 1980, another increase in May and June 1981, a third increase in April 1983, a major increase in fighting in the period from April to July 1984, followed by a longer period of stalemate during which China shifted from infantry attacks to artillery shelling, which at times was intense. The final major shelling and infantry attack by China took place in early January 1987.[16] In March 1988 the two states clashed around the Spratly Islands in the South China Sea. The clashes resulted in China seizing some of the features. During the second half of 1988, tension along the common land border steadily decreased and, by December 1988, border trade resumed.

The normalization process between China and Vietnam began with low-level contacts in the mid-1980s and expanded to high-level meetings in early 1989. In early September 1990 a (then-secret) high-level meeting was held in China. Despite this meeting the normalization process lacked momentum on the political front. This situation prevailed until mid-1991, when the normalization process gained momentum. The increased diplomatic interaction paved the way for a high-level summit in early November 1991, during which bilateral relations were officially fully normalized.[17]

The full normalization of relations between China and Vietnam was made possible by the removal of two deeply divisive issues from the agenda. First, the differences between the two countries regarding relations with the Soviet Union were removed following the Sino-Soviet normalization of 1989. Second, the formal resolution of the Cambodian conflict through the Paris agreements in October 1991 removed that issue from the agenda.

RELATIONS SINCE 1991

During the 1990s the relationship between China and Vietnam was characterized by two contradictory trends; one positive with expanding contacts and cooperation in many fields, and the other negative with continued differences relating primarily to the territorial disputes. The positive trend was prevalent throughout the period but was at times slowed down by the fluctuating levels of tension relating to the territorial disputes. The positive trend has broadly prevailed in the 2000s.

Expanding political, cultural, economic, and military contacts between the two countries illustrate the positive trend in improving and expanding bilateral relations. On a regular basis, official delegations visit the other country to discuss ways of expanding cooperation in various fields. A strong political willingness to strengthen and deepen the overall relationship between the two countries has been displayed. A number of bilateral agreements have been signed following the full normalization of relations in late 1991. The growing economic relations can be seen through the growth in bilateral trade from US$32 million in 1991, to US$692 million in 1995, US$1.42 billion in 1999, to some 9.13 billion in 2005, up to some 16.35 billion in 2007, 20.81 billion in 2009, 27.94 billion in 2010, and 36.47 billion in 2011 — making China Vietnam's major trading partner.[18] China has also provided loans and assistance to upgrade Chinese-built factories in northern Vietnam. In terms of foreign direct investment (FDI) in Vietnam, the number of projects listed as originating from China proper was relatively few in the 1990s and with modest amounts of capital, but in recent years there has been a trend towards increased investment. This can be seen from the following comparison: China's "investment capital" in Vietnam was about US$120 million in the "1990s" and had increased to "nearly" 1.2 billion in the "2006–2007 period".[19] Cumulative figures for the period 1988–2012 show that the number of projects was 893 with a registered capital of US$4,697.2 million.[20] However, if Hong Kong is taken into account, the level of FDI is higher.[21]

In the political field the relationship between the CPC and the Communist Party of Vietnam (CPV) has been expanded through exchange visits at various levels between the two parties. An overview of the outcome of high-level meetings between Vietnam and China during the period 2004–13 demonstrate that the following main issues have officially been included in the joint statements and joint communiqués issued in connection with such high-level meetings:[22] overall relations, economic relations, border issues, Taiwan (i.e., the one-China policy) and international and regional organizations.[23] The contacts between the armed forces of the two countries have also been expanded through regular visits.

Tension in bilateral relations has primarily been caused by differences relating to territorial disputes and to a lesser degree by problems relating to cross-border smuggling. It can be noted that since full normalization of relations in late 1991, sharp differences relating to all the territorial disputes — i.e., overlapping claims to the Paracel and Spratly archipelagos, to water and continental shelf areas in the South China Sea and in the Gulf of Tonkin, and to areas along the land border — were prevalent from May to November 1992. Differences relating to oil exploration in the South China Sea and the signing of contracts with foreign companies for exploration were prevalent during the periods April–June 1994, April–May 1996, and March–April 1997. In 1998 there was no extended period of tension relating to the border disputes, but shorter periods can be noted, such as in January along the land border and in the South China Sea in April, May, July, and September. In 1999, focus was on reaching a settlement of the land border dispute, and this resulted in the signing of a Land Border Treaty on 30 December 1999. In 2000, focus was on settling the Gulf of Tonkin disputes and this resulted in the signing of the Agreement on the Demarcation of Waters, Exclusive Economic Zones and Continental Shelves in the Gulf of Tonkin on 25 December 2000. During both these years there was no noticeable tension relating to the disputes in the South China Sea. Developments from 2001 to 2008 demonstrated that this pattern of interaction relating to the disputes in the South China Sea continued to prevail, with continued dialogue and only limited periods of tension caused by the disputes in the area.[24] In addition the Land Border Treaty was ratified in 2000 while the Tonkin Gulf agreement was ratified in 2004.[25] The demarcation process of the land border was completed at the end of 2008.[26] During the period 2009–11 there were periodic increases in the levels of tensions relating to the disputes in the South China Sea. In response to the fluctuating tensions the two sides have stepped up efforts to manage their disputes in the South China Sea.[27]

ISSUES OF CONTENTION SINCE FULL NORMALIZATION OF RELATIONS IN 1991[28]

After full normalization of bilateral relations the territorial issues have been the major source of controversy, and therefore the major part of the discussion and analysis will be devoted to those disputes. The only other issue officially recognized as a problem has been the smuggling of Chinese goods into Vietnam and its negative impact on the Vietnamese economy. However, the issue of the ethnic Chinese still lingered into the early 2000s and remains a potential source of dispute.

Territorial Disputes[29]

As mentioned above, sharp differences relating to all the territorial disputes — i.e., overlapping claims to the Paracel and Spratly archipelagos, to water and continental shelf areas in the South China Sea and in the Gulf of Tonkin, and to areas along the land border — caused tension from May to November 1992. Differences relating to oil exploration in the South China Sea and the signing of contracts with foreign companies for exploration led to tension during the periods April–June 1994, April–May 1996, and March–April 1997. During 1998 there was no extended period of tension relating to the territorial disputes, but shorter periods can be noted such as in January along the land border and in the South China Sea during the months of April, May, July, and September. During 1999 and 2000 no significant tension was caused by the territorial disputes. As noted above, the period 2001–8 displayed a similar pattern of development, with continued dialogue and only limited periods of tension relating to the disputes in the South China Sea. During the period 2009–11 there were periodic increases in the levels of tensions relating to the disputes in the South China Sea. In response, the two sides have stepped up efforts to manage their disputes in the area.

In order to manage their territorial disputes, China and Vietnam initiated a system of talks and discussions which was both highly structured and extensive. From bottom to top it looks as follows: expert-level talks; government-level talks, i.e. deputy/vice-minister; foreign minister–level talks; and, high-level talks, i.e., presidents, prime ministers, and secretary-generals of the CPC and CPV.[30]

The talks at the expert and government levels deserve further attention in order to ascertain the progress made up to the end of 2000. Talks at

the expert-level were initiated in October 1992; up to late 1995 the talks
focused mainly on the land border and the Gulf of Tonkin issues. The
talks at the government-level began in August 1993 and the thirteenth
round of talks was held in January 2007.[31] Thereafter, there have been
meetings and talks that have not been included in official rounds.[32] The
first achievement was the signing of an agreement on 19 October 1993 on
the principles for handling the land border and Gulf of Tonkin disputes.
It was further agreed to set up joint working groups at the expert level
to deal with the two issues. The joint working group on the land border
held sixteen rounds of talks from February 1994 to the signing of the
Land Border Treaty in December 1999. The joint working group on the
Gulf of Tonkin met seventeen times from March 1994 to the signing of
the Agreement on the Demarcation of Waters, Exclusive Economic Zones
and Continental Shelves in the Gulf of Tonkin in December 2000. Talks at
the expert level on the disputes in the South China Sea proper, the so-called
"sea issues", were initiated in November 1995 and the eleventh round of
talks was held in July 2006.[33]

The negotiation process resulting in the signing of a treaty relating to
the land border on 30 December 1999 reflected the substantially higher
degree of progress made in negotiations on the land border as compared
with talks on other border disputes up to the end of 1999. In 2000 the
negotiations on the Gulf of Tonkin issue was stepped up with a view
to reaching an agreement within that year. This goal was reached on
25 December 2000. Thus, the deadlines for resolving the land border and
the Gulf of Tonkin issues were met in 1999 and 2000, respectively.

Less progress has been achieved with regard to the disputes in the
South China Sea proper, i.e., the competing sovereignty claims to the
Paracel and Spratly archipelagos as well as the overlapping claims to
water and continental shelf areas to the east of the Vietnamese coast. Talks
have been initiated but the parties have yet to agree on which disputes
to include on the agenda, with Vietnam pushing for the inclusion of the
Paracels as an issue alongside that of the Spratlys, whereas China only
wants to discuss the latter issue. To further complicate matters, China
seems to view the disputes over water and continental shelf areas as part
of the Spratly conflict, whereas Vietnam seems to view them as separate
from that conflict. It seems as though Vietnam does not want to initiate
talks relating to the areas of overlapping claims in the South China Sea
proper as it would be interpreted as giving legitimacy to China's claims to

those areas.[34] Thus, of the three South China Sea issues to be addressed by the two countries, there is only agreement on putting one on the agenda for talks, namely the Spratly archipelago, which is a multilateral conflict situation involving other claimants as well.

In response to the periodic increases in the level of tensions relating to the disputes in the South China Sea during the period 2009–11, China and Vietnam reached an "Agreement on basic principles guiding the settlement of sea-related issues" in October 2011.[35] In 2012 and 2013 the two sides have taken steps to implement the agreement, e.g., "departmental level" talks on "demarcation of areas outside the mouth of" the Gulf of Tonkin have been initiated and talks on "co-operation in less sensitive fields at sea" have also been initiated. High-level meetings between the two countries in 2013 have highlighted the continued push for management of the South China Sea situation by the two countries.[36]

The trend towards deepened management and co-operation was brought to an abrupt halt in early May 2014 when Vietnam protested against China's drilling activities in water areas to the west of the Paracel archipelago. The tension related to the incident lasted until mid-July when China announced that the drilling operation had been completed and the rig was withdrawn. The tension lasted longer than in connection with any other incident since the 1990s. The tension brought to the forefront the overlapping claims of the two countries to the Paracel archipelago. In addition, differences relating to claims to maritime zones in the area were displayed.[37]

Smuggling[38]

Although the territorial disputes have been the major source of tension in bilateral relations since full normalization in late 1991, the issue of the smuggling of Chinese goods and its negative impact on Vietnam's economy has also been a source of controversy. And it seems the smuggling and the flooding of the Vietnamese market with Chinese goods was most controversial during the earlier part of the 1990s. Judging by the publicity given to the problem by the Vietnamese side, the situation was most serious in 1993, with renewed attention in 1997.

A closer look at the actions taken to curb the smuggling shows that Vietnam took some unilateral measures in 1993 by introducing tariffs on certain imported goods, and more importantly by tightening control in the border areas. Bilateral moves to address the issue have included discussions at high-level meetings during the Chinese prime minister's visit to Vietnam in late 1992 and during the Vietnamese president's visit to China in late 1993, as well as through such measures as the opening of more border crossings and later by the resumption of direct railway traffic between the two countries.

It seems that smuggling became less of a problem during 1994, at least judging from official statements and contacts. Instead, attention shifted to ways of increasing and expanding economic cooperation, as exemplified by the three agreements signed in November 1994 in connection with the Chinese president's visit to Vietnam. These agreements aimed at increasing trade and economic cooperation, facilitating road transport, and guaranteeing the quality of imported and exported goods. The two sides have continued their efforts to expand economic relations and to enforce control over cross-border trade. The expansion of economic cooperation displayed an expansion in bilateral trade as well as Chinese loans and assistance to upgrade Chinese-built factories in northern Vietnam.

Although economic cooperation between China and Vietnam was expanding, smuggling once again emerged as a major issue of concern in 1997. This was displayed both in connection with the high-level summit in July 1997 and in connection with the visit by the Chinese vice–prime minister in charge of economic affairs to Vietnam in October 1997. The renewed concern about smuggling along the Sino–Vietnamese border can be linked to enhanced efforts on the part of the Vietnamese government to curb smuggling in 1997 and the priority given to the current campaign by the top leadership.[39] Although both China and Vietnam had taken measures to curb smuggling in the border areas, the measures were not to very effective.[40] The October 1997 agreement to initiate negotiations aiming at reaching an agreement on the regulation of cross-border economic activities was a clear indication that both parties were eager to cooperate in order to bring the smuggling along the common border under control. These efforts eventually led to formal agreement on cross-border trade between the two countries, signed on 19 October 1998 in connection with a visit by Vietnam's prime minister to China.[41] Other measures to boost official trade and other aspects of economic co-operation also continued in the late 1990s and the 2000s. Such measures have resulted in a steady growth in bilateral trade.

Ethnic Chinese

The issue of the ethnic Chinese has continued to be a source of controversy in bilateral relations. However, during the process of normalization, the problem did not seem to be related to the ethnic Chinese in Vietnam but to the fate of those who left for China in the late 1970s. At least up to the mid-1990s China persisted in bringing up its demand for their repatriation to Vietnam, whereas the Vietnamese side continued to oppose such repatriation. The Vietnamese stand on the matter was based on economic considerations, i.e., Vietnam could not absorb so many people who, according to the most recent statistics by the United Nations High Commissioner for Refugees (UNHCR), number 301,068.[42] Vietnam also argued that the ethnic Chinese had settled in China and integrated into Chinese society and therefore a repatriation process would disrupt their lives.[43] Vietnam also had security concerns in mind when opposing repatriation given that the large number of ethnic Chinese had been living under the political control and influence of the Chinese authorities since the late 1970s. At least into the 1990s the issue of the ethnic Chinese from Vietnam living in China remained an irritant in bilateral relations. Given the importance of the ethnic Chinese factor in the deterioration of ties in the late 1970s it remains a potential dispute issue in the event of worsening bilateral relations between the two countries.

POTENTIAL ISSUES OF CONTENTION IN CHINA–VIETNAM RELATIONS[44]

Economic Relations[45]

The potential issue of contention in the economic field has moved from smuggling to the trade deficit between the two countries. The growth in bilateral trade has also resulted in a growing Vietnamese trade deficit with China. This trend can clearly be seen when comparing the growth in Vietnam's imports from China with the growth of Vietnam's exports to China. In 1999 Vietnam imported goods with a total value of US$673.1 million from China and exported goods valued at US$746.4 million. In 2002 Vietnam imported goods with a total value of US$2,158.8 million and exported goods with a total value of US$1,158.3 million. In 2003 the corresponding figures were US$3,138.6 and US$1,883.1 million. In 2004, imports had increased to US$4,595.1 million while exports had increased to US$2,899.1 million. The trend continued in 2005 with imports up to US$5,899.7 and exports up to US$3.228.1. The trend of stronger growth in imports from China was further reinforced in 2006 when imports rose to 7,391.3 million, while exports to China increased moderately to US$3,242.8 million. In 2007 imports from China increased to US$12,710 million and exports increased more modestly to US$3,646.1 million. Figures for 2008 display a continued strong growth in imports from China up to US$15,973.6 and also growth of Vietnam's exports to China to US$4,850.1 million. Interestingly, figures for 2009 display a slight decrease in imports from China down to US$15,411.3 while exports from Vietnam grew to US$5,403. However, this decrease in imports from China did not last; instead, imports increased again in 2010 and 2011 to US$20,203.6 and US$24,866.4 million, respectively, while exports from Vietnam continued to grow in both years to US$7,742.9 in 2010 and to US$11,613.3 million in 2011.

These trade figures indicate that bilateral trade between the two countries has increased dramatically during the 2000s. Interestingly, Vietnam had a trade surplus in 1999, but the 2000s has displayed a growing trade deficit for Vietnam with the exception of 2009 when the deficit was slightly reduced. Already in 2002 the Vietnamese trade deficit was about US$1,000 million. The trade deficit increased sharply from 2005 when it was 2,671.6 million to 2008 when it reached US$11,123.5. This suggests that the expansion of bilateral trade during this period was primarily the result of strong growth in Chinese exports to Vietnam. Although the trade deficit for Vietnam hit new heights in 2010 with US$12,460.7 million and in 2011 with US$13,253.1 million, there has also been strong growth in Vietnam's exports to China from US$5,430 in 2009 to US$11,613.3 million in 2011.

The trade deficit issue has been raised in high-level bilateral talks and the two sides seem to agree that the growing imbalance in bilateral trade needs to be addressed. The stated aim is to promote an economic relationship that is mutually beneficial and characterized by a "win-win" outcome.[46] However, the sharply increasing trade deficit of Vietnam indicates that the two sides need to agree on more efficient measures to ensure that a "win-win" outcome is achieved.

Shared Rivers[47]

Chinese development projects upstream along primarily the Mekong River are a concern to Vietnam since its main rice-producing region is the Mekong Delta. Constructions of dams by China upstream along the Mekong River do concern Vietnam due to their possible impact on the water levels downstream. In fact any activity along the Mekong River that would reduce the supply of water downstream would be considered a cause for concern by Vietnam. Thus, activities in China is of considerable interest to Vietnam and such activities could cause tension in bilateral relations if they would be perceived as having an impact on the Mekong River to the detriment of Vietnam.

The issue does not appear to be on the agenda for discussion at high-level meetings. However, Vietnam has raised the issue of shared rivers and the management of waters in both the Red River and the Mekong River in connection with talks with representatives from China's Yunnan province in recent years.[48]

WHAT LEGACY OF HISTORY?

Given the long history of relations between China and Vietnam there are potentially numerous historical events and experiences that can be recalled in modern times, both positive and negative. The perception of the historical interaction between China and Vietnam may differ considerably in the two countries. Given the asymmetric[49] relationship throughout history between the much larger China and the smaller Vietnam, and also the legacy of longer and shorter periods of direct Chinese control over Vietnam, it is safe to argue that China is of greater importance to Vietnam than Vietnam is to China in their respective foreign policies and also that China impacts on Vietnam — in particular in the north of Vietnam — to a larger extent than Vietnam impacts on China. As argued in a recent article, China is Vietnam's most important partner and a geostrategic challenge.[50] The fact that the capital of Vietnam — Hanoi — is located in the north of the country strengthens the importance of China in Vietnam's geostrategic outlook; conversely, with Beijing located in the northeast of China, Vietnam is more peripheral to China's geostrategic outlook compared with the Korean Peninsula, Japan and Russia, which are relatively closer. Having said this, Vietnam does carry importance to China even at the central level for both historical and ideological reasons, i.e., both a long shared history and shared ideological ideals in the form of the ruling Communist parties.

The historical interaction between China and Vietnam can provide both positive and negative references and experiences to the collective memories and to policy formulation in China and Vietnam, respectively, in modern times. Periods of militarized conflicts display animosity and bad relations between the two countries. The interesting thing with the periods of militarized conflicts — in particular the major military attacks or interventions carried out by China after Vietnam regained independence in the tenth century — is that they have all eventually ended with Vietnam preserving or re-establishing autonomy. This is from a Vietnamese perspective considered to be a tradition of "defeating" attacks from China. Such "victories" against China are displayed in the Museum of History in Hanoi and some of them are still commemorated in Vietnam on a yearly basis. Hence, Vietnam does consider itself capable of resisting China and there is no feeling of inferiority. The latter is in sharp contrast to how parts of the Cambodian elite perceive Vietnam and the Vietnamese, i.e., as threatening, and the Cambodians act from a perspective of weakness.[51]

The longer period of direct Chinese control of Vietnam and the shorter one in the fifteenth century are points of reference for those who want to highlight China's past policies of aiming at controlling Vietnam and in fact controlling Vietnam for a very long period — over 1,000 years. Also, in relation to this dimension, the fact that Vietnam has from its own perspective successfully managed to regain its autonomy and independence has contributed to both enhance Vietnam's self-confidence that it can successfully cope with perceived threats emanating from China and to reduce the feeling that China threatens Vietnam's independence.

The legacy of the long period of the tributary relationship between China and Vietnam is not only one of Vietnamese rulers paying tribute to the Chinese emperors, but a much more multifaceted form of interaction between China and Vietnam. Politically, it was not a one-way process in which Vietnam paid tribute to China, but a process in which Vietnamese rulers gained legitimacy through their relationship with the Chinese emperors. Thus, it was beneficial to both parties. The multifaceted interaction between China and Vietnam was evident in political thinking, in the role of Confucianism, and in the cultural sphere. The legacy of this close interaction is a number of similarities between China and Vietnam. The legacy for today's relations between the two countries is not as evident given that it has been shaped more by the close contacts between the two Communist parties and the very close relationship between the DRV and China. Also, in the period since full normalization in late 1991, the party–

party relations combined with expanding collaboration in various fields between the two countries contributed to create a very close relationship. As can be expected in periods of good relations, the official perception and projection of historical relations has been positive and emphasizes the collaborative aspects of the long history of bilateral relations.

Crisis and the Legacy of History: A Case Study of Official Perceptions in 1979

A pertinent question is how is history perceived, remembered and referred to in periods of crisis or when relations are in bad shape. The deterioration in relations of the late 1970s provides an insight into the role of history in a period of deep crisis and open militarized conflict. This was in fact the most recent such crisis and militarized conflict between China and Vietnam. In October 1979 Vietnam's Ministry of Foreign Affairs issued the most authoritative official publication presenting Vietnam's grievances against China. This publication outlined the official Vietnamese position on its relations with China following the deterioration of relations in the late 1970s and the border war of February–March 1979. The publication reflected the perceptions of the Vietnamese leadership within the context of the deterioration of bilateral relations with China. It was also shaped by ideological and nationalistic vocabulary. As it is an evidently subjective publication, it only presents Vietnam's views. However, in the context of identifying Vietnam's official views, the publication is a valuable source of information.

In the publication, little attention is devoted to historical relations, and focus is on developments since 1954, i.e., "Over the Last 30 Years".[52] Only two references are made to events prior to 1954, and they appear towards the end of the publication. The first is an observation that "Over several thousands years in the past, Viet Nam has been invaded scores of times by Chinese emperors."[53] The second states that:

> Viet Nam will stand firm and continue to develop, in spite of all the devilish schemes of the Peking rulers, as it has stood firm and continued to develop over the past 4,000 years in the face of continual invasions by Chinese emperors.[54]

The two quotes display that Vietnam recalled earlier military attacks by China and that the country's intention was to prevail as it had done throughout history. This fits well within the above mentioned Vietnamese interpretation of its "successful" resistance to Chinese military attacks and attempts at domination over Vietnam. However, the fact that the focus of the publication was on developments from 1954 indicates that the grievances Vietnam had against China related to Chinese actions during this modern period of time.

Vietnam formulated three main grievances against China. The first related to China's role at the Geneva Conference in 1954 which resulted in the partition of Vietnam.[55] The second was China's attitude and policies towards the "liberation of South Vietnam and the reunification of the country" during the period 1954 to 1975.[56] The third was China's policy towards Vietnam since 1975, i.e., the end of the Second Indochina War.[57]

According to the Vietnamese, China actively influenced the outcome of the Geneva Conference that led to the partition of Vietnam along the 17th parallel. Although the Vietminh was in a position to liberate the whole country, Vietnam had to accept the division along the 17th parallel due to Chinese pressure to do so. In other words, China worked against the interests of Vietnam at the conference and then pressured Vietnam to accept partition.[58]

The second grievance encompasses accusations against China during different periods of time between 1954 and 1975. From 1954 to 1964, China hampered the "Vietnamese people's struggle for national reunification".[59] From 1965 to 1969, China was accused of "undermining and prolonging" the war of resistance of the Vietnamese people.[60] During the period 1969–73, China was accused of negotiating with the United States behind Vietnam's "back". The focal point being China's improved relations with the United States leading to President Richard Nixon's visit to China in February 1972.[61]

During the period 1973–75, Vietnam accused China of working against the full "liberation" of the south of Vietnam. In fact Vietnam accused China of not honouring its pledge for continued support at the same level as in 1973. China was accused of colluding with the United States and even with the "Saigon regime". Furthermore, China was accused of "Turning Kampuchea into a spring-board for attacking Viet Nam" through support for the actions and policies of the "Pol Pot–Ieng Sary clique".[62]

The third grievance encompasses accusations during the period May 1975 to 1979. The accusations related to "Frenzied but still covert anti–Viet Nam activities". First, against the South of Vietnam through the activities of the "Pol Pot–Ieng Sary clique" during the period 1975 to 1977. Second, by using the "Hoa (Chinese) nationals" to "undermine" Vietnam "from inside". Third, by using aid to increase the pressure on Vietnam both by rejecting Vietnam's request for "further aid" in 1975 and by delaying the delivery of already committed aid to Vietnam.[63] According to the Vietnamese, China then proceeded to implement a policy aimed at "Systematically and openly opposing" Vietnam. First, Vietnam claimed that China "fabricated the so-called problem of 'victimized residents' to openly start a large-scale campaign against" Vietnam. Vietnam put the blame on China for the exodus of "Hoa" (ethnic Chinese) from Vietnam starting in the spring of 1978. Second, China cut off aid and withdrew its experts in an effort to hurt Vietnam. Third, China was accused of creating a tense situation in the north along the land border between China and Vietnam, in the southwest along the border between Cambodia and Vietnam by supporting the "genocidal Pol Pot–Ieng Sary clique", and in the west by putting pressure on Laos to distance itself from Vietnam. Fourth, China was accused of escalating its policies against Vietnam by attacks from two directions in the southwest through the "genocidal Pol Pot–Ieng Sary clique" and in the north where China launched a "war of aggression" against Vietnam on 17 February 1979. Vietnam defeated both attacks. Finally, China continued to "oppose Viet Nam by all means".[64]

China responded to the Vietnamese publication by producing a publication of its own. This publication was specifically aimed at refuting Vietnam's claims.[65] As in the case of Vietnam's publication, the Chinese publication outlined China's views on the relationship between the two countries. Thus, it was also subjective as it was aimed only at outlining China's views from China's perspective. However, in the context of this study — since the specific aim is to identify China's official views and policies — the publication is a useful source of information.

The Chinese publication is divided into three parts: the first more general in character entitled "Confession and Scandal",[66] the second dealing with the first two main grievances of the Vietnamese book, i.e., up to 1975,[67] and the third dealing with accusations in the post-1975 period.[68]

The first part refutes all accusation made by Vietnam and also highlights that China and Vietnam had earlier enjoyed a very good relationship and that China had provided Vietnam with extensive support in the struggle against both France and the United States. It puts the blame for the deterioration of bilateral relations on Vietnam. It argues that the book shows that Vietnam's "attempt to achieve hegemony in Southeast Asia and its anti-China policy are two aspects of one and the same thing". Vietnam is accused of not only turning to the Soviet Union for aid but also to "follow Moscow more closely in hostility to China, acting as the 'Cuba of Asia'".[69]

The second part refutes the accusation of Vietnam relating to the "Anti-French and Anti-American Struggle" and outlines in details the extent of China's support to Vietnam during this long period of struggle. China refutes the claim that the outcome of the Geneva Conference of 1954 was reached against the will of the Vietnamese.[70] In addition to rejecting the accusations relating to the 1954–75 period, the Chinese publication also outlines the amount of support China provided to Vietnam in terms of civilian and military aid as well as diplomatic support.[71]

The third part refutes the Vietnamese claims and accusations and outlines a number of accusations against Vietnam's behaviour and policies during the second half of the 1970s. First, China outlines that despite its internal problems it continued to provide aid to Vietnam after 1975.[72] Second, China claims that Vietnam "embarked on a course of aggression and expansion, trying to rig up an 'Indochina federation', dip its finger in the Gulf of Thailand and dominate Southeast Asia".[73] Third, Chinese territory had also "become a target for Vietnamese aggression"; first, in 1975, Vietnam had sent troops to "occupy six islands in China's Nansha island group", i.e., in the Spratlys. Furthermore, Vietnam had created disputes along the land border between the two countries.[74] Fourth, beginning in April 1978 Vietnam was accused of having launched a "large scale campaign against China and Chinese nationals"; this had resulted in over 200,000 refugees being "driven into China", among them "many Chinese residents".[75] Fifth, in February 1979 the "armed intrusions into Chinese border areas" by Vietnam "had taxed China's forbearance to the limit and forced the Chinese frontier guards to undertake a necessary while at the same time limited counter-attack in self-defence".[76] Finally, it is argued that,

> It is easy to see that the policy for regional hegemony pursued by Hanoi at the instigation of the Soviet Union is the root cause of the hostilities in Indochina, the unrest in Southeast Asia and the deterioration in Sino–Vietnamese relations during the past few years.[77]

The accusations and counter-accusations presented in the two publications clearly display the extent to which the relations between China and

Vietnam deteriorated during the second half of the 1970s. The Vietnamese publication was formulated as a "White Book" about negative aspects of China's policies towards Vietnam, and thus it did put emphasis primarily on negative aspects of China's policies and actions throughout the period since 1954. The Chinese publication was partly formulated as a response to the Vietnamese publication, and thus one aim was to refute the Vietnamese claims and accusations. The Chinese publication did put emphasis on positive aspects of its policies throughout the periods since the 1950s and on the good bilateral relations up to 1975. In relation to the post-1975 period, the Chinese publication focused on negative aspects of Vietnam's policies and actions.

CONCLUDING REMARKS

China and Vietnam share a long history of relations marked by extended periods of collaboration and shorter periods of military conflict. Vietnam was for more than a thousand years a part of the Chinese empire before regaining independence in the tenth century AD. The independent Vietnam remained under Chinese cultural and political influence and a tributary relationship developed. The period of French colonial rule in Vietnam during the second half of the nineteenth century and the first half of the twentieth ended this close relationship.

After Vietnam regained independence from France in 1954, relations between China and Vietnam were officially very close up to the end of the Second Indochina War in 1975. Thereafter, relations deteriorated into open hostilities in early 1979, and tension remained high for most of the 1980s. From the late 1980s relations started to improve, leading to full normalization in November 1991. The 1990s were characterized by two contradictory trends: expanding and improving relations in most fields on the one hand, and recurring periods of tension relating to border disputes on the other. Both countries are making considerable efforts to manage and eventually settle the border disputes. The major part of the first decade of the 2000s was characterized by less tension compared to the 1990s, relating to territorial issues and expanding political and economic relations. During the period 2009–11, tension periodically increased, and in response the two countries moved to step up their dispute management efforts.

The future development of the relationship between China and Vietnam will be determined by how successfully the two sides handle disputed issues. Deepening bilateral cooperation in different fields and expanding economic interaction has contributed to building a more stable bilateral relationship. The progress in managing the territorial disputes has also positively contributed to the prospect of long-term stability in the bilateral relationship.

Despite these positive developments, the disputes in the South China Sea remain a threat to a stable relationship, both through the overlapping sovereignty claims to the Paracel and Spratly archipelagos and the disputes over resources in maritime areas. Potential future challenges to the bilateral relations include risks associated with economic competition and uneven trade relations, as well as risks associated with developments affecting the Mekong River.

The long historical relationship will continue to have a strong legacy on China–Vietnam relations, mainly a positive one given that the relationship has been characterized by long periods of collaboration. However, in periods of bilateral tension, less harmonious periods in the history of relations will be highlighted, although the main factors in, for example, the deterioration of relations in the late 1970s, were directly connected with the then ongoing developments and the grievances articulated by Vietnam related to events from 1954 onwards.

The official bilateral relationship is of course elite driven and there is a mutual interest in promoting good relations and expanding these relations. Thus, there is an interest in promoting a positive image of the relationship between the two countries. This extends to how the historical interaction is being portrayed. The elites also have an interest in managing and containing disputed issues, and the territorial issues have been a particular challenge since full normalization of relations in late 1991. Notable progress has been made by settling the land border and Tonkin Gulf issues and also in better managing tension in the South China Sea, although the latter remains a source of controversy and leads to periodic tension. Of interest is of course the fact that the sovereignty claims of both China and Vietnam to the Paracel and Spratly archipelagos are based on historical arguments.

Although the official relationship is elite driven, it would be wrong to assume that there is limited people-to-people contact. The land border between the two countries is the scene of extensive contact between the populations on both sides. Trade has grown considerably over the last two decades. There is also considerable Chinese tourism in Vietnam, in particular in the northern part of Vietnam. The exchanges and interaction in the fields of education and culture can also be noted. In other words, the relationship between the two countries is multifaceted.

Notes

1. Information derived from Ramses Amer, "Vietnam–China Relations", in *Berkshire Encyclopedia of China*, vol. 2, *Tangshan Earthquake, Great to ZUO Zongtan*, edited by Karen Christensen and Linsun Cheng (Great Barrington, MA: Berkshire, 2009), p. 2394; Ramses Amer, "Indochina–China Relations", in *Berkshire Encyclopedia of China*, vol. 3, *Huai River to Old Prose Movement*, edited by Karen Christensen and Linsun Cheng (Great Barrington, MA: Berkshire, 2009), p. 1154; Ramses Amer, "Sino–Vietnamese Relations", in *Southeast Asia: A Historical Encyclopedia, From Angkor Wat to East Timor*, vol. 3, R–Z, edited by Ooi Keat Gin (Santa Barbara, CA: ABC-CLIO, 2004), p. 1213; and Ramses Amer, "Sino–Vietnamese Wars", in ibid., p. 1216. References will be made to more detailed studies in the section.
2. For a detailed study on developments up to the sixth century, see Jennifer Holmgren, *Chinese Colonisation of Northern Vietnam: Administrative Geography and Political Development in the Tonking Delta First to Sixth Centuries A.D.*, Oriental Monograph Series no. 27, Faculty of Asian Studies (Canberra ACT: Australian National University, 1980).
3. Ibid., pp. 171–73.
4. Joseph Buttinger, *A Dragon Defiant: A Short Story of Vietnam* (Newton Abbot, Devon: David & Charles, 1972), pp. 36–37.
5. For more details about the interaction between China and Vietnam, see Gabriel Devéria, *Histoire des relations de la Chine avec L'Annam – Vietnam du XVI au XIX siècle* [History of the relations of China with Annam – Vietnam from the 16th to the 19th centuries] (Paris: Ernest Leroux éditeur, 1880); *Historical Interaction of China and Vietnam: Institutional and Cultural Themes*, compiled by Edgar Wickberg, International Studies, East Asian Series Research Publication no. 4 (Center for East Asian Studies, University of Kansas, 1969); and Alexander Barton Woodside, *Vietnam and the Chinese Model: A Comparative Study of the Nguyên and Ch'ing Civil Government in the First Half of the Nineteenth Century* (Cambridge, MA: Harvard University Press, 1971).
6. The patterns of Chinese migration and the policies of Vietnamese dynasties towards the migrants is analysed by Riichirio Fujiwara, "Vietnamese Dynasties' Policies toward Chinese Immigrants", *Acta Asiatica*, no. 18 (March 1970), pp. 43–69. For a detailed analysis of the role of Chinese migrants in expanding Vietnamese control in the Mekong River delta, see Paul Boudet, "La conquête de la Cochinchine par les Nguyên et le rôle des émigrés chinois" [The conquest of

Cochinchine by the Nguyens and the role of the Chinese migrants], *Bulletin de l'École Française d'Extrême-Orient* 42 (1942): 115–32. See also Émile Gaspardone, "Un chinois des mers du sud: Le fondateur de Hà-tiên" [A Chinese from the South Seas: The founder of Hatien], *Journal Asiatique* [Asiatic journal] vol. 240 (1952): 363–85.

7. For a detailed analysis of the Geneva Conference of 1954 with a focus on the role played by China, see François Joyaux, *La China et le règlement du premier conflict d'Indochine (Genève 1954)* [China and the settlement of the First Indochina Conflict (Geneva 1954)], Série internationale – 9, Université de Paris-I Panthéon-Sorbonne, Institut d'histoire des relations internationals contemporaines (IHRIC) (Paris: Publication de la Sorbonne, 1979).

8. Information derived from Amer, "Vietnam–China", p. 2394; Amer, "Indochina–China", p. 1155; and Amer, "Sino–Vietnamese", pp. 1213–14. More detailed studies on China–Vietnam relations and key issues and dimensions during this period include: W.R. Smyser, *The Independent Vietnamese: Vietnamese Communism between Russia and China 1956–1969*, Papers in International Studies, Southeast Asia, no. 55 (Athens: Centre for International Studies, Ohio University, 1980) and Victor C. Funnell, "Vietnam and the Sino–Soviet Conflict 1965–1976", *Studies in Comparative Communism* 11, nos. 1–2 (1978): 42–169. Two more recent studies are Lien-Hang T. Nguyen, "The Sino-Vietnamese Split and the Indochina War, 1968–1975", in *The Third Indochina War: Conflict between China, Vietnam and Cambodia, 1972–79*, edited by Odd Arne Westad and Sophie Quinn-Judge (London: Routledge, 2006), pp. 12–32; and Jian Chen, "China, the Vietnam War, and the Sino–American rapprochement, 1968–1973" in ibid., pp. 33–64.

9. For details on the claims made by Vietnam in the late 1970s, see *The Truth About Viet Nam–China Relations over the Last 30 Years* (Hanoi: Ministry of Foreign Affairs, Socialist Republic of Vietnam, 1979) (hereafter *The Truth About*). For China's response, see *On the Vietnamese Foreign Ministry's White Book Concerning Viet Nam–China Relations*, by *People's Daily* and Xinhua News Agency Commentators (Beijing: Foreign Languages Press, 1979) (hereafter *On the Vietnamese*).

10. The information in this section is derived from Ramses Amer, "Sino–Vietnamese Normalization in the Light of the Crisis of the Late 1970s", *Pacific Affairs* 67, no. 3 (1994): pp. 358–66; Ramses Amer, "Sino–Vietnamese Relations: Past, Present and Future", in *Vietnamese Foreign Policy in Transition*, edited by Carlyle A. Thayer and Ramses Amer (Singapore: Institute of Southeast Asian Studies; New York: St Martin's Press, 1999), pp. 69–102; and Ramses Amer, "Assessing Sino–Vietnamese Relations through the Management of Contentious Issues", *Contemporary Southeast Asia* 26, no. 2 (2004): 320–21.

11. The deterioration of relations between China and Vietnam, the conflict between Vietnam and Cambodia and the interlinkages between the two conflicts and

their regional and international ramifications created what has been termed the "Third Indochina Conflict" and the "Third Indochina War". The developments have been the subject of attention in the scholarly literature; see, for example, Nayan Chanda, *Brother Enemy: The War after the War: A History of Indochina since the Fall of Saigon* (Orlando: Harcourt Brace Jovanovich, 1986); Grant Evans and Kelvin Rowley, *Red Brotherhood at War: Indochina since the Fall of Saigon* (London: Verso Editions, 1984); Steven J. Hood, *Dragons Entangled: Indochina and the China–Vietnam War* (Armonk: East Gate, 1992); Robert R. Ross, *The Indochina Tangle: China's Vietnam Policy 1975–1979* (New York: East Asian Institute, Columbia University, Columbia University Press, 1988); *The Third Indochina Conflict*, edited by David W.P. Elliot (Boulder, CO: Westview, 1982); and Westad and Quinn-Judge, eds., *The Third Indochina War*. For more specifically on China–Vietnam, see, for example, William J. Duiker, *China and Vietnam: The Roots of Conflict*, Indochina Research Monograph no. 1 (Berkeley: Institute of East Asian Studies, University of California, 1986); and Anne Gilks, *The Breakdown of the Sino–Vietnamese Alliance, 1970–1979*, China Research Monograph no. 39 (Berkeley: Institute of East Asian Studies, University of California, 1982).

12. In this study, the Soviet Union is used as synonymous with the Union of Soviet Socialist Republics (USSR).

13. The term Cambodia is used in this study unless the name of the country is included in a quotation from a primary source using a different terminology.

14. For details on talks relating to the ethnic Chinese, see Ramses Amer, *The Ethnic Chinese in Vietnam and Sino–Vietnamese Relations* (Kuala Lumpur: Forum, 1991), pp. 57–76.

15. For a detailed study of the Chinese attack, see King C. Chen, *China's War with Vietnam, 1979: Issues, Decisions, and Implication* (Stanford: Stanford University, Hoover Institution Press, 1987).

16. For a detailed overview relating to military activity along the land border during the 1980s, see Edward C. O'Dowd, *Chinese Military Strategy in the Third Indochina War: The Last Maoist War* (London: Routledge, 2007), pp. 89–107.

17. For a theoretical analysis of the normalization process in terms of conflict resolution, see Ramses Amer, "Explaining the Resolution of the China–Vietnam Conflict: How Relevant is Zartman's 'Ripeness Theory'?", *Asian Journal of Political Science* 12, no. 2 (2004): 109–25.

18. Total figures for bilateral trade for 1995, 1999, 2005, 2007, 2009, 2010, and 2011 are derived from "Imports of Goods by Country Group, by Country and Territory", from the website of the General Statistics Office of Vietnam <http://www.gso.gov.vn/default_en.aspx?tabid=472&idmid=3&ItemID=14 606> (accessed 26 February 2014) (hereafter "Imports of Goods") (the table evidently displays the figures over total imports from China in 2011 under

India — as available information indicates continued growth in imports from China and not a sharp decline as displayed in the table); and from "Exports of Goods by Country Group, by Country and Territory", from the website of the General Statistics Office of Vietnam <http://www.gso.gov.vn/default_en.asp x?tabid=472&idmid=3&ItemID=14611> (accessed 26 February 2014) (hereafter "Exports of Goods").

19. "Vietnam–China Economic Ties Continue Growth", from the website of Viet Nam Ministry of Foreign Affairs <http://www.mofa.gov.vn/en/ nr040807104143/nr040807105001/ns080602095212/newsitem_print_preview> (accessed 25 September 2012).

20. Figures derived from "Foreign Direct Investment Projects Licensed by Main Counterparts (Accumulation of projects having effect as of 31/12/2012)", from the website of the General Statistics Office of Vietnam <http://www. gso.gov.vn/default_en.aspx?tabid=472&idmid=3&ItemID=14606> (accessed 13 August 2012).

21. This can be illustrated by the following figures from up to the end of 2012 that the cumulative number of project listed under "Hong Kong SAR (China)" was 705 but the cumulative registered capital was US$11,966.7 million (see ibid.).

22. In the context of this study, high-level meetings include meetings between or in connection with visits by presidents, prime ministers, and the secretary generals of the CPC and CPV, respectively. They are listed in the order that they have been featured in joint statements and joint communiqués issued in connection with high-level meetings.

23. The following key documents have been consulted: The joint communiqué from the then prime minister Wen Jiabao's visit to Hanoi on 6–7 October 2004 ("China–Vietnam Issues a Joint Communiqué", from the website of the Ministry of Foreign Affairs of the People's Republic of China <http://www.fmprc.gov. cn/eng/wjb/zzjg/gjlb//2792/2793/t163759.htm> [accessed 3 June 2008]). The Joint Statement issued in connection with the visit of the then president of Vietnam, Tran Duc Luong, to China on 18–22 July 2005 ("Vietnam and China Issue Joint Statement", from the website of Viet Nam Ministry of Foreign Affairs <http://www.mofa.gov.vn/en/nr040807104143/nr040807105001/ ns050726144049/view#ccLEVPzhsk9a> [accessed 26 July 2005]). The joint communiqué issued in connection with the visit by Nong Duc Manh the then secretary general of the CPV to China on 22–26 August 2006 ("Vietnam–China Joint Communiqué", from the website of *Nhan Dan* <http://www.nhandan.com. vn/english/news/250806/domestic_commu.htm> [accessed 26 June 2008]). The joint statement issued in connection with the visit to Vietnam by China's then president Hu Jintao on 15–17 November 2006 ("Vietnam–China Joint Statement", from the website of *Nhan Dan* <http://www.nhandan.com.vn/

english/news/171106/domestic_vnchi.htm> [accessed 26 September 2007]). The joint press communiqué issued in connection with the visit by Vietnam's then president, Nguyen Minh Triet, to China on 15–18 May 2007 ("Vietnam and China Issue Joint Press Communiqué", from the website of *Nhan Dan* <http://www.nhandan.com.vn/english/news/190507/domestic_pr.htm> (accessed 26 September 2007) (hereafter "Vietnam and China Issue"). The joint statement issued in connection with the visit to China by the then secretary general of the CPV, Nong Duc Manh, from 30 May to 2 June 2008 ("Vietnam and China Issue Joint Statement", from the website of *Nhan Dan* <http://www.nhandan.com.vn/english/news/020608/ domestic_vn.htm> [accessed 4 June 2008]). The joint statement issued in connection with the visit to China by Vietnam's Prime Minister Nguyen Tan Dung on 22–25 October 2008 ("Vietnam, China Reach Awareness to Enrich Partnership", from the website of Viet Nam Ministry of Foreign Affairs <http://www.mofa.gov.vn/en/ nr040807104143/nr040807105001/ns081027154132> [accessed 27 October 2008]). The joint statement issued in connection with the visit to China by the secretary general of the CPV, Nguyen Phu Trong, on 11–15 October 2011 ("Vietnam–China Joint Statement", Communist Party of Vietnam Online Newspaper <http://www.cpv.org.vn/cpv/Modules/News/NewsDetail. aspx?co_id=30107&cn_id=48489> [accessed 14 August 2013]). The joint statement issued in connection with the visit to China by Vietnam's president Truong Tan Sang on 19–21 June 2013 ("Viet Nam, China Issue Joint Statement", from the website of Viet Nam Ministry of Foreign Affairs <http://www.mofa. gov.vn/en/nr040807104143/nr040807105001/ns130624152141/newsitem_ print_preview> [accessed 28 June 2013]) (hereafter "Joint Statement — June 2013"). The joint statement issued in connection with the visit to Vietnam by China's Prime Minister Li Keqiang on 13–15 October 2013 ("VN, China Issue Joint Statement", from the website of Viet Nam Ministry of Foreign Affairs <http://www.mofa.gov.vn/en/nr040807104143/nr040807105001/ ns131016041515/newsitem_print_preview> [accessed 1 November 2013]) (hereafter "Joint Statement – October 2013").

24. For an overview of incidents during this period, see Ramses Amer, "The Sino–Vietnamese Approach to Managing Border Disputes: Lessons, Relevance and Implications for the South China Sea Situation", in *The South China Sea: Cooperation for Regional Security and Developments, Proceedings of the International Workshop, Co-organized by the Diplomatic Academy of Vietnam and the Vietnam Lawyers' Association, 26–27 November 2009, Hanoi, Vietnam,* edited by Tran Truong Thuy (Hanoi: The Gioi Publishers and Diplomatic Academy of Vietnam, 2010), pp. 264–67.

25. Information derived from Ramses Amer and Nguyen Hong Thao, "Vietnam's Border Disputes: Legal and Conflict Management Dimensions", in *The Asian*

Yearbook of International Law, vol. 12 (2005–2006), edited by B.S. Chimni, Miyoshi Masahiro and Thio Li-ann (Leiden: Nijhoff, 2007), pp. 117–21.

26. "Joint Statement: On the completion of the demarcation and markers placement on the entire land border line between Vietnam and China", from the website of Viet Nam Ministry of Foreign Affairs <http://www.mofa. gov.vn/en/cn_vakv/ca_tbd/nr040818094447/ns090106100042> [accessed 8 January 2009]). See also "China–Vietnam, Land Boundary Survey Work Completed 2008/12/31", from the website of the Ministry of Foreign Affairs, People's Republic of China <http://www.fmprc.gov.cn/eng/zxxx/t530192. htm> (accessed 8 January 2009); and "Vietnam and China Fulfil Land Border Demarcation", from the website of *Nhan Dan* <http://www.nhandan.com. vn/english/news/life/010109/ life_biengioi.htm> [accessed 8 January 2009]).

27. For an overview of incidents in 2009 and 2010, see Ramses Amer, "Vietnam in 2009: Facing the Global Recession", *Asian Survey* 50, no. 1 (2010): 215–16; Ramses Amer, "Vietnam in 2010: Regional Leadership", *Asian Survey* 51, no. 1 (2011): 200; and Ramses Amer, "Dispute Settlement and Conflict Management in the South China Sea: Assessing Progress and Challenges", in *The South China Sea: Towards A Region of Peace, Security and Cooperation*, edited by Tran Truong Thuy (Hanoi: The Gioi Publishers and Diplomatic Academy of Vietnam, 2011), p. 266. For details about developments in 2011, see Ramses Amer and Jianwei Li, "Recent Developments in the South China Sea: An Assessment of the Core Bilateral Relationship between China and Vietnam", in *Maritime Security Issues in the South China Sea and the Arctic: Sharpened Competition or Collaboration?* edited by Gordon Houlden and Nong Hong (Beijing: China Democracy and Legal System Publishing, 2012), pp. 43–59. For developments up to 2013, see Ramses Amer, "China, Vietnam and the South China Sea. Disputes and Dispute Management", *Ocean Development and International Law* 45, no. 1 (2014), pp. 17–40.

28. The approach used in this section is derived from Amer, "Sino–Vietnamese Relations", pp. 108–14; and Amer, "Assessing Sino-Vietnamese", pp. 328–37. For a broad overview on the border issues in Sino–Vietnamese relations, see Ramses Amer, "Sino–Vietnamese Border Disputes", in *Beijing's Power and China's Borders: Twenty Neighbors in Asia*, edited by Bruce Elleman, Stephen Kotkin and Clive Schofield (Armonk, New York: Sharpe, 2012), pp. 295–309.

29. For a more detailed analysis of the events relating to the territorial disputes in Sino–Vietnamese relations from late 1991 to the end of 2000, see Ramses Amer, *The Sino-Vietnamese Approach to Managing Boundary Disputes*, Maritime Briefing 3, no. 5 (Durham: International Boundaries Research Unit, University of Durham, 2002), pp. 8–35, 49–58. Unless otherwise stated, information is derived from ibid., pp. 8–58.

30. See ibid., pp. 9–14, 50–58; Amer, "Assessing Sino–Vietnamese", pp. 329–31; Amer and Nguyen, "Vietnam's Border Disputes", pp. 118–22; Ramses Amer and Nguyen Hong Thao, "The Management of Vietnam's Border Disputes: What Impact on Its Sovereignty and Regional Integration?", *Contemporary Southeast Asia* 27, no. 3 (2005): 433–34; and Ramses Amer and Nguyen Hong Thao, "Vietnam's Border Disputes: Assessing the Impact on Its Regional Integration", in *Vietnam's New Order: International Perspectives on the State and Reform in Vietnam*, edited by Stéphanie Balme and Mark Sidel (Houndmills, Basingstoke: Palgrave Macmillan, 2007), pp. 74–76.

31. The thirteenth round of government-level talks were held in Beijing on 19–20 January 2007 ("Vietnam and China Issue"; and "Viet Nam, China Hold Government-level Border Negotiations", from the website of Viet Nam Ministry of Foreign Affairs (<http://www.mofa.gov.vn/en/nr040807104143/nr040807105001/ns070122102447>) [accessed 3 June 2008]).

32. For details, see Amer and Li, "Recent Developments", pp. 60–62; and Amer, "China, Vietnam", pp. 20–28.

33. The eleventh round of talks on "sea issues" was held on 10–12 July 2006 ("Vietnam and China Show Goodwill on Sea Issues," from the website of *Nhan Dan* (http://www.nhandan.com.vn/english/news/130706/domestic_vn.htm) (accessed 8 August 2008)). At a meeting in Hanoi on 27–29 November 2007 between the Vietnamese and Chinese delegations to the "Sino–Vietnamese Government Border and Territory Negotiation" it was agreed that the twelfth round of talks on the "Sea Issues" would be held in 2008 (*Viet Nam, China*).

34. Author's discussions with Vietnamese officials in Hanoi in September and November 1997, in December 1998, and in May 1999.

35. "VN-China Basic Principles on Settlement of Sea Issues," from the website of Viet Nam Ministry of Foreign Affairs (http://www.mofa.gov.vn/en/nr040807104143/nr040807105001/ns131016150351/newsitem_print_preview) (accessed 28 February 2014). The text has also been reproduced in Amer, "China, Vietnam", pp. 39–40.

36. For details, see ibid., pp. 26–28. For the high-level meetings in 2013, see "Joint Statement – June 2013"; and "Joint Statement – October 2013".

37. On the drilling rig incident, see Ramses Amer, "China–Vietnam Drilling Rig Incident: Reflections and Implications", Policy Brief no. 158 (2014), Nacka: Institute for Security and Development Policy; Carlyle A. Thayer, "4 Reasons China Removed Oil Rig HYSY-981 Sooner Than Planned", *The Diplomat* (2014) <http://thediplomat.com/2014/07/4-reasons-china-removed-oil-rig-hysy-981-sooner-than-planned/> (accessed 25 July 2014); and Carlyle A. Thayer, "Vietnam, China and the Oil Rig Crisis: Who Blinked?", *The Diplomat* (2014) <http://thediplomat.com/2014/08/vietnam-china-and-the-oil-rig-crisis-who-blinked/> (accessed 6 August 2014).

38. Information up to 1998 is derived from Amer, "Sino–Vietnamese Relations", pp. 113–14.

39. For reports on the renewed priority given to the fight against smuggling in late 1997, see "PM Khai Orders an All-Out War against Smugglers", *Viet Nam News* (18 October 1997), p. 1; "Smuggling, Fraud Still Rampant in 1997", ibid., p. 3; and "Ministry to Intensify Smuggling Fight", *Viet Nam News* (13 November 1997), p. 2.

40. Author's discussions with officials and researchers in Hanoi in September 1997.

41. *British Broadcasting Corporation Summary of World Broadcasts Part Three Far East*/3363 G/1 (21 October 1998) for a report carried by Xinhua News Agency; and ibid., 3364 G/1 (22 October 1998) for a report carried by the website of Vietnam News Agency (VNA).

42. The figure is derived from "2013 UNHCR Regional Operations Profile: East Asia and the Pacific. China. Statistical Snapshot", from the website of the United Nations High Commissioner for Refugees (UNHCR) <http://www.unhcr.org/cgi-bin/texis/vtx/page?page=49e487cd6&submit=GO> (accessed 21 January 2014).

43. Author's discussions with officials and researchers in Hanoi and Ho Chi Minh City in February–March 1992, November 1993, December 1994, December 1995, and November–December 1996.

44. The approach used in this section is derived from Amer, "Sino-Vietnamese Relations", pp. 108–14.

45. Figures for trade between China and Vietnam derived from "Imports of Goods" and from "Exports of Goods".

46. See note 23.

47. For a study on the relations between China and Vietnam focusing on the Greater Mekong Sub-region, see Oliver Hensengerth, *Regionalism in China–Vietnam Relations: Institution-Building in the Greater Mekong Subregion* (London: Routledge, 2009).

48. In connection with the visit of Governor Qin Guangrong of Yunnan Province to Hanoi in April 2004, he met with Vietnam's Prime Minister Nguyen Tan Dung. The prime minister "urged the Chinese official" to, among other things, "cooperate in using water of the Hong and Mekong rivers" ("PM Urges Cooperation between Border Provinces and Yunnan", from the website of Viet Nam Ministry of Foreign Affairs <http://www.mofa.gov.vn/en/nr040807104143/nr040807105001/ns070405094302/view#Gl6avVNV6Jnm> (accessed 3 June 2008)). Furthermore, when the Vietnamese prime minister visited Yunnan province on 29 October 2007, he asked "the locality to cooperate with Viet Nam in exploiting the water resources of the Hong (Red) and Mekong Rivers for mutual development" ("PM asks Yunnan to Cooperate in Using River

Water", from the website of Viet Nam Ministry of Foreign Affairs <http:// www.mofa.gov.vn/en/nr040807104143/nr040807105001/ns071030081930/ view#TXubLkSkHFBR> (accessed 3 June 2008)). More recently, in early April 2012, in connection with the visit by the governor of Yunnan Province to Hanoi, it was agreed that the two sides "should mobilise their current cooperation mechanism and make sustainable use of water resources in the two countries' border areas" ("President Hails Stronger Ties with Yunnan", from the website of Viet Nam Ministry of Foreign Affairs <http://www.mofa.gov.vn/en/ nr040807104143/nr040807105001/ns120404145555/newsitem_print_preview> [accessed 1 October 2012]).

49. For a detailed study on China–Vietnam relations focusing on the asymmetry dimension, see Brantley Womack, *China and Vietnam: The Politics of Asymmetry* (New York: Cambridge University Press, 2006).

50. For a discussion along these lines, see Amer, "Vietnam in 2009", pp. 211– 17.

51. For details about Cambodia–Vietnam relations and Cambodian elite perceptions of Vietnam, see Ramses Amer, "Cambodia and Vietnam: A Troubled Relationship", in *International Relations in Southeast Asia: Between Bilateralism and Multilateralism*, edited by N. Ganesan and Ramses Amer (Singapore: Institute of Southeast Asian Studies, 2010), pp. 92–116.

52. *The Truth About.*

53. Ibid., p. 92.

54. Ibid., p. 95.

55. Ibid., pp. 17–26.

56. Ibid., pp. 27–84.

57. Ibid., pp. 64–84.

58. Ibid., pp. 17–26.

59. Ibid., pp. 28–35.

60. Ibid., pp. 35–45.

61. Ibid., pp. 45–56.

62. Ibid., pp. 56–63.

63. Ibid., pp. 67–72.

64. Ibid., pp. 72–84.

65. *On the Vietnamese.*

66. Ibid., pp. 1–10.

67. Ibid., pp. 11–27.

68. Ibid., pp. 28–38.

69. Ibid., p. 9.

70. Ibid., pp. 14–17.

71. Ibid., pp. 11–27.

72. Ibid., pp. 29–39.

73. Ibid., p. 30.
74. Ibid., pp. 32–33.
75. Ibid., p. 33.
76. Ibid., p. 34.
77. Ibid., p. 35.

5

LEGACY OR OVERHANG:
Historical Memory in
Myanmar–Thai Relations

Maung Aung Myoe

History has often been used and misused by statesmen and political leaders to serve their national, regime or personal interests. Historical lessons are, rightly or wrongly, employed to guide the nation's domestic and foreign policy. In countries with nation-building projects, history is presented, in different formats, with a particular nationalist discourse to inform the general public of their roles and duties and to imagine their nations through lenses of a specific socio-political context. In many cases, a particular historical juncture serves as the basis for creating collective memories, shaping perceptions of self and others, framing issues and prescribing particular courses of action. In the introductory chapter to this book, N. Ganesan conceptually defines historical overhang as "a negative perception that derives from historical interactions and subsequently becomes embedded in the psyche of a state, both at the levels of the elites and the citizen body". In the context of bilateral relations in Asian countries, he argues that the historical overhangs or legacies have been kept alive and consciously cultivated and embellished in order to make them more durable and invoke emotional responses.

In Myanmar, in terms of framing a nationalist discourse, the most important historical juncture is the period of British colonial rule from 1885 to 1948. For several hundreds of years, under different dynasties, yet on more or less the same area of land, Myanmar had remained an independent polity. At one stage, Myanmar under King Bayint Naung (1551–81) extended its influence over most of present-day mainland Southeast Asia. King Sinphyu Shin (1763–76) of the Konebaung dynasty was famous for his victories over Qing troops in four military encounters (1765–69) and his subjugation of the Kingdom of Ayutthaya in 1767. Beginning with the defeat and the loss of coastal provinces in the first Anglo–Burmese War (1824), followed by yet another defeat and the loss of lower Myanmar in the second Anglo–Burmese War (1852), Myanmar eventually lost its independence in 1885. This was the most humiliating moment for the very proud people of Myanmar. Therefore, the anti-colonial struggle or national liberation movement has been the epitome of Myanmar's historiography. In a way, the modern history of Myanmar is essentially a history of national struggle against colonialism/imperialism and of endless efforts to forge a sense of unity among the people "living on the same stretch of land for immemorial time through thick and thin".

Myanmar's historical enemy, ever since it entered the modern world of nation-states in the post-colonial period, therefore, has been the British imperialists (*byi-ti-sha-nae-chae*) or "White Face imperialists" (*myet-hnar-phyu-nae-chae*), and, by extension, neo-imperialists or neo-colonialists. The negative and stereotypical image of the British imperialist was constructed and socialized to the public particularly through the national education system. However, the success or failure of such a process depends on several factors that are beyond the scope of this chapter.

As far as Myanmar–Thai relations are concerned, there is little evidence to suggest that the people of Myanmar hold strong anti-Thai sentiments and perceptions. It is basically from the perspective of the Thai people that Myanmar is considered a historical enemy of the Thai nation.

In this chapter it will be argued that a historical overhang or legacy does indeed exist in Myanmar–Thai relations, albeit mostly emanating from the Thai side. It is the Thai political elites who cautiously nurture anti-Myanmar sentiments among the Thai public and purposely employ such sentiments in Thai policy towards Myanmar. This historical overhang or legacy on the part of Thailand is more like a overhang from its historical past. This point will be illustrated in the long-lasting buffer-zone policy of the Thai government.

BRIEF OVERVIEW OF MYANMAR–THAI RELATIONS

The historical narrative and historiography of Myanmar–Thai relations is full of conflicting and controversial issues since legends became history and fictions became facts. Moreover, when history is employed as an important instrument in the making and shaping of a nation, the historical narrative tends to become a distorting mirror. The first military encounter between the two polities (or kingdoms), Myanmar and Siam, according to *Thai Rop Phama* (Thai punch Myanmar), took place near Chiang Kran in the year 1539, soon after the conquest by Myanmar of the coastal city of Martaban. Although Myanmar's chronicles do mention King Tabin Shwehti's subjugation of Martaban in the year 1540, they do not mention anything about battles in Chiang Kran. As far as Myanmar's sources are concerned, the first (major) military encounter with the Thais took place in 1548 during the reign of King Tabin Shwehti.

Historically, the extent and influence of the Bagan (Pagan) Empire, which existed from the eleventh to the thirteenth century, according to an inscription dated 1196, reached as far south as Cape Salang or Junk Ceylon in the northern part of the Malay Peninsula. The inscription mentioned that Dawei (Tavoy) and Thanintharyi (Tennasserim) were within Bagan's orbit.[1] Therefore, Myanmar's rulers in later dynasties appeared to have held a view that the whole stretch of the Thanintharyi coast, where many important commercial port cities facing the Indian Ocean are located, was part of Myanmar's sphere of influence. As these port cities generated a vast amount of revenue in "the age of commerce", control over them was important for both the Thais and Myanmar. It was in the context of struggle for domination of these port cities that military confrontations arose between the two polities. For a young, energetic and ambitious king like Tabin Shwehti, it was an indisputable fact that Myanmar exercised suzerainty over these port cities and that the attempts by the Thais to get control over Dawei in 1546–47 was nothing but a challenge to Myanmar's authority that should not be tolerated.

One of the most important and dramatic events in Myanmar–Thai relations is the "War of 1548", which marked a turning point in the bilateral relationship. The outcome of the war completely reshaped Myanmar's perception of the Thais and Ayutthaya. Until the outbreak of the "War of 1548", Myanmar had never considered the Kingdom of Ayutthaya as part of their sphere of influence. The military campaign against the Thais, which resulted in the death of Chief Queen Phra Suriyothai and the capture of the brother, son (Crown Prince Phra Ramesuan) and son-in-law (Maha Thammaracha — Viceroy of Phitsanulok) of King Phra Maha Chakkraphet, ended with the submission of the Thai king to Myanmar. He was obliged to swear an oath of allegiance, to deliver thirty war elephants and about 450 kilograms of silver per year and to surrender the custom duties collected at Thanintharyi port, in addition to immediately presenting two elephants, among other things, to obtain early release of his royal family members. As a result of this solemn promise, Tabin Shwehti called off his military expedition against Kamphaengphet, Phisanulok and Sukhothai, and returned to his capital, Hanthawaddy, by the middle of 1549. In short, Maha Chakkraphet offered to make Ayutthaya a tributary state of Myanmar (Hanthawaddy) in exchange for the release of his relatives. For the next fifteen years, Hanthawaddy was preoccupied with the issue of the royal succession and wars of pacification. Barely a year after his Ayutthaya campaign, Tabin Shwehti was assassinated and Hanthawaddy plunged into chaos. Taking advantage of the situation, Myanmar's chronicles claim that the Ayutthaya king failed to send annual tribute to the court of Myanmar.

Bayint Naung became the King of Hanthawaddy in January 1551. After several years of war for internal pacification, King Bayint Naung firmly established his authority over a vast area of the Ayarwaddy (Irrawaddy) river basin and Shan plateau. Meanwhile, he learned about the existence of four white elephants in the possession of the Thai king and, according to Myanmar's sources, he asked for two of them. When this request was refused by Maha Chakkraphat, King Bayint Naung marched his army into Ayutthaya in 1563. While the Thai king's refusal to surrender two "white elephants" was the official reason for the use of force against Ayutthaya, the real motive was undoubtedly to reassert Myanmar's authority and suzerainty over the Thai polity. Bayint Naung marched his battle-hardened and fully equipped army, with its massive firepower, into Ayutthaya in 1563, via Mae Lamao, after securing supplies from Chiang Mai and subjugating the important Thai provincial cities of Sokhothai, Phitsanulok, Sawankhalok, and Phichai. After months of siege warfare accompanied by fierce fighting and an artillery barrage by Myanmar, Chakkraphat finally surrendered in 1564. Bayint Naung installed Phra Mahin, son of Chakkraphat, as new ruler of Ayutthaya. Chakkraphat and his family, including a nine-year-old grandson, Naresuan, were taken to Hanthawaddy. (Nowhere in the Myanmar chronicles, however, one can find any mention of Naresuan [also known as Phra Naret] being taken to Hanthawaddy as a hostage.) At the request of Chakkraphat, Bayint Naung allowed the ex-king to become a monk, and, about five years later, to go on a pilgrimage to Ayutthaya. Once he reached Ayutthaya, the former Thai king, together with his son Phra Mahin, revolted against Myanmar suzerainty. Against this background, Bayint Naung marched his army to Ayutthaya for the second time in May 1568. The Viceroy of Phitsanulok, Maha Thammaracha — Phra Mahin's brother-in-law and Chakkraphat's son-in-law — fought alongside Myanmar's army. Ayutthaya put up a desperate defence against Myanmar's offensive and the siege lasted until July 1569. Bayin Naung refused Phra Mahin's offer of peace negotiations. The Thai king had proposed these when he lost his father, former king Chakkraphat. Ayutthaya finally fell to Myanmar's forces on 31 July 1569. Bayint Naung firmly reasserted Myanmar's suzerainty over Siam and, on 29 September, installed Maha Thammaracha as the vassal ruler of Ayutthaya. At least until the death of Bayint Naung in 1581, Ayutthaya did not raise the standard of revolt again.

Meanwhile, according to Thai sources, soon after he became the king of Ayutthaya, Maha Thammaracha presented his seventeen-year-old daughter Suphankalaya (Phra Suvanadewi, or Phra Suwan in Myanmar's sources)[2] to Bayint Naung to become a royal consort and to secure an early return of Naresuan, who by then was a fifteen-year-old boy. Once Naresuan arrived back at the Ayutthaya court he was made the crown prince and was sent to Phitsunalok as the viceroy. In 1590, at the age of 35, Naresuan became the King of Ayutthaya.

In the post–Bayint Naung period, Ayutthaya began to challenge Myanmar's authority. King Nanda Bayin was obliged to send his army to Ayutthaya five times, in 1582, 1585, 1586, 1590 and 1592: Myanmar's troops suffered heavy losses in every battle. In his fifth campaign against Ayutthaya, following the advice from one of his ministers, Nanda Bayin sent his crown prince to the battlefield. Myanmar's army left the capital on 5 November 1592. In the Myanmar chronicles, it is mentioned that, on 30 December 1592, during the chaos of the battle, the crown prince was hit by a canon shell and died over the neck of his war elephant.[3] (According to the Thai chronicles, this event occurred on 25 January 1593. The Thai version of this event will be explained later.) The Myanmar account is further corroborated by a contemporary record in the form of a memorandum, written by a Jesuit monk by the name of Father Nicholas Pimenta and published in 1601. The memo stated that the crown prince was shot and killed by a lead bullet, or *plumbea glande*. On the basis of this evidence, Victor Lieberman, a scholar of the history of Myanmar, claimed that the crown prince of Myanmar was indeed killed by gunshot, not by King Naresuan in an elephant duel as claimed by some Thai historical texts. When the Myanmar commanders learned of the death of the crown prince, they called off the campaign and returned home.

In 1596 Naresuan attacked Hanthawaddy but abandoned the campaign after four months. However, in 1600, when he heard that the kings of Taungoo and Rakhine had attacked Hanthawaddy, Naresuan once again marched his army to the capital. When he found out that Nanda Bayin had been taken to Taungoo as a prisoner of war, Naresuan led his troops to Taungoo, but was forced to withdraw them after a month of encampment. There were no more armed clashes between Myanmar and the Thais until the death of Naresuan in 1605. Meanwhile, in Myanmar, the early kings of the Nyaungyan dynasty were preoccupied with wars of national pacification. In fact, there was no more military conflict between the two polities for about seventy-five years. The counter-attacks by Myanmar against the alleged Thai invasions in 1675 and 1700 ended in humiliating defeats and were repelled by Thai troops.

Preoccupied with domestic issues and matters relating to the threat of invasion by Qing troops for their failure to surrender the last Ming Emperor who had taken refuge in Innwa, the kings of the Nyaungyan Dynasty did not have time to launch any military adventures against Ayutthaya. The year 1752 witnessed the fall of the Nyaungyan Dynasty and the birth of a new dynasty, known as Konebaung, in Myanmar. This also marked the resurgence of a powerful kingdom in Myanmar and the reassertion of Myanmar's suzerainty over its traditional sphere of influence. In 1759, after six years of pacification campaigns, the founder of the Konebaung Dynasty, King Alaungpaya, marched his army into Siam as Ayutthaya attacked Dawei, a town of Myanmar in the south. Yet Alaungpaya failed to reassert Myanmar's authority over Ayutthaya.

It was his son and successor, King Sinphyushin, who sent Myanmar's army into Siam, completely destroyed Ayutthaya in 1767, and made the Thais feel the full force of Myanmar's power. These events occurred because in the early days of Sinphyushin's reign the Thai king had helped Chiangmai to rebel against Myanmar and had instigated the governor of Dawei to declare independence from the Konebaung court. In response, the king ordered his armies to re-take control of these two polities and then go on to attack Ayutthaya itself. It took the two armies over a year to reach their destination. They met before the gates of Ayutthaya in January 1766. The siege of Ayutthaya lasted for almost sixteen months. Meanwhile, since 1765, the court of Myanmar at Innwa had been forced to counter invasions from Qing China. In this situation, Myanmar's forces at the gates of Ayutthaya wanted to end their siege as soon as possible so that they could reinforce the Chinese front. In April 1767 Myanmar's troops dug tunnels below the city walls and, filling them with firewood and setting them on fire, brought them down. Myanmar's troops then entered the city and captured the palace. On 9 April 1767, the Thai king, Ekatat, was found dead. The city was stripped of all valuables and all the prisoners, including Utumporn the deposed king and other members of the royal family and court officials, were taken back to Innwa. No doubt the fire destroyed much of the city. Contrary to accounts given in many Thai sources, however, many scholars of Myanmar believe that there was no massacre of the inhabitants. The city, however, did suffer heavy structural damage and remained in ruins. The fall of Ayutthaya had a deep impact on Thai perceptions of Myanmar.

FICTIONALIZED FACTS

In this brief narrative of Myanmar–Thai relations from 1548 to 1767, there are to be found at least two historical figures that have been popularized in Thai history textbooks and various Thai historical novels. While King Naresuan has been seen, undisputedly, as the most important national hero for a very long time, his grandmother Queen Suriyothai has also recently received much attention in modern Thai popular literature, movies and television series. Both of them belong to the same category of historical personages: defenders of the Kingdom of Ayutthaya in the long Thai struggle against the arch-enemy, Myanmar. Another newcomer to this heroic pantheon is Naresuan's elder sister, Princess Suphankalaya.

Myanmar's chronicles do not record the death of Queen Suriyothai in the battle. In the *Chronicle of Ayudhya*, one of the most authoritative chronicles in Thailand, however, the battle scene is vividly described in detail. Here, Suriyothai, having dressed herself as a viceroy or a crown prince (*Uparat*), accompanies her beloved husband King Chakkraphat to the battlefield and fights along with him. When she finds out that the king's elephant has made a false move in the duel, Suriyothai sacrifices her life for her king and husband, and, by extension, for her kingdom. The chronicle relates:

> Queen Suriyothai, seeing that her royal consort had lost his position and would not escape the hands of the enemy, manifested her faithfulness and, weeping, drove her royal male elephant, Song Suriya Kasat, out to rescue him. The royal elephant of the King of Pyay [Governor of Pyay] handily got its head up and lost its position. The King of Pyay reached down and slashed with his war scythe, struck Queen Suriyothai on the shoulder and cut down to about her breast. Prince Ramesuan and Prince Mahin forced their royal elephants in to intervene and save their mother but were not in time. As soon as their mother died on the neck of her elephant, the two brothers retreated to engage the enemy and were able to protect the entrance of the corpse of their mother into the capital. The troops of the capital were routed by the enemy and died in great numbers.[4]

Thai historical books, novels and movies — notably the movie titled *Suriyothai* — have all praised the heroism of the queen. The historicity of this figure, however, is questionable. Sunait Chutintaranond, a prominent Thai historian at Chulalongkorn University, pointed out that "the name [Suriyothai] undoubtedly derived from the story compiled or perhaps written by early Bangkok chroniclers",[5] indicating that this historical figure could not be found in earlier Thai chronicles. Putting this question aside, however, as Thailand entered into the modern world of nation-states in the latter half of the nineteenth century, Suriyothai's image as a faithful royal consort who devoted her life to her husband had been eventually transformed into that of a queen who sacrificed her life for the king, for the nation and for Buddhism.

While the actual nature of the battle and the circumstances surrounding the death of the crown prince of Myanmar have been subjected to different interpretations, Thai sources have described the event in eloquent terms. The noises of the battlefield are deafening, with the trumpeting of elephants and the clashing of swords and other weapons. Naresuan and his brother, mounted on elephants in must, ride ahead of their army. Soon they discover that they are alone in the midst of Myanmar's troops, accompanied only by a handful of their attendants. When the dust clears, Naresuan sees, to his surprise, the crown prince of Myanmar, whom he knew as his childhood playmate at the court of Myanmar, mounted on an elephant, resting under the shade of a tree. Naresuan then challenges the crown prince to a duel. "The Crown Prince could have ordered his arrest", wrote M.L. Manich Jumsai in his *Popular History of Thailand* published in 1976, "but feeling ashamed, he accepted the challenge and got killed at the hand of Naresuan".[6] Prince Chula Chakrabongse gives a more fascinating account in his book entitled *Lords of Life: A History of the Kings of Thailand,* published in 1960:

> They themselves [Naresuan and his brother Ekatotsatort] were riding on the necks of their elephants which were at the time in must. This made them more ferocious than usual. Hearing the tumult of the shouting, the shots fired, the clashing of naked weapons, the animals went mad and ran off in the direction of the Crown Prince of Burma, setting up such a curtain of dust in that dry season that none could see whither they were going. When the elephants did come to a halt and the dust cleared, the two brothers saw that, but for a handful of their personal guards in their red coats, who had managed somehow to follow them on foot, they were alone in the midst of the enemy.... He [Naresuan] saw the Crown Prince sitting on his elephant in the shade of a large tree, and he hailed him in a loud voice: "Elder Brother, why do you sit thus under that tree. Drive your elephant out, and let us join in single combat as we used to do in practice when we were students. Let it be a sight for our troops to see, so that it will be known that brave deeds have not yet deserted princes, nor have they lost their skill, and they can still perform the noble art of single combat on elephants."... The Crown Prince could have ordered his troops to kill or capture the Thai King and his brother, but he had the noble and royal blood of Burmese warriors in his veins, so he drove his elephant out into the open.... As the Crown Prince swept with his sabre attached to the long pole, the Black Prince [Naresuan] ducked and only the brim of his leather hat was cut off in the shape of a crescent moon. After the two elephants disengaged, they charged one another again and this time it was the Thai animal which got in below, and the hapless Crown Prince was cut in half from his shoulder to his waist. The bulk of Thai troops now arrived and a confused melee followed,

but Naresuan gave an order to permit the enemy to carry the body of
their valiant prince off the field.[7]

Many scholars of Myanmar have questioned the authenticity of this
account. Myanmar's sources do not mention any single combat or the
crown prince resting in the shade of a tree. There was confusion, and one
of Myanmar's war elephants in must, instead of attacking Naresuan's
elephant, turned to gore that of the crown prince. The crown prince
grappled to control his elephant but he received a gunshot wound
and died, still mounted on his beast. In this state of sudden confusion,
Naresuan, according to Myanmar's chronicles, not knowing of the death
of the crown prince, broke off the engagement when he became aware
that some of Myanmar's commanders were pursuing him and withdrew
to his fortress. Myanmar's chronicles state that "Naresuan lost no time
and fled to the confines of his fortress city."[8] Myanmar's commanders
decided to call off the campaign against Ayutthaya since they had lost
their crown prince.

In the context of Thai history, it was because he slew the crown prince
of Myanmar in battle and defended the Kingdom of Ayutthaya that King
Naresuan became a national hero. As far as the people of Myanmar are
concerned, however, the crown prince was killed in action by a gunshot
wound, and the elephant duel with Naresuan is merely a myth. For Thais,
however, the legendary duel is a great historic moment.

The news of the death of the crown prince reached his father Nanda
Bayin and saddened him. While standard chronicles in Myanmar do not
mention any particular reaction on the part of the king, *Yodaya Yazawin*, a
largely apocryphal account based on testimony given by people of the old
Thai capital Ayutthaya, states that the king "put to death the commanders
who accompanied the Crown Prince by putting them in a clamp and
grilling them over a fire. The anger of the king of Hanthawaddy did not
abate, and he struck and killed with his sword the *young* daughter which
Phra Naresuan's *younger sister* [sic] Chantakalya had borne by the King
of Hanthawaddy"[9] (italics in the original; it should be noted that the Thai
princess at the court of Myanmar is described as the "elder sister" of
Naresuan in other Thai historical sources). Yet, Myanmar scholars believe
that the princess was alive when Hanthawaddy fell in 1599 and that she
spent the rest of her life at the Rakhine court where she was taken after
the fall of the capital.

What is interesting is that the name and the story of the princess has never been found in Thai chronicles or in any other official Thai records. The *Yodaya Yazawin* does not identify the princess by the name of Suphankalaya, but as Chantakalya. The sudden rise of Suphankalaya's fame in the late 1990s has perplexed both Thai and Myanmar scholars. This phenomenon might be attributed to two individuals. One is a cosmetic firm owner and the other is a Thai Buddhist monk who authored a pamphlet and has claimed to have distributed 50,000 copies for charity. According to his version:

> Like his father before him, Nanda Bayin tried to subjugate Ayutthaya, now ruled by King Naresuan, the Princess' [Suphankalaya] brother. He did not succeed but during the course of this war, one of Nanda Bayin's sons was killed. Enraged, Nanda Bayin took revenge. He unsheathed his sword and killed the princess who was then eight months pregnant with his child. The implication is that Nanda Bayin suspected the princess of being a spy.

The recent glorification of Suphankalaya, who was once merely a footnote to her younger brother Naresuan, occurred at a time when the Thai people were reflecting on the economic hardships experienced in the wake of the 1997 financial crisis. People threw themselves into frenzy, purchasing memorabilia bearing her [imagined] portraits, amulets, calendars and books, in the belief that her spirit would help them overcome all their difficulties. In this context, a myth was created and a history invented, centring on the colourful story of Suphankalaya, in the tradition of what James Taylor has called "salvation histories", which tend to occur in times of Thai national crises. A central theme in this newly emerging story of Suphankalaya is that Ayutthaya was redeemed by the selfless sacrifice of the princess. Naresuan was freed from captivity and Ayutthaya subsequently regained its independence from Myanmar. Suphankalaya has consequently become a symbol of anti-Myanmar sentiment. It was perhaps in this context that, in late 1998, the Thai Third Army erected a monument to the princess in front of its headquarters in Phitsanulok and commissioned a biography.[10]

In other words, the stories of Queen Suriyothai's tragic death, of King Naresuan's slaying of the crown prince of Myanmar in a duel fought on elephants, and of Suphankalaya's sacrifice for her brother have become fictionalized in a most sensational manner.

THAI PERCEPTION OF MYANMAR

The perception and construction of Myanmar as an arch-enemy of the Thai nation in Thai historiography and in various literary works, as correctly argued by Sunait Chutintaranond, is a relatively modern phenomenon, coinciding with the age of nation-states. He points out that earlier Thai chronicles paid little attention to the wars between Siam and Myanmar. It was only after the tragic fall of Ayutthaya in 1767, that the chroniclers in the Bangkok period carefully reconstructed the events surrounding the Myanmar–Thai wars and commissioned a nationalist discourse with an anti-Myanmar theme. Sunait Chutintaranond observes:

> It was not until the fall of Ayudhya in 1767 that Siam's political and intellectual leaders started to realize the unbridled violence of the Burmese and the resultant perils to Thailand, and showed more concern for investing and reconstructing the past circumstances of their hostilities with this neighbour.... After the war, the Thai rulers totally changed their political attitude toward the Burmese. The Burmese, who since the death of King Naresuan in 1605, had never been perceived as a dangerous and implacable enemy, were now regarded as Siam's most threatening hostile neighbor.[11]

Thai chroniclers and scholars took the liberty of characterizing and stereotyping Myanmar as evil and inhumane. The dehumanization of Myanmar has thus become a recurrent theme in Thai historiography since the early Bangkok period; it has become an important intellectual exercise. There was a subtle shift in the projection of Myanmar's image from being an enemy of Buddhism to an enemy of the Thai nation as Thailand entered into the modern world of nation-states. The emergence of modern Thai nationalism and the centrality of "nation-religion-monarch" in the Thai identity or "Thainess" have further strengthened this trend. It is in this context that Prince Damrong Rajanubhab undertook a study on Myanmar–Thai relations. He analysed the wars between the Thais and Myanmar and penned a manuscript titled *Thai Rop Phama* (later translated into English as "Our Wars with the Burmese"), first published in 1917. His book has subsequently become one of the most influential works shaping Thai perceptions of Myanmar and popularized the image of Myanmar as an enemy of the Thai nation.[12]

After the 1932 Siamese revolution, during the first Phibunsongkhram government (1938–44), the Thai government initiated a nation-building project and made conscious attempts to instil the image of Myanmar as an enemy of the Thai nation in the minds of the Thai people on a nationwide scale through state-sponsored socialization and propaganda, most importantly through school textbooks and historical novels. Luang Wichitwathakan, the most important propagandist of Phibunsongkhram, was instrumental in this project. As the image of evildoing Myanmar as an enemy of the Thai nation, which has formed "an invariable ingredient in modern Thai historiography",[13] gradually became embedded, Thais begin to imagine their nation through the lens of anti-Myanmar sentiment. Sunait Chutintaranond's insightful analysis is worth quoting at length as it clearly demonstrates and neatly captures the content and context of Thai perceptions of Myanmar. In his words:

> The negative attitude of the Thai towards the Burmese is a deliberate, not a chance, happening.... The governments of both the traditional and the modern Thai state play very important roles in instilling a hostile image of the Burmese in the minds of the people, aiming at the benefits of their political legitimacy and social integration. The image of the Burmese as an evil enemy of the "Thai nation", popularly understood and accepted, is, of course, the result of a powerful "institutionalizing" and "socialization" process built and developed mostly in the world of the ruling class before being distributed for public consumption. In other words, sanctions against the Burmese are inspired by political and intellectual leaders. Prejudicial feelings toward the Burmese are widely and effectively ingrained in the minds of the Thai people through the channels of oral tradition, historical literature, textbooks, plays, music and movies, especially during and after the nation-building period, the time when the idea of nationality came to be emphasized.[14]

Even at the turn of the twenty-first century, Thai propaganda on anti-Myanmar themes or negative images of Myanmar has persisted and assumed a life of its own. Thai history textbooks continue to portray Myanmar as evil and as an enemy of the Thai nation. Several films were produced on similar themes in recent years. *Bang Rajan*, a Thai movie based on the struggle of villagers who tried to fend off the Myanmar invasion in 1767, released in 2001, has generated intense anti-Myanmar sentiment among the Thai public and "made many Thai eager for revenge for Burma's destruction of Ayudhaya 234 years ago."[15] *The Legend of Suriyothai* released in August 2001was reportedly sponsored by Queen Sirikit with huge production costs. Another movie on the same theme and of the same epic proportions was *King Naresuan*, the most expensive film ever made in Thailand; parts one and two of the movie were released in early 2007 while part three was initially scheduled to be released in 2010.

Employing statue building as an effective instrument in nation building, the Thai authorities commissioned a number of monuments to commemorate Thai heroes and heroines. The most magnificent and prominent King Naresuan Monument is in Ayutthaya. Statues of King Naresuan in different postures and sizes can be found all over Thailand. In 1995, the Queen Suriyothai Monument, a decade in the making, was unveiled in Ayutthaya. Over the years some local people have come to believe that Suriyothai's face resembles the features of Queen Sirikit herself and that the four soldiers guarding the elephants are those of four military commanders behind the 1991 coup. A recent addition to this trend is the commemoration of a Suphankalaya statue in Phitsunulok. The Third Army in Phitsunulok erected a monument to the princess in front of its headquarters and commissioned a biography in late 1998. The so-called biography mentioned, among other things, that "the princess was unfairly killed while lying on her bed by a cruel husband [a Myanmar king]."[16] One of the most recent developments in this fashion in Thailand was the decision to erect a statue of King Naresuan in Mae Sai, just opposite Tachilek, a Myanmar border town, when the two countries were locked in border skirmishes. Although the Thai foreign minister Surakiart Sathirathai argued that it was done only to honour the king's contribution to the Thai nation and not to confront any country,[17] the proposed site clearly signalled that the statue is intended to affront Myanmar. Through the production of literary works and entertainment on anti-Myanmar themes, the politics of statue building, and the introduction of history textbooks that dehumanize Myanmar in schools, the Thai general public has been socialized to view Myanmar as an enemy of the Thai nation.

MYANMAR'S PERCEPTIONS OF THAILAND

To the best of my knowledge, Myanmar nationals do not hold any strongly negative images of Thai people except the belief that they are spiritually and physically weak and, to a lesser extent, ungrateful and insincere. The author strongly suspects that a majority of the people of Myanmar do not know the real reason behind their ancestors calling Siam "Yodaya". Many people mistakenly believe that *Yodaya* was the corrupted form of *Ayutthaya* (former royal capital of Siam). *Ayutthaya* is a Sanskrit term to mean "the city that could not be conquered". Thus, it was in accordance with occult practice and with the intent to degrade the Thais that the ancient people of Myanmar called the metropolis *Yutthaya*, meaning "the city that could be conquered". As time went by, Yutthaya became Yodaya.

There is little evidence to suggest that Myanmar has any historical overhang or legacy with Thailand. Dr Ma Tin Win, a specialist in the pedagogy of history, has correctly noted that history textbooks in Myanmar have rarely paid attention to the importance of Myanmar–Thai relations.[18] Only in 2002 did the government of Myanmar produce three history textbooks on Myanmar–Thai relations for primary, lower-secondary and upper-secondary classes. Nevertheless, history textbooks in the past sixty years have inevitably covered Myanmar–Thai relations as part of national history. Yet they have rarely attempted to instil a negative image of the Thai people in the minds of school children. The wars have basically been portrayed as wars between two kingdoms, and Ayutthaya has usually been blamed as having been the first to infringe the territory of Myanmar and to challenge Myanmar suzerainty. Therefore, they were just wars, from the point of view of Myanmar. Toe Hla, a prominent historian in Myanmar, analysing Thai behaviour, has noted that whenever the kings of Myanmar were preoccupied with domestic affairs, Ayutthaya invariably took control of the country's frontier. These acts were inevitably followed by the kings of Myanmar marching their armies to the capital of the Thai kingdom. This is the pattern of Myanmar–Thai relations in the pre-colonial period.[19] Little anti-Thai sentiment can be found in Myanmar popular literature or films dealing with Myanmar–Thai relations.

During the 1990s, however, the government of Myanmar did engage in the politics of statue building. This had more to do with promoting regime legitimacy than with attempting to irritate its eastern neighbour. In the early 1990s the government commissioned two statues of King Bayint Naung in Tachilek and Kawthaung, border towns situated at the two ends of the Myanmar–Thai boundary. While some people have viewed this as an unfriendly gesture towards Thailand, the author believes that the intention was more to command respect from the Thais than to threaten them. After all, Bayint Naung is a respectable figure for Thai people as well. If the government of Myanmar had really wanted to send provocative signals towards Thailand, it could have erected statues of Alaungpaya or Sinbyushin. The politics of statue building in Myanmar has been, however, driven by its particular socio-political context. Prior to 1988, the building of Aung San statues was more common. Since 1988, due to the irreconcilable political outlook and policy preferences between the military regime and Aung San Suu Kyi, daughter of Aung San, the military elite has not allowed this trend to continue and has commenced a different statue or monument building programme. To place themselves in the history of nation/state-building in Myanmar and to claim historical and institutional legitimacy, the Tatmadaw (military) leaders have commemorated monuments glorifying three "Empire-builder" warrior kings — Anawrahta, Bayint Naung and Alungphaya.

In short, the people of Myanmar do not hold negative images of Thai people except that they tend to regard them as physically and mentally weak. Their historical fault was that they failed to acknowledge Myanmar's suzerainty over Ayutthaya or to respect the territorial integrity of the ancient kingdoms of Myanmar. On the contrary, they continually infringed Myanmar's frontiers and instigated peripheral political communities to rise up against the authority of Myanmar. The kings of Myanmar had therefore to discipline them. That Thais are ungrateful and insincere is another widely held perception among the people of Myanmar. However, these images have never been systematically instilled in the minds of the public. Most of these images of Thai people are basically presented at the individual level in a selected manner. There are no state-sponsored projects to propagate them. As Sunait Chutintaranond has correctly pointed out, "there is almost no anti-Thai sentiment in Myanmar popular culture, and Thailand is never mentioned as an enemy, which is a stark contrast to the heavy dose of anti-Myanmar sentiment in Thai textbook, films and media reports."[20] Even when the government of Myanmar renamed "Victoria Point" in Kawthaung as "Aung Zeya Point" (in honour of King Alaungpaya) in the early 1990s, following informal requests by local Thai authorities across Kawthaung, it changed the name to "Bayin Naung Point" for the simple reason of promoting bilateral friendship. The government of Myanmar has never projected Thailand as a national enemy. But it does not consider Thailand as a trusted friend either.

THE BUFFER ZONE POLICY

The most obvious case of historical overhang or legacy in Myanmar–Thai bilateral relations is the Thai government's security policy of creating a buffer zone between the two countries. The Thai government's buffer zone policy has been largely driven by the Thai perception of Myanmar as a perpetual enemy of the Thai nation, cautiously constructed by the Thai political elite and the strategic vision and geopolitical realities of Thailand defined within the global and regional security structure.

The Thai strategic vision has been historically influenced by what is commonly known as the "Bending with the Wind" policy, meaning, in the simplest terms, seeking protection from and cultivating favour with whichever country is the most powerful at any given time. Therefore, the Thai willingly sent tribute to the *Son of Heaven* for centuries, bowed to colonial powers in the late nineteenth century, allied with the Japanese in the early part of World War II, and kowtowed to the United States during the Cold War. When it observed the U.S. disengagement from Southeast Asia in the early 1970s, the Thai government secretly established ties with China. It is this approach of "bending with the wind" that has shaped Thailand's policy towards its neighbouring countries. Thus, while Thailand pursued anti-communist policies as a close U.S. ally during the Cold War, it ended up supporting the most radical communists of all, the Khmer Rouge, when the Cold War structure began to break down and Bangkok drifted towards Beijing.

Supporting anti-government insurgents of neighbouring countries and creating buffer zones along bilateral borders have been a persistent policy of successive Thai governments since the late 1940s. It is a well-known fact that Thai security forces and authorities had turned a blind eye to the Malayan Communist Party's activities in Southern Thailand, since the establishment of its first main base in Betong in 1953 to its final days in 1989, despite formal arrangements for security cooperation between the two countries. Critics have pointed out that the MCP/CPM's survival was due to the lack of enthusiasm on the part of the Thais in resolving the issue. Cross border raids and ambushes by the MCP from bases in southern Thailand in the late 1960s touched off the second Emergency period in Malaysia. Chin Peng stated that, "as long as we stayed in the hinterland and caused no trouble, the Siamese troops and police left us alone. If they didn't see us, as far as the Siamese authorities were concerned, we were not there. Besides, there was a *quid pro quo* in it for them."[21] The Thai government also established a buffer zone between Laos and Thailand, by arming Hmong minorities and supporting [rightist] "white" Laos to contain the incumbent Communist Lao government and prevent the expansion of Communism into Thailand. For about fifteen years after the leftist Laos People's Revolutionary Party (LPRP) came to power in 1975, there were tensions and skirmishes along the bilateral border. Only after the shift in the global balance of power, together with the withdrawal of Vietnamese forces from Laos, did relations between the two countries improve. Similarly, throughout the 1980s, the Thai government supported the Khmer Rouge against the government in Phnom Penh and provided sanctuary for anti-Cambodian government forces.

Official diplomatic relations between Myanmar and Thailand were inaugurated in August 1948, a few months after Myanmar's independence. Myanmar by then had begun to enter a state of civil war. Law and order was eventually restored in major cities, but many rural and border areas remained under various insurgent forces. Ethnic minorities, such as the Kayin and Shan, who fought against the government in Yangon (Rangoon), were supported by the Thai government's security policy. Since the late 1940s successive Thai governments have created a buffer zone between the two countries so as to contain any hostile acts initiated by Myanmar and limit the expansion of communism into Thailand. As noted earlier, this buffer zone policy was partly driven by the Thai perception of Myanmar as a perpetual enemy of the Thai nation, cautiously constructed by the Thai political elite and the traditional establishment.

Defined on the basis of what is not Thai as the construction of the virtuous self and the stereotypical other, the concept of "Thainess", which has never been precisely defined, has been an essential and crucial element in the Thai perception and negative identification of Myanmar as a perpetual enemy. Thus Pavin Chachavalpongpun argues that "Thai–Burmese relations have been entangled in this complex process of the creation of Thainess".[22] In the simplest sense, being Thai means being anti-Myanmar. However, Thainess may include being anti-foreign, being anti-communist, and subscription to other (indigenous) social and international norms. Therefore, the social construction of "Thainess" is dynamic and elastic (or plastic if I may borrow the term from Pavin), subjected to manipulation by powerful elites, causing "confusion, ambiguity and discrepancy" in the way Thailand conducts its diplomacy with Myanmar.[23]

The negative identification of Myanmar, therefore, has been a cornerstone of the Thai buffer zone policy towards Myanmar since the late 1940s. As Alfred McCoy comments:

Most Thai leaders have deep traditional distrust for the Burmese, who have frequently invaded Thailand in past centuries. No Thai student graduates from elementary school without reading at least one gruesome description of the atrocities committed by Burmese troops when they burned the royal Thai capital at Ayuthia in 1769. Convinced that Burma will always pose a potential threat to its security, the Thai government has granted asylum to all of the insurgents operating along the Burma–Thailand border and supplied some of the groups with enough arms and equipment to keep operating. This low-level insurgency keeps the Burmese army tied down defending its own cities while the chaotic military situation in Burma's borderland regions gives Thailand a reassuring buffer zone.[24]

However, according to Pavin Chachavalpongpun, the imprecise and elastic nature of defining Thainess, as Thai political elites in power consciously select certain values and norms at different times to serve their personal or perceived national interests, has produced inconsistency in Thailand's Myanmar policy, especially since the late 1980s.

The successive Thai governments have consistently supported armed anti-Myanmar government organizations. This included Thai support for the Kuomintang (KMT) remnants residing in the border area of Myanmar in the 1950s, former Prime Minister U Nu's rebel forces in the 1970s, and various ethnic-based insurgent groups, such as the Kayin (Karen), Shan and Mon, since the late 1940s. Moreover, it is a well-known fact that most of the arms supplied to anti-Yangon insurgents along the Myanmar–Thai border came from warehouses under the control of a Thai military unit known as *Sopokotobo-315* (Special Operation Division 315), which operated secretly and independently. Some weapons originated from stocks of the Thai military.

Thailand has benefitted enormously from the buffer zone policy. The country has exploited Myanmar's natural resources by entering into business deals with insurgents. Meanwhile, whilst it was busy fighting the Burma Communist Party (BCP) insurgency, the government of Myanmar could not pay much attention to ethnic-based insurgencies along the Myanmar–Thai frontier. However, since the mid-1980s, the Tatmadaw has given much more attention to counter-insurgency operations targeting ethnic insurgencies. More operations have been conducted with greater intensity against insurgent groups, such as the Kachin Independence Army (KIA), the Shan State Army (SSA), the Shan United Revolutionary Army (SURA), the New Mon State Party (NMSP) and the Karen National

Liberation Army (KNLA). In 1984 and 1987 the Tatmadaw formed two new infantry divisions and put them on operations against insurgents along the Myanmar–Thai border. By 1987 the Tatmadaw confidently declared that it would eliminate the KNLA insurgency within two years. Therefore, for the first time in forty years, the Tatmadaw began to seriously challenge the Thai government's buffer zone policy. In the course of this development, the Myanmar government has made diplomatic efforts to prevent further Thai involvement in supporting insurgents. At the invitation of the Myanmar government, Thai Crown Princess Maha Chakri Sirindhorn paid a ten-day state visit to Myanmar in March 1986. This was followed by the visit of Thai Crown Prince Maha Vajiralongkorn in March 1988.

In January 1987, during General Chavalit Yongchaiyudh's — commander-in-chief of the Royal Thai Army — visit to Yangon, General Saw Maung, chief of staff of the Tatmadaw, raised issues concerning Thailand's policy towards insurgents. Saw Maung made four requests to Thailand in connection with the insurgents along the Myanmar–Thai border. The first request was for the Thai government to take measures to prevent foreigners from gaining access to the insurgents. The second was for the Thai government to take measures to prevent arms, ammunition and other war materials from reaching the insurgents. Saw Maung told his counterpart that he was surprised to learn that insurgents had so many weapons, ammunition and other war materials without having facilities for their production. The third request was for the Thai authorities to disarm and detain those insurgents who retreated from battles into Thai territory and, if possible, to hand them over to the Myanmar authorities. The fourth request was an understanding on the part of the Thai government that Myanmar had no intention to occupy Thai territory. Saw Maung promised that the Tatmadaw would try as much as possible not to infringe Thai territory but, as he admitted, sometimes shells inevitably landed on Thai soil. Obviously, the visiting Thai general categorically denied that the Thai government allowed anti-Yangon insurgents to use Thai territory. At the same time, however, Chavalit Yongchaiyudh surprised the Myanmar generals by saying that the two armed forces should cooperate to suppress the insurgency. When Saw Maung paid a reciprocal visit to Thailand in July 1987, General Chavalit Yongchaiyudh once again said that Thailand saw no threat from Myanmar and was looking forward to enjoying good coordination and cooperation at every level of command. When he came to Myanmar again in April 1988, Chavalit Yongchaiyudh further discussed the feasibility of cooperation and coordination. Still, the Tatmadaw commanders were unconvinced.

Meanwhile, Thai Prime Minister Chatichai Choonhavan laid down the foreign policy principles governing Thailand's relations with its neighbours, including Myanmar. His most well remembered slogan was that Indochina should be transformed "from battlefield into marketplace". In this context, the Thai government laid down basic objectives in its policy towards Myanmar that included promotion of a close relationship with Myanmar and encouragement of Myanmar to be a good and stable neighbour.[25] Based on these objectives, the Thai government pursued a foreign policy towards Myanmar which came to be known as "constructive engagement". At about the same time, on 25 January 1989, echoing Chatichai's vision, Chavalit Yongchaiyudh suggested the creation of *Suvannaphume* (Golden Land), which encompassed mainland Southeast Asia. The plan was to make Thailand the economic centre of mainland Southeast Asia. This plan, however, did not go very far as neighbouring countries saw it as resonant of Thai hegemony. Myanmar was also sceptical about the plan as it seemed redolent of the Greater Thailand Policy of the 1930s.

Under the rubric of constructive engagement, the Thai government appeared to relax its buffer-zone policy towards Myanmar. Yet, in reality it did not abandon the policy at all. Throughout 1989 and 1990, the Thai government had tolerated, to a certain extent, artillery shells fired by the Tatmadaw landing on Thai soil. In some instances, it had also turned a blind eye to intrusion by Myanmar's troops into Thailand to encircle insurgent strongholds from the rear. At the same time, the Thai army had provided supporting fire and sanctuary for insurgents. For example, during the Tatmadaw offensive in May 1989, the Tatmadaw found out that the Thai Army provided supporting fire for the KNLA. And in December 1989, when the Tatmadaw captured the KNLA's Phalu camp, all the KNLA troops crossed into Thailand without any trouble. However, by mid-1992, it became clear that the Thai government was not prepared to abandon its long-standing buffer-zone policy. In connection with the capture of a disputed area known as Hill Point 1542 by the Tatmadaw, relations between the two countries began to turn sour and tension escalated into skirmishes. This incident occurred at the time of Anand Panyarachun's interim government and Chuan Leekpai's Democrat government. The tension was eventually defused in December 1992. However, signs of uneasy relations between the two countries began to surface again. By 1995 it was clear that the Thai government had firmly reinstated its buffer-zone policy. In early 1995, during operations against the KNLA's strongholds, Myanmar's troops encountered Thai Army artillery fire. The Tatmadaw also found out that the Thai Army had given protection to Khun Sa's Mong Thai Army (MTA) and even allowed them to use Thai soil to attack Tatmadaw positions. In short, throughout the early 1990s Myanmar's army repeatedly encountered instances where Thailand had not abandoned its buffer-zone policy. In 1995 a Thai police general explained the Thai government's policy towards Myanmar:

> The Thai government ... did not want it [Myanmar] to have unity and peace. Thus the Thai government supported minority groups and provided them with arms. However, the Thai government did not trust the minorities either. Thailand did not want the minorities to win for fear that the conflicts among themselves would have a negative impact on Thailand. In other words, the Thai government did not want any party to win the war.... There should be no complete peace in Myanmar. In this way Thailand would achieve security and freedom from the Myanmar threat.[26]

This statement, without any doubt, clearly illustrated the Thai historical overhang or legacy of Myanmar as an enemy of the Thai nation.

Until the mid-1990s, Thailand had an effective buffer zone along the Myanmar–Thai border. However, Thailand has lost this formidable barrier as the government of Myanmar has increasingly asserted its control over border areas. Only when the Tatmadaw gained "border dominance", by capturing insurgent strongholds and bases along the bilateral border and entering ceasefire agreements with other insurgents, did Thailand begin to restore some form of a buffer zone between the two countries. On 14 August 1996, Chulalongkorn University held a seminar on Thai national security issues. The panel at the seminar concluded that "although there was no imminent threat to Thailand's security in the 21st century, border problems, especially on the Burmese side, could turn into hot spots in the future."[27] This conclusion, without any doubt, reflected Thai anxiety over the loss of its buffer zone between Myanmar and Thailand. According to Surachat Bumrungsuk from Chulalongkorn University, "in the next five to ten years, Thailand's security problem will shift from its eastern flank to its western one (Myanmar–Thai border)." He further stated that "as the *Burmese forces are consolidating their hold in minority-controlled areas along the border*, which stretches more than 2,400 kilometers, chances of armed confrontations between the two countries will increase" (italics in the original).[28]

Despite the lack of clear security threats from Myanmar, further steps were subsequently taken to secure or restore a buffer zone along the Myanmar–Thai border. The year 2000 witnessed major developments in Thai security policy along the Myanmar–Thai border. On 6 January 2000, in his lecture to 200 officers at the National Defence College and Joint Staff College, Thai supreme commander General Mongkol Ampornpisit warned that "Thailand should remain vigilant with Burma posing a potential security threat."[29] Although this kind of message is no doubt quite common in the National Defence College, what was significant this time was the fact that it became a public statement. On 10 March 2000 the Thai National Security Council sponsored a seminar on "Security Policy towards Burma". Kachadpai Burusphat, the secretary general of the council, told the audience that there were no major changes in Thai security perceptions and policy towards Myanmar, and he hoped that the government of Myanmar would compromise with the opposition. Yangon interpreted this to mean that Thailand would continue to host and support anti-Yangon insurgent and political organizations.[30]

In April 2000 the Thai Ministry of Defence asked the Thai government to amend Ministerial Regulation No. 45 — which was jointly drafted by the Ministry of Defence and Ministry of the Interior — and Article 13 of the 1954 Conscription Act, which prohibited tribal people living in 500 villages in the twenty-six border provinces of Thailand from entering military service.[31] Major General Saksin Thipayakesorn, chief of the army's Reserve Affairs Department, argued that "times had changed and rural areas, especially in the North, were not what they were five decades ago".[32] Though his remark was somewhat vague, the Myanmar authorities interpreted it to mean that Thailand felt that it had lost a buffer that had been in place for about five decades, and as a result it had to create another one. In December 2000 the Thai army planned to build up to fifty new villages for the hill tribes to control them more effectively and for border security. Major General Pradit Boonkerd, the army's chief of the Directorate of Civil Affairs, explained that the new villages, known as "self-defence villages", would be built in Tak province, next to the Myanmar–Thai border. A three-phase programme was developed as the basis for the self-defence of the villages.[33] According to the programme,

All villagers would register with the authorities and be issued with household registration documents and ID cards; villagers would be trained to defend themselves and use firearms while information centres and bunkers are established; and villagers would be encouraged to find production opportunities and boost productivity.[34]

The Thai army also planned to form a so-called "civilian army", with about 5,000 members along the Myanmar–Thai border. This was to be set up under the "territorial defence training scheme" supervised by the 3rd Army. By May 2000, 120 villages in Chiangmai, Chiangrai, Tak, Mae Hong Son, Phayao, Nan, Uttaradit and Phitsanulok districts were already organized under the programme. According to the Thai army, by 2001 the number of villages established under this programme would have grown to 529. The training programme included instruction on the use of various kinds of weapons, explosives and communication equipment. A Thai source revealed that even though every village under this programme had been registered and recognized by the local administration authority, ninety-nine per cent of the villagers were not Thai and did not have identification cards.[35] With regard to the Thai policy of building a buffer zone along the Myanmar–Thai border, an article in a state-owned newspaper in Myanmar commented,

> With the surrender or return to legal-fold of armed national groups and capture of KNU strongholds along the Myanmar–Thai border by the Tatmadaw, Thailand lost its front-line defensive positions. In this situation, as tactical commitment, Thailand made arrangements in a harmonious way to put its northern region under the command of special administration department, to transform villages of hill tribes into defence villages, to enlist members of the hill tribes for military service and to deploy special forces along the border in a bid to substitute its lost domains along the border and to gain control of the border area.

> The matter of enlisting hill tribes into military service is also interesting. As the past successive governments of Thailand never acknowledged the hill tribes as citizens, tribesmen of over 500 hill villages of 26 provinces were totally barred from joining the army under the 45th Ministerial Regulation and the 1954 Conscription Act. Now, members of the hill tribes are lured with various kinds of inducement to enlist in the army. Included in the inducements is the pledge that they will be issued national registration cards as soon as they join the army. According to a report

by the Thai ministry of defence, if these tribesmen can be recruited into [the] army, Thailand will get braver and tougher soldiers who know the territory very well.[36]

In sum, the government of Myanmar was not convinced that Thailand had abandoned the buffer zone policy. In 1991, in connection with the prolonged insurgency in Myanmar, Sithu Aung wrote: "some countries, under the pretext of border problems, usually encourage the insurgents of their neighbors who have taken up strongholds on the border. Their motive is to make the border their buffer zone. Some countries make contacts with their neighbors' insurgents on the border for their economic gains."[37] In an article published in 2001 in one of Myanmar's newspapers, it was stated that one of the cornerstones of the Thai security policy was to "build a buffer zone between the potential threat nation and itself by supporting any organization ... opposed to the government of that nation".[38]

It was only in early 2002 that the Thai government under Thaksin Shinawatra openly admitted that Thailand has been practising a buffer-zone policy in regards to Myanmar. Thaksin said that Bangkok would abandon its policy of supporting ethnic rebels. His statement drew a barrage of criticism from the Thai political establishment. As far as the Myanmar government is concerned, Thailand has continued its buffer-zone policy, yet the degree of activism depends very much on who is in control of the policy-making process.

An interesting case in connection with the Thai buffer-zone policy was the tension and armed conflicts that occurred in 2001. The fundamental cause of this tension was the Democrat-led Thai government's decision to restore a buffer zone along the Myanmar–Thai border during the late 1990s. By 1996 Yangon had entered ceasefire agreements with a number of insurgent groups and had taken control of major insurgent outposts along the bilateral border. The Tatmadaw captured KNLA strongholds in military operations, while it took over MTA bases from Khun Sa when he unconditionally surrendered to the government. In other words the Tatmadaw had gained border dominance and now faced Thai troops directly. As a result, the Thai military began to reactivate its long-standing policy of having a buffer zone.

In February 2001, during the SURA's attacks on Tatmadaw outposts and Tachilek, a border town, the authorities of Myanmar believed they had evidence that Thai troops were involved. The government of Myanmar was convinced that Thai troops provided artillery support for SURA from Aung Zeya Hill, located inside Thailand. Again, in April 2001, Thai troops were involved in SURA's attacks on the Tatmadaw outpost at E-7 hillock and other areas. Thai troops not only supported the insurgents, but also participated in combat activities. The Thais helped SURA to secure bases along the border so that it could serve as a buffer. The border incident further escalated into armed conflicts between the two military forces in May and June 2001. During this crisis, both sides engaged in a war of words and published provocative and finger-pointing articles. For instance, when Bangkok accused Yangon of protecting drug trafficking, the Myanmar newspaper responded as follows:

> They [the Thais] have never dared to shout about the narcotic drug problem for long[,] the way as a thief being bitten by a dog dared not shout but now they say the problem poses danger to the nation. It is absurd for a nation where no law has been introduced to seize precursor chemicals used in manufacturing narcotic drugs to suggest so. If the Thai government authorities are perturbed by the production of narcotic drugs along the borders of Myanmar, Thailand and Laos and would like to announce it to the world in an attempt to make themselves heroes, they should recall the nation's history concerning production, sale and distribution of narcotic drugs. The government of Thailand permitted the Chinese merchants to monopolize the opium trade beginning in 1852 but in 1907 it revoked the opium licence granted to the Chinese merchants. From then on the [Royal] government took charge of the business itself [as a monopoly]. Deny if it dares to do so. Then I shall reveal all those involved[,] including members of the royal family.[39]

Several other articles followed in a similar vein. As the drug issue came to the centre stage of the tensions between the two countries in early 2001, a series of articles in Myanmar's newspapers attacked the Thai government for blaming the government of Myanmar for everything that goes wrong in Thailand. This finally led to a strong diplomatic protest from Bangkok as some articles implicitly accused a Thai king (of the eighteenth century) of being responsible for the opium trade in Southeast Asia. Three articles, namely "In Spite of Our Good Will", "How Did Opium Arrive at the Golden Triangle Region?" and "Never Been Enslaved but Real Slaves", by Dr Ma Tin Win, which consecutively appeared in Myanmar's newspapers on 16–18 May 2001, drew serious protests from the Thai government.

One article explained that the British and Siam signed the Treaty of Friendship and Commercial Agreement in 1855, before the former fought the second Sino–British (opium) war. In the treaty, the Royal Government of Siam allowed the British to import opium without customs duty or tax, a concession that could not be found in the Anglo–Burmese treaty of 1826 or even in the Sino–British treaty concluded at the end of the Opium War. But the Siamese government allowed tax-free opium trade. In addition to this, treaties with various colonial powers included a clause that allowed the citizens of those countries to travel freely in Siam, including along the Mekong River. This situation gave the British access to the Golden Triangle region for opium-growing poppies. The author concluded:

> I would like to tell the Siamese who are accusing Myanmar of refining opium, that even the most inferior king of our nation had never let the nation fall under total subjugation without a fight[,] though your king Maha Mongkut had done so. We had never signed any agreement with any nation to import opium.[40]

Other articles in Myanmar's newspapers criticized King Naresuan of Thailand and portrayed him as someone of mediocre quality and his father Maha Thammaracha as devious. Ma Tin Win wrote that Phra Naret could not defeat Myanmar even when the country had been thrown into disunity and that he had failed to really succeed in any of his endeavours.[41]

The tension and armed conflicts were finally resolved through diplomatic means by late 2001 only after Prime Minister Thaksin Shinawatra firmly established his authority over the policy-making process and transferred some senior military officers from key positions responsible for Myanmar policy. Today, it appears that the Thai buffer-zone policy still exists, but the degree of implementation depends on how the dominant groups within the political elite define their personal, regime and national interests. Nevertheless, the negative image of "Myanmar as an enemy of the Thai nation" continues to shape the strategic vision and security perception of the Thai political elites.

CONCLUSION

It is obvious that historical overhangs or legacies do exist in Myanmar–Thai bilateral relations and that they play an important role in setting foreign and security policy agendas, especially on the part of Thailand.

For Thailand, the 220 years extending from 1648 to 1767 constitutes the historical period that underpins thinking about relations with Myanmar. The dramatic fall of Ayutthaya in 1767 and its subsequent destruction, in fact, was a turning point in Thai perceptions of Myanmar. The history of Thailand was rewritten to present Myanmar as a historical enemy. Dehumanization of Myanmar became, and remains, a recurrent theme in Thai popular culture. The Thai public has been socialized with negative images of Myanmar, leading to the general understanding that to be Thai means to be anti-Myanmar. Therefore, it can be said that the fall of Ayutthaya is the critical juncture that triggered a historical overhang or legacy in Myanmar–Thai relations. This dramatic event is clearly employed by the Thai elite to frame a particular political discourse that serves their interests.

The historical overhang or legacy in Thailand's Myanmar policy is an elite-driven phenomenon. It is closely related to how "Thainess" is defined by those in power. The imprecise nature of this definition allows the Thai elite ample room to manipulate the concept. While the basic norm of anti-Myanmar sentiment remains at the core of Thainess, prioritization of various indigenous Thai social values and international values is subjected to manipulation by the Thai elites.

The most obvious case of historical overhang or legacy in Myanmar–Thai relations is the Thai buffer-zone policy towards Myanmar. Supporting various anti-Yangon armed organizations has been a policy of Thailand since the late 1940s. Negative images of the people of Myanmar and Thai perceptions of Myanmar as an historical enemy are the cornerstones of this policy. Throughout the period of the Cold War, the policy was further supported by the strategic vision of the Thai government. In the late 1980s, while the fundamental nature of the buffer-zone policy remained unchanged, the Thai government began to relax its application. This was due to the strong business interest represented by the political elite then in power. This trend was reversed by the subsequent Democrat-led government, which ostensibly paid more attention to international values of respect for human rights and democracy. The additions of respect for human rights and democracy as important components of Thainess, overlaying traditional anti-Myanmar sentiments, enabled "undemocratic" Myanmar, with its poor human-rights record, to consolidate its position as an enemy of the Thai nation. Therefore there is a strong correlation between the Democrat-led government and Thailand's confrontational policy towards Myanmar. In other words, the historical overhang or legacy was further strengthened when the Thai political elites were convinced that the leaders of Myanmar's regime did not share similar international values. In some ways this was a convenient choice for the Thai political elites at the time of national soul searching after the 1997 economic crisis and the hardships it generated. Therefore, "Myanmar as national enemy of Thailand" was invoked in an attempt to overcome the national crisis.

On the part of Myanmar the story is somewhat different. Since the people of Myanmar do not hold any particularly strong negative images of the people of Thailand, it is rather difficult to determine when and under what circumstances the government of Myanmar invokes the historical overhang or legacy. In fact, there is little evidence to suggest that an historical overhang or legacy exerts any influence in Myanmar's policy towards Thailand. For Myanmar, it is the Thai overhang from their historical past, and the fact that the Thai political elites tend to consciously cultivate and embellish this, that constitutes the core of the problem.

Notes

1. U Nyein Maung, *Shaehaung Myanmar Kyauksar Myar* [Ancient Myanmar stone inscriptions] (Yangon: Department of Archaeology, 1972), p. 66.
2. Ukala, *Maha Yazawungyi* [Great chronicle], vol. 2 (Yangon: Yarpyae Publishing House, 2006), p. 327. (However, it was also stated on page 296 in the same chronicle that Maha Thammaracha, the governor of Phitsunalok, presented his daughter Phra Eindadevi to Bayint Naung in January 1567.)
3. Ukala, *Maha Yazawungyi* [Great chronicle], vol. 3 (Yangon: Yarpyae Publishing House, 2006), p. 94.
4. Quoted in Sunait Chutintaranond, *Suriyothai in the Context of Thai–Myanmar History and Historical Perspective*, vol. 1, *Views and Vision* (Yangon: Universities Historical Research Centre, 2001), pp. 74–75.
5. Ibid., p. 75.
6. M.L Manich Jumsai, *Popular History of Thailand* (Bangkok: Chalermnit, 1976), p. 240.
7. Prince Chula Chakrabongse, *Lords of Life: A History of the Kings of Thailand*, 3rd ed. (Bangkok: DD Books, 1982), pp. 49–50.
8. Ukala, *Maha Yazawungyi* [Great chronicle], vol. 3 (Yangon: Yarpyae, 2006), p. 94.
9. Tun Aung Chein, "Translation of the Yodaya Yazawun" (draft manuscript), p. 38. Actually, Suphankalaya was the elder sister.

10. *The Nation*, 1 March 1999.

11. Sunait Chutintaranond, "The Image of the Burmese Enemy in Thai Perceptions and Historical Writings", in *On Both Sides of the Tenasserim Range: History of Siamese–Burmese Relations*, edited by Sunait Chutintaranond and Than Tun (Bangkok: Chulalongkorn University, 1995), pp. 2–7.

12. Ibid., p. 24.

13. Ibid., p. 19.

14. Ibid., p. 31.

15. *Bangkok Post*, 25 March 2001.

16. *The Nation*, 1 March 1999.

17. *Bangkok Post*, 5 May 2001.

18. Tin Win Ma, "A New Tune from Ayutthaya", in *So Bold the Courage as Blood Red*, edited by Tin Win Ma (Yangon: News and Periodical Enterprises, 2002), p. 47.

19. Hla Toe, *Bayint Naung Mintaragyi Bawa Atwe Akhaw Yonekyichet Hnit Saung Ywethmu Myar* [Philosophy of life and activities of King Bayint Naung] (Naypyitaw: Department of Historical Research, 2010), p. 51.

20. Asia Times Online, 7 March 2001.

21. Karl Hack, "The Long March Peace of the Malayan Communist Party in Southern Thailand", in *Thai South and Malay North: Ethnic Interactions on the Plural Peninsula*, edited by Michael J. Montesano and Patrick Jory (Singapore: NUS Press, 2008), pp. 173–98.

22. Pavin Chachavalpongpun, *A Plastic Nation: The Curse of Thainess in Thai–Burmese Relations* (Lanham: University Press of America, 2005), p. 6.

23. Ibid., pp. 22–24.

24. Alfred W. McCoy, *The Politics of Heroin in Southeast Asia* (Singapore: Harper & Row, 1972), pp. 335–36.

25. Venika Boonma-klee, *Burma: Thai Foreign Policy Under Chatichai Chunhavan's Government* (Bangkok: Thailand Research Fund, 1997), p. 140.

26. Pasuk Phongpaichit, Sungsidh Piriyarangsan and Nualnoi Treerat, *Guns, Gambling, Ganja: Thailand's Illegal Economy and Public Policy* (Bangkok: Silkworm Books, 1998), p. 129.

27. *The Nation*, 15 August 1996.

28. Ibid.

29. *Bangkok Post*, 7 January 2000.

30. Thadinhtauk Thet Shey, "*Hma Tapa Achar Mashi*" [No other things], *Myanma Alin* (newspaper), 2 April 2001.

31. *Bangkok Post*, 14 April 2000.

32. *Bangkok Post*, 13 April 2000.

33. *Bangkok Post*, 12 April 2000.

34. Ibid.

35. *Bangkok Post*, 14 May 2000.

36. Nga Khin Nyo, "*Ayaekyone Thetlone kaunghma*" [Only the stamina is essential in time of emergency], *Kyemon* (newspaper), 2–3 March 2001.

37. Sithu Aung, "Internal Insurgency and Outside Interference", *Working People's Daily*, 8 March 1991.

38. Myint Soe (Natala), "*Lu Meik Hnar Yan Mashipa*" [No henchmen available for hire], *Kyemon*, 9 March 2001.

39. Kappiya Kan Kaung, "Latest Cheap Jokes of Sukhumbhand", *New Light of Myanmar*, 21 May 2000; *Kyemon*, 19 May 2000.

40. Ma Tin Win, "How Did Opium Arrive at the Golden Triangle Region?" *New Light of Myanmar*, 17 May 2001; *Kyemon*, 17 May 2001.

41. Tin Win Ma, "Phra Narit Did Not Amount to Much", *New Light of Myanmar*, 28 May 2001; *Kyemon*, 28 May 2001; Tin Win Ma, "Will Tell All That Is True, Barring None", *New Light of Myanmar*, 30 May 2001; *Kyemon*, 30 May 2001.

6

GLORIFYING THE INGLORIOUS PAST:
Historical Overhangs or Legacies in Thai–Cambodian Relations[1]

Pavin Chachavalpongpun

In 1978, American political scientist Walter Vella stated, "Like any system of loyalty, nationalism has its virtues and its faults. Its good lies in its power to unite; its bad lies in its power to divide."[2] This assessment of nationalism has never gone out of fashion. The current state of Thai–Cambodian relations has been ostensibly moulded by the powerful, yet dangerous, sentiment of nationalism which has its deep roots in the bitter historical intercourse between the two kingdoms. In their modern-day context, the ransacking of the Royal Thai Embassy in Phnom Penh in January 2003 and the recent eruption of armed conflicts between Thailand and Cambodia over the Hindu Temple of Preah Vihear, known in Thai as *Phra Viharn*, exemplifies the work of nationalism and the impact caused by historical overhangs or legacies on this fragile relationship. Nationalism has over the years been exploited by the two countries' political leaders to fulfil a myriad of their own political interests. Nationalism has been capable in many instances of driving them into confrontations, and even war. While the rationale behind nationalism might be discursive, nationalism in itself is a systematic construct. Countries fabricate history to celebrate their past, using nationalism as a political tool in their manipulation of public opinion. As history is remodelled for political agendas, old wounds are reopened. Past bilateral conflicts are refreshed. It is evident that contemporary Thai–Cambodian relations have become a casualty of the remade past.

This chapter examines how history has been distorted and nationalism employed to serve the power interests of the Thai and Cambodian leaders. It discusses the implications of the historical overhang or legacy on today's interactions between Thailand and Cambodia, and elucidates why and how such a phenomenon has endured despite the fact that the international environment has consistently changed. The chapter argues that historical overhangs or legacies have been firmly sustained and have frequently emerged as a primary determining factor in Thai–Cambodian relations, particularly whenever their political leaders encountered legitimacy crises at home. To divert the people's attention from domestic issues, leaders fanned the flame of nationalism while making enemies across the border. In the process, they rekindled bitter memories of the historical past to justify their foreign policy towards the enemies in the neighbourhood, as reflected in the state's perception of the virtuous self versus the stereotypical other. Recently, non-state actors in Thailand, such as the People's Alliance for Democracy (PAD), also took advantage of the contentious history between Thailand and Cambodia to unseat the Thaksin-backed governments.[3] In other words, domestic politics has been the main source of bilateral tensions between Thailand and Cambodia. To demonstrate the nexus between the distortion of history and foreign relations, this chapter investigates two major events that have severely deteriorated Thai–Cambodian ties, namely, the conflict over the disputed Preah Vihear Temple and the clash between the Thaksin–Hun Sen alliance and the Abhisit Vejjajiva government. It concludes that although history and nationalism can produce devastating effects on bilateral relations, they have remained useful apparatuses for political leaders in achieving their much-needed legitimacy and strengthening their power positions.

EMBITTERED HISTORY ENLIVENED

Thai historian Charnvit Kasetsiri once wrote:

> Among the neighbouring countries of Southeast Asia, none seems more similar to Thailand than Cambodia (perhaps not even excluding Laos and the "Tai" people scattered throughout such countries as Burma, Vietnam, and southern China). Both nations share similar customs, traditions, beliefs, and ways of life. This is especially true of royal customs, language, writing systems, vocabulary, literature, and the dramatic arts. In light of these similarities, it seems surprising, therefore, that relations between Thailand and Cambodia should be characterised by deep-seated "ignorance, misunderstanding, and prejudice." Indeed, the two countries have what can be termed "a love-hate relationship".[4]

Thailand and Cambodia share an approximately 800-kilometre-long border. Historically, their respective peoples, the Siamese and Khmers, had continually interacted through the exchange of culture, marriage and trade. Such interaction even predated the Sukhothai Kingdom, supposedly the first Thai kingdom, that came into being in 1238. From the period of Sukhothai to the rise of Ayutthaya, another supposedly Thai kingdom founded in 1351, the Siamese looked up to their Khmer neighbours and embraced their advanced civilization. Successive Siamese kings were filled with tremendous admiration for anything Khmer, ranging from the art, architecture, language and royal rituals. David Wyatt said that Ayutthaya inherited much from Angkor as the former was rising to become a major power in mainland Southeast Asia.[5] But the Khmer civilization eventually sank into decline. In 1431 Ayutthaya's army invaded and destroyed Angkor, the seat of the Khmer Empire, transforming this ancient kingdom into one of Siam's vassals.[6] The collapse of Angkor can be compared to the fall of Ayutthaya in 1767, but Thai historians have been reluctant to make this analogy as it would cast Thais in the role of "villains".[7]

The love-hate relationship between the Siamese and Khmers persisted after the end of the Angkor era. As Siam was busy fending off Burmese incursions, the Khmers often took the opportunity to attack Ayutthaya from the east. In revenge, according to the Thai chronicles, King Naresuan of Ayutthaya (1590–1605) ordered the capture of Lovek, the capital of the Khmer kingdom at the time, and beheaded its ruler, Phraya Lovek. Naresuan then washed his feet with Phraya Lovek's blood.[8] While the

Siamese perceived Lovek as a rebel against Ayutthaya's monarch, he was considered by Cambodian historians as a hero who fought for the kingdom's freedom. The unequal relations between Siam and Cambodia which had lasted throughout the pre-colonial period profoundly deepened the feelings of mutual distrust. But Siam was not the only eminent power in this sub-region. Vietnam also expanded its influence over Cambodia. As a result, Cambodia often found itself squeezed between two powerful overlords, Siam and Vietnam. Thongchai Winichakul asserted that the contest between the two overlords over Cambodia was further intensified and complicated by factional fighting within the Cambodian court from the eighteenth to nineteenth centuries. Whenever a faction sought support from one overlord, the loser sought the other's protection. In the meantime, the Cambodian kings always attempted to create a balance of the overlord's power by blurring the line of allegiance in order to make the kingdom somewhat independent.[9] It is therefore convenient for the Thais to conclude, based on their arbitrary historical perspective, that the Khmers were cowardly but opportunistic, striking only when Siam was in trouble.[10]

With the advent of colonialism, King Norodom of Cambodia (1860–1904) signed an agreement with France in 1863 to institute a protectorate over his vulnerable kingdom against the two oppressive neighbours — Siam and Vietnam, and eventually became a part of French Indochina. The new international order based on colonial politics served as a catalyst to an already ongoing process of overhangs or legacies. The force of colonial politics pressured Siam to conclude a treaty with France in 1907. Consequently, Siam ceded the Cambodian provinces of Battambang, Sisophon and Siem Reap to the French protectorate of Cambodia (as it had done in the 1890s with the Lao vassal territories on the eastern side of the Mekong River). The Siamese–Cambodian border was demarcated based on the watershed as indicated in a map sketched in 1904 by the supposed "joint committee" consisting of Siamese and French surveyors.[11] Siam's loss of the Cambodian provinces to the French has been played up, until today, as a major theme of Thai nationalism — the theme which centres upon the loss of "Thai territories" to greedy foreign powers and opportunistic neighbours. The discourse of lost territories remains authoritative and is a key ingredient of Thailand's nationalistic foreign policy. It has also entrenched the historical overhangs or legacies in bilateral relations, especially since Thailand has made repeated claims of its ownership of the Preah Vihear Temple which is located in its supposedly lost territories.

Ascending to power in 1938, Field Marshal Plaek Phibun Songkhram began the process of re-glorifying Siam's history and revived the issue of lost territories in order to legitimize his military regime. Because such an issue dealt with national security, strong governments, like that of Phibun, were supposedly imperative in navigating the country out of these precarious environments, thus emphasizing the relations between regime type and the impact on bilateral overhangs or legacies. Phibun embarked on the campaign to recover the lost provinces from the French. He closely collaborated with Luang Wichit Wathakan, a prolific nationalist writer and composer, to reconstruct Thai history, one that portrayed the country's vulnerability and at the same time its greatness in the past. The Phibun government, for example, printed the Thai map which showed Cambodia as being historically part of Thai territory. It also claimed that the Thais and Khmers were one and the same people. France had to warn Phibun against harbouring any designs on Cambodia.[12] Phibun's irredentist claims effectively stirred up anti-French sentiment in Bangkok, subsequently leading to a series of skirmishes with French troops on the Thai–Cambodian border. In the meantime, Phibun forged intimate ties with Japan and implemented a pro-Japanese foreign policy. The Franco–Siamese conflict allowed Japan to demonstrate its amicable relationship with the Phibun regime. Japan, in 1941, decided to step in to mediate in the conflict and the final settlement gave the disputed areas in Cambodia and Laos back to Thailand.[13] Not until 1947, two years after Japan lost the war, was Thailand forced to return the Cambodian provinces to France.[14] King Norodom Sihanouk mentioned in his book *Sweet and Sour Memories* that Cambodia's territory had become "whole again".[15]

The Thai political domination of Cambodia throughout the course of history had an enormous effect on their bilateral relationship in the post–World War II period. In 1950, as Cambodia obtained independent status within the French Union, Thailand became the first country to establish diplomatic relations with Phnom Penh. In 1953 Cambodia fully regained its independence, and two years later King Sihanouk abdicated in favour of his father and elections were held. This marked the beginning of the "Sihanouk era" in Cambodian politics. But this era was marred by heightened mutual suspicion. Cambodia eventually broke off its diplomatic relations with Thailand twice, in 1958 and 1961, purportedly as a protest to the Thai claim on the Preah Vihear Temple. In Thailand the Foreign Ministry unleashed its own propaganda against Cambodia. It said in 1958:

> With the support and approval of the Cambodian Government, campaigns for the cession of Khao Phra Viharn began in the Cambodian press and radio. The Cambodian people were told that Thailand was their enemy and was trying to destroy their newly-gained independence by occupying Khao Phra Viharn and by coveting other parts of their country as well.... How could we think, for one moment, what useful purpose would serve Thailand to look upon our neighbour as an enemy.[16]

In retaliation an article in *La Dépêche du Cambodge*, a newspaper under the political direction of the then Cambodian prime minister Sim Var, said that the Garuda on the Thai national emblem should be replaced by the vulture.[17] The tension caused by mutual insults against their national dignity and the ongoing conflict over the temple ownership pushed Thailand and Cambodia further to the brink of a full-scale war. In 1962 they took the temple dispute to the International Court of Justice (ICJ). Thai Prime Minister Field Marshal Sarit Thanarat (1959–63) called on Thais to display their love for the nation in the battle to regain Thailand's lost property. His government urged each Thai to donate one baht towards the expense for the court case.[18] The ICJ finally ruled the case in Cambodia's favour. Sarit, in his nationalistic response to the ICJ ruling, said, "With blood and tears, we shall recover the Phra Viharn one day."[19]

Thailand's relations with Phnom Penh became more complicated following the outbreak of the Cambodian–Vietnamese war. The Khmer Rouge regime founded Democratic Kampuchea in 1975, even though its core ideology was rigidly communist. The Khmer Rouge reign characterized the tragic era of Cambodian history in which up to three million might have been killed under the leadership of Pol Pot.[20] Only after Vietnam invaded Cambodia in 1978 did the genocide stop. It is important to note that the Sino–Soviet ideological split deeply polarized the communist division in Indochina. Whereas China backed the Khmer Rouge in tackling the Vietnamese, the Soviet Union aligned itself with Hanoi. Thailand was aware of the possibility of becoming the last domino in mainland Southeast Asia. Thus, such external factors, in many ways, provided the long-lasting role for historical overhangs or legacies in Thai–Cambodian ties. Thailand went ahead with establishing its diplomatic relations with China in 1975.

It hoped that the détente with China and the support given to the Khmer Rouge would contain the military advancement of communist Vietnam in the region. The Khmer Rouge survived their expulsion from Cambodia thanks to a steady supply of arms from Vietnam's traditional enemy, China, delivered to the Khmer Rouge by the Thai forces who wanted a buffer against the Vietnamese.[21] In the context of the Association of Southeast Asian Nations (ASEAN), Thailand exploited its position as a frontline state vis-à-vis the communist threat while successfully Aseanizing its anti-Vietnam policy.

This brief overview of Thai–Cambodian history reveals the linkage between the mutual negative perceptions, and how they were fed into the formulation of certain policies and the prescribed behaviour of their respective leaders. It also identifies the many critical historical junctures that led to the crystallization of the overhangs or legacies in the bilateral relationship. When the issue of the claim over Preah Vihear was recently resurrected, leaders repeatedly referred to history, stirred up nationalism and reassigned their neighbour as the enemy. The end result may reassure a number of political objectives among Thai and Cambodian elites, but it has proven extremely harmful to bilateral relations as well as regional peace and security. Ouk Sophoin, chargé d'affaires of the Cambodian Embassy in Bangkok, for example, responded to an article published in the *Bangkok Post*, "Do you know the name of the neighbouring country which helped and sheltered the Khmer Rouge in the 1980s and for most of the 1990s?"[22] Obviously Sophoin refreshed the past in order to justify his government's current policy towards Thailand. Sophoin's method of lifting history out of its rightful context to explain contemporary relations between Thailand and Cambodia is however not an innovation. For both countries, nation building is a never-ending process. Throughout the twentieth century the elites had been preoccupied with constructing their countries' identities based on unreasonable patriotism and the presence of enemies. Cambodia has been made one of Thailand's traditional enemies and arbitrarily used to legitimize the regime of the day, and vice versa. The available literature on the construction of Thai identity demonstrates how the process can be arbitrary, self-serving and politically motivated. Thongchai, for example, argued that the appearance of "Thainess", or *khwampenthai*, depends much upon what is not Thai. This analysis revolves around the creation of positive and negative identifications of Thainess; thus the image of a Cambodian adversary emerged. Meanwhile, Matthew Copeland asserted that during the years of absolute monarchy, Thai nationhood was created as an intellectual product of the royal court, an overarching discourse which a handful of kings and their loyal courtiers disseminated to a passive and for the most part receptive populace in such a way as to pre-empt the spread of rival ideas, symbols, and imagery.[23] This discourse can be useful in calling for public sacrifice should the kingdom be thrown in jeopardy. Similarly, Cambodian nation building was also politically driven. Ian Harris unveiled that the Cambodian identity building also had its anti-foreigner dimension.[24] This identity creation was in response to political repression and economic injustice Cambodians felt under foreign occupation, according to Penny Edwards.[25] The nation-building process has continued to breathe new life into the historical overhang or legacy in the Thai–Cambodia relationship.

FACTORS UNDERPINNING HISTORICAL OVERHANGS OR LEGACIES

Historical events have become a convenient tool for modern-day leaders to implement antagonistic foreign policy towards each other. This section discusses three factors that have fortified the power of historical overhangs or legacies in Thai–Cambodian relations. First, it looks into the concept of lost territories both in the historical and contemporary contexts in order to understand today's bilateral tensions arising from the contentious Preah Vihear Temple. Second, it examines the impact of the legitimacy crises, especially in Thailand, on the conduct of bilateral diplomacy. Claiming to protect its own national interests, Thailand became entangled in the Cambodian conflict throughout the 1970s to 1980s. Likewise, Cambodia has become actively and daringly engaging in the political turmoil in Thailand, using the history of Thai involvement in Cambodian politics to legitimize its position in the Thai crisis of the present day. Third, the state propaganda devices, such as education and the media, represent one of the root causes of the historical overhangs or legacies in the relations between Thailand and Cambodia. They have become a part of the process of nation building — the building of a nation that is supposedly superior to its neighbour.

The Lost Territories Enigma

Nidhi Eoseewong argued that Thai historiography as it has been produced over the last two centuries originated out of a desire on the part of the

Thai elite to define a Thai self that has been periodically threatened by outsiders.[26] The threat usually pertained to the nation's territorial integrity. Many countries around the world have claimed to have lost some of their territories unjustly to foreign powers or immoral neighbours. Thongchai Winichakul observed, "Lao nationalists talk about losing the *Isaan* (northeast) region to Thailand. Cambodian ones talk about losing territories to Thailand and Vietnam. They produce maps of lost territories like Thai nationalists did for generations. Thais have been taught that their territories were lost as well. Every country lost territories. The idea of loss is a powerful tool used to whip up nationalism, especially in domestic politics."[27] In the Thai case, official history tells the tale of the loss of the supposedly Thai territories to Britain (northern Malay states) and France (Cambodian provinces).[28] Accordingly, the concept of lost territories has constantly been backdated as though Siam had originally been a bounded kingdom with a precise territorially based sovereignty. Sukhothai, Ayutthaya and Thonburi were all made Thailand's old capitals even when the notion of sovereignty only arrived with the Western mapping technology during the colonial period. In reality, the Siamese and Khmers had been in contact for centuries with the absence of the modern concept of a clear-cut boundary. Thailand's reinvention of history was designed to justify its current campaign to recover lost territories. Similarly, Cambodia has reconstructed its own version of history to invalidate the Thai claim. At the height of their dispute over the Preah Vihear temple in 2009, many Cambodian patriots expressed their anger at Thailand's claim of ownership of the temple. For instance, a Cambodian wrote in an online public forum:

> Thais are thieves who stole Khmer creations and claimed them as Thai. Even *Muay Thai* (Thai boxing) has its Khmer creation. Khmer alphabets, Khmer vowels and Khmer numerals are today used by Thais. Thais have never given the credit or mentioned the Khmers who helped Thai ancestors from the Mongol killing or helped Siam from the Burmese occupation, but to claim every Khmer creation belonged to Thais. Yet, Thais were the destroyers of Khmer temples and now they are collecting tourist money from Khmer temples. Thais are the shameless people on earth.[29]

The need to highlight the issue of lost territories in the country's history has been to provoke a sense of nationalism among the people, and to seek their support, compliance and submission in regards to the state's policy. In reality, leaders could have been facing a legitimacy crisis and thus exploiting the issue of lost territories to cover up their shortcomings. In 1893 the French threatened Siam to surrender its control over the left bank of the Mekong River. They sent gunboats to block the mouth of the Chao Phraya River. This was known as the *Pak Nam* crisis. While Thai history paints the French as an aggressor, it exhibits the vulnerable side of the Siamese kingdom. But Thongchai provocatively argues that rather than seeing the 1893 incident as the Siamese "lamb" being terrorized by the French "wolf" leading to the "loss" of part of "Thailand"; the incident should be interpreted as the "big wolf" of France and the "small wolf" of Siam fighting over the "lambs" of Lao and Cambodian territories.[30] The distortion of history has become normalized throughout various regimes of the Thai state. Hence, the loss of the Preah Vihear Temple to Cambodia in 1962 played into the hands of the authoritarian regime of Sarit. Sarit immediately lit the fire of nationalism among the Thais by underlining the theme of lost territories. He took advantage of the ICJ ruling by constructing a new history for the Preah Vihear Temple. Sarit saw the loss of the temple, which, he claimed, had been fiercely defended throughout history by courageous Thai ancestors, as the loss of another piece of Thai territory. He urged the Thais to always remember that the temple was stolen by the enemy who lacked dignity and legitimacy with its abhorrent tactics.[31] Yet, successive Thai governments never challenged the ICJ verdict simply because they were unable to find new evidence to counter the earlier ruling.

In January 2003 the Royal Thai Embassy in Phnom Penh was burned down by so-called Cambodian nationalists. A few days earlier a local Cambodian newspaper reported that Suvanand Kongying, a famous Thai actress, declared that the Angkor Wat belonged to Thailand. Her alleged statement immediately stirred up great resentment inside Cambodia. Hun Sen angrily responded, "Suvanand was not even worth a blade of grass at Angkor."[32] However, the underlying message might not really be about protecting the dignity of Cambodia's territorial integrity. A Cambodian general election was around the corner and the conflict with Thailand could have been used to favour or undermine certain political factions. The opposition party blamed Hun Sen for his plot to divert public attention away from his government's inability to wipe out corruption and its willingness to allow Vietnamese candidates to run in the election under his party, the Cambodian People's Party (CCP). The Thaksin government, despite enjoying intimate relations with the Cambodian leaders, felt that it had done absolutely nothing to merit such a shocking violation of international law tacitly encouraged by the Cambodian authorities, and that the elites in Phnom Penh should be condemned for entertaining the theme of territorial integrity and jeopardizing bilateral ties. Meanwhile, the Thai media reported that Thai King Bhumibol Adulyadej said to a group of furious Thai protesters gathering in front of the Cambodian Embassy in Bangkok, "Do not forget who we are. We are *phu dee* (those of high class)."[33]

Internal Crisis and Foreign Policy

Domestic politics shapes the face of a country's foreign policy. This "linkage politics", or the nexus between the internal political situation and how it dictates foreign policy and the leaders' worldview, is a useful theoretical framework in assessing Thai–Cambodian relations.[34] As history has shown, the realm of foreign relations has consistently been exploited by political players to realize their own political purposes, which do not necessarily reflect the interests of their own countries. As mentioned earlier, the types of regime also play a vital part in the moulding of foreign policy and perceptions towards neighbours. Whereas during the Cold War years a series of Thai military regimes defined foreign policy so intimately with the notion of national security, thus supporting and sheltering the Khmer Rouge against communism *à la* Vietnam, the Thaksin government implemented a business-oriented policy, imitating the policy of Prime Minister Chatichai Choonhavan (1988–91) of turning the battlefield in Cambodia into a marketplace for Thai products.[35] Different political groups have incessantly sought to hegemonize their views both on domestic and foreign policies. They have competed with one another for ultimately the complete control of foreign policy. This study argues that foreign policy has been taken up as a self-legitimizing mechanism for political players. The present-day regime attempts to delegitimize past foreign policy so as to reconstruct its own legitimacy and strengthen its mandate to rule. Meanwhile, political opposition groups use the same tactic to demoralize the ruling regime, turning foreign policy into a powerful political weapon to achieve a similar outcome. The emergence of non-state actors, including the PAD and the red-shirted protesters under the guise of the National United Front of Democracy against Dictatorship (UDD), is seriously challenging the state's authority in the foreign policy decision-making process.[36] They have rewritten history to fit in with the political agendas of the power-holders, and in this case manipulated the issue of Preah Vihear. Hence, the deep polarization in Thai politics effectively constitutes the antecedent conditions for the worsening relations between Thailand and Cambodia. Both the pro- and anti-Thaksin factions have introduced their own versions of nationalism to undermine each other.

Hun Sen, in defending his leadership, decided to play the Thaksin card, by appointing him as Cambodia's economic adviser, refusing to extradite him despite repeated requests by the Abhisit government, and even allegedly granting him a Cambodian passport.[37] Supalak Ganjanakhundee has pointed out that this was the first time in modern history that a Cambodian leader has openly played internal Thai politics. Normally it has been the Thai side that influenced Cambodian domestic politics. In the past, Thailand supported the Cambodian opposition's efforts to destabilize the regime in Phnom Penh. Hun Sen himself had gained first-hand experience as Thailand backed the Khmer Rouge and the coalition against him in the 1980s. Many of his political enemies sought refuge in Thailand. Supalak said, "Hun Sen probably thinks now is the time to pay back."[38] Charnvit added that during the Cambodian conflict, Thailand supported the Khmer Rouge, but now Hun Sen is doing the same thing by supporting the Thai Rouge (the red shirts).[39] From this perspective, Hun Sen is crafting his country's foreign policy towards Thailand, using the historical context in which the Thais were heavily involved with the Khmer rouge in order to rationalize his inimical attitude towards the incumbent Abhisit government.

Distorted Textbooks and Provocative Media

Historical overhangs or legacies have been kept alive, replicated and refined in part by state education and the media. Instead of using them to ameliorate relations damaged by the bitter past, the Thai and Cambodian states continue to produce arbitrary textbooks and have manipulated the media in order to underline the greatness of their nation at the expense of belittling their neighbour. But are they really fighting to preserve the nation's identity and its historical significance? Or in fact, are they fighting to preserve their political hegemony within the domestic realm as well as in the domain of foreign relations?

In Thailand, the state has promoted Thai history through school textbooks under an overriding royalist-nationalist theme (*prawathisat baeb rachachatniyom*), forming a superior ideology vis-à-vis its neighbours. Thai students learn how the Siamese kingdom had to succumb to foreign invaders throughout its history, but the nation survived because of the wisdom and farsightedness of the Thai monarchs. The number-one enemy of the Thai kingdom has been the Burmese, who sacked the old Ayutthaya kingdom not once, but twice. While the tale of Siam being a ruthless destroyer of Angkor is missing in Thai textbooks, humiliating images of the Cambodians, such as the cowardly and opportunistic Khmer King Lovek, are particularly highlighted to make the Thai superiority apparent.[40] The issue of lost territories is also included in the historical textbooks, including the loss of Preah Vihear Temple to Cambodia in 1962. Indeed, only the Thai name of Phra Viharn appears in school textbooks, since it is generally believed that the name was linked to ownership. The name Preah Vihear/Phra Viharn posed a major stumbling block during the Thai–Cambodian Joint Boundary Commission (JBC) meeting in February 2009; each side insisted on using their own dialect in reference to the disputed temple. But textbooks are not the only means employed to inculcate a sense of Thai nationhood and to construct Cambodia as the enemy. State agencies in Thailand have issued countless press releases attacking the Cambodians when bilateral problems arose, thus shaping the contours of their relationship. Thai leaders talked about history, often discursively and arbitrarily, to contest the Cambodian leadership through bureaucratic channels. In 1961 the Thai Foreign Ministry declared in its press release, "As a matter of fact, Thailand has been in possession of Khao Phra Viharn since 1941 and, although France protested in 1949, Thailand has continued to be in possession of it without interruption."[41] In recent times Hun Sen's statement, appearing in a Cambodian press release, said, "If you [Prime Minister Abhisit] say the Thai army did not invade Cambodia on 15 July 2008, I wish all the evil things befall on you."[42] Moreover, leaders also turn to new media as their latest political instrument. Abhisit has launched his own interactive media channel called "AbhisitOrg" to communicate with his supporters. He often discusses Thailand's relations with Cambodia through this channel. On 6 January 2010, Abhisit defended his foreign policy towards Cambodia and vowed that he would not allow Hun Sen to take advantage of Thai interests.[43] Some of his interviews were posted on Youtube. Thaksin adopted a similar strategy. He has his own website and accounts with Facebook and Twitter. On the eve of him being appointed as Cambodia's economic adviser, Thaksin tweeted in Thai from Dubai, where he had spent much of his time since being ousted in a 2006 coup, "I thank Hun Sen for giving me such an honour. But I would have more enjoyment if I could work to eradicate Thai people's poverty."[44] Meanwhile, Hun Sen has relied on his Cambodian People's Party (CPP) blogs to confront the Thai leadership.[45] On 10 February 2010, the Cambodian government sent a strongly worded letter to the Internet giant Google, complaining that its online Google Earth map incorrectly places parts of the eleventh century Preah Vihear temple in Thailand. It lambasted the map for being "devoid of truth and reality and professionally irresponsible, if not pretentious".[46]

Charnvit argued that the Thai media has upheld tightly its perception of the traditional discourse of nationalism which underscores the inviolable national dignity. Thai feelings of "not wanting to be humiliated by Cambodia's victory" over the temple powerfully shaped Thai media coverage following the appointment of Thaksin as Cambodia's economic adviser.[47] But such a perception is uni-dimensional and fails to acknowledge other equally important aspects in the Thai–Cambodian relationship, such as economic ties and regional cooperation.[48] He also stressed how Preah Vihear has haunted the Thais in different stages of history. Charnvit asserted, "Thai bitterness over the Preah Vihear stemmed largely from what can be termed as 'inadequate history' — history learning that is distorted by a sense of nationalism."[49] In sum, problems in Thai–Cambodian relations have been sustained largely by the nationalist history taught in the schools and popularized through state channels, and by products of the commercial media as a dominant mode of reproduction of historical knowledge.[50] These factors have eclipsed the work of bilateral mechanisms such as the Thai–Cambodian Joint Commission, designed to promote good ties between the two countries through cultural contacts. It was founded in the aftermath of the attack on the Royal Thai Embassy in Phnom Penh in 2003, and consisted of several sub-committees covering culture, history and tourism.[51] But its activities have been suspended since the conflict over the Preah Vihear temple complex broke out in 2006.

OBSCURE PAST, TROUBLESOME PRESENT

Recently, two pressing issues have greatly put Thai–Cambodian relations to the test; the contentious Preah Vihear temple and the war of words between the governments of Abhisit and Hun Sen. They have been intensified and highly politicized by the forces of nationalism and the inimical attitudes towards each other as a result of their resentful past. This chapter will demonstrate how historical overhangs or legacies have come to play their role in these issues, leading to an even more acrimonious relationship, apparently to fulfil certain political objectives for the leaders in Bangkok and Phnom Penh.

The Temple of Doom

The dispute over the Preah Vihear temple was reignited in 2008, forty-six years after the ICJ ruling, as part of a plot to remove the government of Samak who was the self-proclaimed political nominee of Thaksin. The royalist PAD and the opposition Democrat Party saw the opportunity to politicize the Preah Vihear issue, to rewrite Thai–Cambodian history and to unleash the forces of nationalism, following the appointment as foreign minister of Noppadon Pattama, Thaksin's former personal lawyer. In May 2008 Noppadon, on behalf of the Thai government, signed a joint communiqué with Cambodia's deputy prime minister Sok An in Paris to confirm the Thai support for Cambodia's request to the United Nations Educational, Scientific and Cultural Organisation (UNESCO) to have the temple listed as a World Heritage Site. Upon returning to Bangkok, Noppadon was greeted by infuriated PAD nationalists at the airport. They shouted, "Noppadon is a traitor."[52] The PAD and the Democrat Party used the joint communiqué, which was later declared unconstitutional by the Constitutional Court because of the lack of parliamentary approval, to delegitimize the Samak government. Thailand, since the military coup of 2006, has been intensely polarized. The coup makers, with the support of the royalists, wanted to get rid of Thaksin because he posed a threat to the power position of the old establishment. But Thaksin still remained popular among his supporters in the rural regions and has been able to contest the traditional power holders through his political proxies. In an attempt to erode Thaksin's popularity and to keep up the momentum of their demonstrations against the Thaksin-backed Samak regime, the PAD and the Democrat Party endorsed a nationalistic strategy, accusing Samak and Noppadon of selling out the motherland to Cambodia. At the same time, the PAD and the Democrat Party refreshed indignant historical relations between Thailand and Cambodia in the following manner.

First, they aroused a sense of nationalism among the Thais. Proclaiming themselves as defenders of the Thai nation, the PAD and the Democrat Party reproached Thaksin and his cronies for their willingness to sacrifice Thai territories in exchange for personal benefits. They then connected the Preah Vihear issue to the loss of Thailand's territorial integrity and the failure of the state. They deliberately obscured the fact that UNESCO earlier clarified that Cambodia's request had nothing to do with remaining boundary disputes or overlapping sovereignty between the two countries, especially the contentious 4.6 square kilometres that surround the temple.

The theme of the loss of territories propagated by the anti-Thaksin forces was constructed on fabricated memories of the Thais being robbed of their lands by greedy *farang* (or Westerners, without specific race or nationality) powers in the past and by sinister Cambodians in the modern day. False memories and the rise of paranoid nationalistic anxiety convinced many Thais that the country was poised to lose its sovereignty over the surrounding areas because of the traitorous joint communiqué. It can be observed that the myth of lost territories was still thriving among many Thais. In response, Noppadon claimed that while his government worked conscientiously towards building up amicable relations with Cambodia, the PAD and the opposition party wanted to turn this friendly marketplace back into a battlefield.

Second, the PAD and the Democrat Party resurrected the Thai taboo of *khai chat*, or selling the country, to rationalize their scheme to overthrow the Samak government. *Khai chat* is a serious accusation in Thailand. The notion has no place in Thai history. Siamese monarchs have been incessantly extolled because they cherished the kingdom's territorial integrity and the inherent sacredness of the motherland soil (*phaendin*). But Thaksin, Samak and Noppadon, according to the PAD and the Democrat Party, betrayed their own nation by cooperating with Cambodian Hun Sen. The PAD, in particular, revealed that Thaksin had recently signed a commercial deal with Hun Sen for a development project in Cambodia's Koh Kong, and that the Thai support for the World Heritage Listing of the temple was a part of such a deal.[53] Cambodian Defence Minister General Teah Banh subsequently confirmed that Thaksin was planning large-scale investments in Cambodia, with Koh Kong serving only as the first step in his business ventures in the country.[54] It was reported that Thaksin eyed Koh Kong as a prime location for his casino and entertainment complex, purportedly called "Modern City".[55] Besides the Koh Kong project, Thaksin also planned to develop new tourist attractions in Phnom Penh and other major cities. Hun Sen was said to be pleased with Thaksin's proposal and was keen to work with him because Thaksin was "trustworthy".[56] Meanwhile, during the parliamentary no-confidence debate, from 23 to 25 June 2008, Abhisit, leader of the Democrat Party, further provoked nationalist feelings by stressing: "I hope that all Thai MPs will show distrust of this government. I call on all MPs who are "Thai" to vote against Prime Minister Samak and Foreign Minister Noppadon for abusing their constitutional power involving the Preah Vihear issue. It is time for the Thais to have a government that is grateful to its Thai ancestors and knows how to prioritize the nation's interests".[57] Under extreme pressure, Noppadon was forced to resign from the post of foreign minister. During his farewell at the foreign ministry, Noppadon announced, "I did not sell my country."[58]

Here, it is imperative to note that the role of the monarchy has been important, alongside the taboo of *khai chat*, in inculcating a sense of nationalism against foreign threats. Then and now, the monarchy exploited nationalism to strengthen its endorsed regimes and certain kinds of ideology that alienated its enemies. Now and then, the monarchy has continued to play a significant part in maintaining the image of foreign rivals to suppress internal enemies supposedly represented by Thaksin and his tainted regime. Protecting the Thai nation became equal to protecting the monarchy, since both are fundamental identities of the Thai nationhood.

Third, together the PAD and the Democrat Party reinvented the image of Cambodians as Thailand's adversaries. This negative depiction was once again made relevant to explain away Cambodia's involvement in Thai politics, especially at the time when Thailand was weak. Sondhi Limthongkul, leader of the PAD, recommended a resolution of the conflict by force. He said, "Our sacred mission is to protect our motherland and take back Thai territory." He also proposed that:

> A commission must be set up to invite Cambodia to bilateral negotiations. If the dispute cannot be settled, Thailand would, temporarily adhering to the ICJ's ruling, mobilise Thai troops, push Cambodians back from Thai territory, and formally inform Cambodia that, apart from the Preah Vihear temple, the surroundings belong to Thailand, and Thailand would pay any price to protect its sovereignty, even at the cost of war.[59]

The PAD's wish came true. One Thai and three Cambodian soldiers died in an exchange of rifle and rocket fire when their troops clashed on the border in October 2008. This was not the last armed clash between the two countries. As the conflict became more intense, Thailand and Cambodia engaged in a series of armed skirmishes. Throughout 2009–10, such actions between the armies of the two countries occasionally occurred, leading to a number of deaths and casualties on both sides.

Relentless War of Words

While making Cambodia the enemy of the state, some Thai political figures tried to demonize the Cambodian leaders at a personal level. In October 2008, Kasit Piromya of the Democrat Party, a well-known sympathizer of the PAD, appeared on the televised political talk show *Kom Chad Luek* and insulted Hun Sen. He called Hun Sen a *kui*, a derogatory term meaning a tramp, a vagrant or a gangster. He thought Hun Sen was *bah,* meaning deranged or mentally imbalanced. Kasit believed Hun Sen did not want good relations with Thailand and speculated that he was a *khikha*, or slave, of Thaksin. These disparaging terms were used against Hun Sen in order to satisfy the nationalistic needs of the PAD and the Democrat Party. At various points in the interview, Kasit characterized Thailand as belonging to a higher class, in contrast to the "unrefined" Hun Sen. To him, Cambodia was sullied with corruption and Hun Sen was the gangster of Southeast Asia.[60] Kasit also reportedly said, "I will use Hun Sen's blood to wash my feet."[61] His statement reminded many Cambodians of the tragic death of their king, Lovek. Hun Sen responded to Kasit with equally provocative language. He challenged, "What if I insult your king? What would you say if I insulted your prime minister and your ancestors? I'm not angry with you, but please use dignified words".[62]

After the Democrat Party formed the government in December 2008, Hun Sen immediately challenged Abhisit's leadership. Abhisit has largely suffered a legitimacy problem since his party had never won the majority vote but was only able to set up a coalition government following the dissolution of the Thaksin-backed People's Power Party. The game of retaliation thus began again, with Hun Sen working intimately with Thaksin in order to discredit the Abhisit regime. It also responded to Hun Sen's own interests. He has never been fond of the Abhisit government. Hun Sen realized that not only had Thaksin long been his business partner, but the former Thai premier still commanded loyalty among his rural supporters. Thus, Thaksin represents Hun Sen's long-term interests. First,

Hun Sen directly criticised Thailand's political instability and its failure of internal political reconciliation. He suggested that Thailand should be bypassed for the ASEAN chairmanship because of its internal political bickering (Thailand was Chair of the ASEAN Standing Committee from July 2008 to December 2009). In March 2009, Hun Sen proudly declared, "I am the leader of Cambodia who was elected by the will of the people, not by robbing power."[63] Chronic political divisions in Thailand, symbolized by the standoff between the PAD and the Democrat government against Thaksin and his red-shirted supporters, left an opening for Hun Sen to intervene in Thai politics. Cambodian diplomats also followed up Hun Sen's policy of legitimizing Cambodia's involvement in Thai politics. You Ay, former Cambodian Ambassador to Bangkok, criticized the *Nation*'s recent commentary on Cambodia,

> When you stated that the … Cambodia premier thought he was still leading some Khmer Rouge faction … you are absolutely dead wrong. It was Samdech Techo Hun Sen, who struggled and brought the demise of the Khmer Rouge. Prime Minister Hun Sen could have done it much earlier, if a neighbouring country had not given shelter to the Khmer Rouge. It was also Samdech Techo Hun Sen who brought the Khmer Rouge leaders to the Extraordinary Chamber of Courts of Cambodia (ECCC).[64]

In November 2009, Hun Sen provocatively expressed how he felt Thaksin was unfairly treated by the Thai government and that he would offer one of his luxurious mansions to receive Thaksin if the latter wanted refuge in Cambodia, and would not extradite him.[65] A few days later during the ASEAN Summit in Hua Hin, Hun Sen further irritated Thai patriots by announcing that Thaksin would be appointed as his government's economic advisor. The appointment was made official by virtue of a Royal Degree in the Cambodian capital on 4 November 2009. The Cambodian leader carried on releasing contentious statements to disparage the Thai government and question its legitimacy. Hun Sen compared Thaksin with Nobel laureate Aung San Suu Kyi, leader of the National League for Democracy of Burma. He said on behalf of his wife, Bun Rany, "Though I am not Thai, I am hurt by what has happened to him. My wife even cried on learning about it and has an idea to build a home for Thaksin to come and stay honourably." Furthermore, Hun Sen also offered his support to the red-shirted protesters in Thailand. He stated, "This is just moral support from me. As one million Thai people of the red-shirted group support Thaksin, why cannot I, as a friend from afar, support Thaksin?"[66]

Hun Sen's offensive move sorely raised the political temperature in Thailand and was once again inflated by the PAD nationalists. The PAD condemned Hun Sen for meddling in Thailand's internal affairs and impugning its judicial system. Major-General Chamlong Srimuang, one of the PAD's leaders, accused Thaksin of treachery in using a neighbouring nation to push his personal political agenda in Thailand.[67] At the same time, the government adopted harsher diplomatic measures against Cambodia. On 6 November 2009, The Thai Foreign Ministry recalled its ambassador to Phnom Penh to protest against Cambodia's official appointment of Thaksin. It also decided to review all bilateral agreements with Cambodia and pull out of maritime talks, which would have covered potential rich supplies of oil and gas in a disputed area of the eastern Gulf of Thailand. Cambodia retaliated by recalling its ambassador to Bangkok. However, border trade continued as usual with no restrictions on Thais visiting Cambodia, although the situation along their common border had been tense. The Thai military, exploiting the notion of national security and nationalism, depicted a deadly scenario of a possible new round of armed clashes. It has built 340 bunkers in two schools and several villages in Si Sa Ket near the site of the Preah Vihear Temple as a sign of unease that has swept through this border town.[68]

Portraying Thailand as a nation under attack by the enemy, the Abhisit government regained some popularity due to the decisive reaction to Thaksin and Hun Sen's actions, thus demonstrating that nationalism was once again politically useful. According to the ABAC (Assumption University) Poll conducted from 25 October to 5 November 2009, Abhisit's popularity had almost tripled from 23.3 per cent in September 2009 to 68.6 per cent in its later poll; this was due to the increase in support for the government in the aftermath of Hun Sen's attack on the Thai judicial system and the appointment of Thaksin.[69] Countering the rise of Abhisit's popularity in Thailand, Thaksin paid a visit to Cambodia on 12 November 2009 at the invitation of Hun Sen and gave a lecture to Cambodian government officials. He later travelled to Siem Reap to play golf with the Cambodian leader and met with a group of his red-shirted supporters with the intent to aggravate the Abhisit administration. On top of this, Hun Sen deepened the degree of "awkwardness" in his relations with Thailand by arresting a thirty-one-year-old Thai engineer, Sivarak

Chutiphong, an employee of Cambodia Air Traffic Services, on the charge of spying on the fugitive former premier Thaksin for Thailand. He was later released, apparently thanks to Thaksin's help in negotiating with Hun Sen. Then, the pro-Thaksin opposition party, the Puea Thai (For Thai), and Cambodia's Hun openly joined forces in contesting Abhisit's legitimacy. In particular, Hun Sen took every opportunity to label the Abhisit government as his country's foe, just as Abhisit and the PAD had earlier labelled the Khmers as Thailand's enemy. Hun Sen said in December 2009, "I am not the enemy of the Thai people. But the Prime Minister [Abhisit] and the Foreign Minister [Kasit] look down on Cambodia extremely. Cambodia will have no happiness as long as this group is in power in Thailand."[70] The Cambodian premier, again, made headlines across the region in February 2010, when he launched crude remarks against Abhisit:

> I am angry at a few people in Thailand. I am not angry at the whole Siamese people and two lousy English-language newspapers, the *Nation* and *Bangkok Post*.... You [Abhisit] are a thief who stole power [from Thaksin]. If you don't believe me, then lets hold an election and you will lose.... If you don't speak the truth about Siamese troops invading Cambodia on 15 July 2008, let the sacred powers break your neck, let you be shot dead, be crushed to death by a car, be electrocuted or shot dead by a stray bullet.... Not only that Thailand invaded [Cambodia], but they also invaded and cheated in history by changing the name of Prasart Preah Vihearn into Phra Viharn.... If Thai troops did not intrude into Wat Keo Sekkha Kiri Savarak, let bad luck befall on me.... I have chided you many times before. Do you feel hurt? If you retaliate, I will hit back at you again.... I have sent a letter to tell the Siamese people that there has never been a period when the Siamese society is so chaotic as the period under Abhisit. Thai foreign relations are also bad.... You ordered the yellow shirts [PAD] to stage the coup and to seize the airports.... Would Abhisit take an oath that his family will perish in a plane crash that the Siam troops did not invade Cambodia?... He [Abhisit] is crazy, confused and deserves to be eliminated. This guy has no honour for his family.[71]

Not only was Hun Sen ready to savage Cambodia's relations with Thailand due to his personal animosity against the Abhisit government, he also used history to validate his accusation against Thailand. Hun Sen has continued to call Thailand "Siem", a term used by Cambodians in reference to Siam, which often connotes a sense of historical antipathy. Here, an amalgam of false history, nationalism and political crises at home combined into a heady cocktail leading to the deterioration of the bilateral relationship. Negative memories between the two countries have never been erased, but instead celebrated for some political purposes, even at the expense of further damaging bilateral ties.

CONCLUSION

The Preah Vihear issue truly reflects the fragile relations between Thailand and Cambodia. The bitter historical background — coupled with the nationalist sentiment used as a tool of the unfinished nation-building processes in both Thailand and Cambodia — has proven to be a tangible obstruction to any sense of neighbourliness. In the case of Thai–Cambodia relations, the nationalist bias in each country's history has not ended, but on the contrary has even been reproduced and has recently re-emerged.[72] The manner in which history has been recreated as a political weapon, either to undermine domestic opponents or foreign enemies, has led to perpetual suspicion on the part of Thailand and Cambodia towards each other. Thailand's domestic crisis has harmfully affected its relations with Cambodia since various factions have continued to treat this neighbour as their political hostage. Hun Sen's involvement in Thai politics has also deepened the already frail foundation of mutually peaceful co-existence. The territorial disputes over the Preah Vihear temple have become a test case to evaluate the stability of bilateral relations. Evidently, it attests to the fact that their similar cultural and religious backgrounds have failed to withstand the occasional storms in their bilateral relationship, mainly due to political leaders aggravating bilateral conflicts for their own power interests.

There have been numerous critical junctures throughout their mutual history that have unveiled the unattractive side of Thai–Cambodian relations. Indeed, they are not the only countries in the world to have experienced a shared traumatic history. A more important message is that the leaders have never ceased taking advantage of this controversial history, which has continued to sour bilateral ties. Factors behind the persistent historical overhangs or legacies derive from both within and beyond the borders. From 2008, bilateral relations have been much dictated by the domestic situation in Thailand. Internal crises have continued to set the conditions for hostile relations. The anti-Thaksin forces manipulated the Preah Vihear issue to impair Thaksin-backed regimes, while fully realizing that their provocative acts could cost Thailand in its relations with Cambodia. When the anti-Thaksin forces were in power, Thaksin took up the same strategy of internationalizing the domestic situation, by conspiring with Cambodia to destabilize the Abhisit government. Nationalistic foreign policy was implemented; it was also buttressed by the obscure history in which both Thailand and Cambodia, by each identifying its virtuous self, stereotyped the other in a negative light. State channels, such as education and the media, have nurtured the negative stereotypes. This elucidates why the portrayal of Cambodia as Thailand's historical arch-enemy has been frozen in aspic. The current spat between Thailand and Cambodia indicates that the two countries are still haunted by their mutual hatred, which is not necessarily a vestige of their historical past, but rather a product of political manipulation of the more recent elites.

Notes

1. The author would like to express his sincere thanks to *Asian Affairs* for its kind permission to reproduce parts of this chapter. It was first published as an article in *Asian Affairs*. See Pavin Chachavalpongpun, "Embedding Embittered History: Unending Conflicts in Thai–Cambodian Relations", *Asian Affairs* 43, no. 1 (2012): 81–102.
2. Walter F. Vella, *Chaiyo! King Vajiravudh and the Development of Thai Nationalism* (Honolulu: University Press of Hawai'i, 1978), p. x.
3. The PAD, formed in February 2006, is a coalition of royalists, Bangkok elites, factions in the military and powerful business interests, with an aim to deracinate Thaksin's legacy in politics. The Thaksin-backed governments were led by Samak Sundaravej (January–September 2008) and Somchai Wongsawat (September–December 2008).
4. Charnvit Kasetsiri, "Thailand–Cambodia: A Love-Hate Relationship", *Kyoto Review of Southeast Asia* 3 (March 2003) <http://www.charnvitkasetsiri.com/PDF/Thailand-Cambodia.pdf>.
5. See Chris Baker, "Ayutthaya Rising: From Land or Sea?" *Journal of Southeast Asian Studies* 34, no. 1 (February 2003): 41–62.
6. After the collapse of Angkor, a new capital was built at Phnom Penh. Phnom Penh remained the royal capital for 73 years, from 1432 to 1505, when it was abandoned for 360 years, from 1505 to 1865, by subsequent kings due to internal fighting between the royal pretenders. Later kings moved the capital several times and established their royal capitals at various locations in Tuol Basan (Srey Santhor), Pursat, Lovek, Lavear Em and Oudong.
7. Charnvit, "Thailand–Cambodia: A Love-Hate Relationship", p. 3.

8. Ibid., pp. 4, 8. Charnvit referred to the work of three Thai historians, Janchai Phakatimkom, Boonteun Srivorapong and Santi Pakdeekham, who argued that King Naresuan did not kill the Cambodian ruler, and the ritual in which the blood of Phraya Lovek was used to wash Naresuan's feet did not occur. These writers contended that Phraya Lovek fled to Laos where he lived out the rest of his days.

9. Thongchai Winichakul, *Siam Mapped: A History of the Geo-Body of a Nation* (Honolulu: University of Hawai'i Press, 1994), pp. 84–85. Also see David P. Chandler, *A History of Cambodia*, 4th ed. (Boulder, CO: Westview, 2007); and Walter F. Vella, *Siam under Rama III 1824–1851* (New York: Association for Asian Studies, 1957).

10. Ibid., p. 166.

11. See Pavin Chachavalpongpun, "The Temple of Doom: Hysteria about the Preah Vihear Temple in the Thai Nationalist Discourse", *Legitimacy Crisis and Conflict in Thailand*, edited by Marc Askew (Chiang Mai: Silkworm Books, 2010). Also see Michael Wright, "Khao Phra Viharn: Some Historical Background", Matichon Online, 31 July 2008 <http://www.matichon.co.th/news_detail.php ?newsid=43665&grpid=04&catid=01> (accessed 28 March 2009); and Anucha Paepanawan, *Exclusive: Kanmuang Ruang Khao Phra Viharn* [Exclusive: The political case of Khao Phra Viharn] (Bangkok: Kleung Aksorn, 2008).

12. Scot Barme, *Luang Wichit Wathakan and the Creation of a Thai Identity* (Singapore: Institute of Southeast Asian Studies, 1993), p. 64.

13. For further discussion, see Kobkua Suwannathat-Pian, "Thai Wartime Leadership Reconsidered: Phibun and Pridi", *Journal of Southeast Asian Studies* 27, no. 1 (March 1996): 166–78.

14. In 1941, Cambodia was occupied by the Japanese. As Japan was losing the war, it decided to arrest French officials and declare Cambodia independent. But when the Japanese surrendered, the French took over again, in 1945.

15. Quoted in Michelle Vachon, "Building History: Researchers Surprised by Battambang Finds", *Cambodian Daily*, 16 August 2003.

16. Ministry of Foreign Affairs of Thailand, *Relations between Thailand and Cambodia* (Bangkok: Prachandra Press, 1959), p. 2.

17. Ibid., 4. *La Dépêche du Cambodge*, published on 19 June 1958: "Pendant sept siècles, et aujourd'hui encore, nous avons payé cher l'expérience de la déloyauté des chefs e'Etat et des Gouvernement de cette nation rapace dont le vautour remplacerait plus judicieusement le Garouda sur ses armoires."

18. Benchapa Krairiksh, *Nao Khmer* [Being in Cambodia] (Bangkok: Matichon Books, 2004), p. 94.

19. Bunruam Tienchan, Praphat Chaleimak and Saranya Wichatham. *Khrai Dai Khrai Sia Khwam Khat Yaeng Thi Ban Plai: Prasad Khao Phra Viharn* [Who won who lost, the uncontrollable conflict: Khao Phra Viharn] (Bangkok: Animate, 2008), p. 90.

20. Various studies have estimated the death toll at between 740,000 and 3 million, most commonly between 1.4 and 2.2 million, with perhaps half of those deaths being due to executions, and the rest from starvation and disease. For example, the U.S. Department of State–funded Yale Cambodian Genocide Project gives estimates of the total death toll between 1.2 and 1.7 million. Amnesty International estimates the total death toll as 1.4 million. Pol Pot gave a figure of 800,000, and his deputy, Khieu Samphan, said 1 million had been killed. See Bruce Sharp, *Counting Hell: The Death Toll of the Khmer Rouge Regime in Cambodia*, 1 April 2005 <http://www.mekong.net/cambodia/deaths. htm> (accessed 3 January 2010).

21. An Asia Watch Report, *Khmer Rouge Abuses along the Thai–Cambodian Border* (Washington: Asia Watch Committee, 1989), p. 6.

22. "Cambodia Pours Scorn on Thai Scholar's Article", *Bangkok Post*, 11 January 2010.

23. See Thongchai, *Siam Mapped*. Also see Matthew Phillip Copeland, *Contested Nationalism and the 1932 Overthrow of the Absolute Monarchy in Siam* (PhD Dissertation, Australian National University, 1993), p. 3.

24. Ian Harris, *Cambodian Buddhism: History and Practice* (Honolulu: University of Hawai'i Press, 2005), p. 132.

25. Penny Edwards, *Cambodge: The Cultivation of a Nation, 1860–1945* (Honolulu: University of Hawai'i Press, 2007), p. 6.

26. Quoted in Patrick Jory, *Problem in Contemporary Thai Nationalist Historiography* (Kyoto: Centre of Southeast Asian Studies, March 2003) <http://kyotoreview. cseas.kyoto-u.ac.jp/issue/issue2/article_251.html>.

27. Thongchai Winichakul, "Preah Vihear Could Be a Time Bomb", *The Nation*, 30 June 2008.

28. Thailand claimed to have lost Kedah, Perlis, Kelantan, and Terengganu to Britain and Battambang, Sisophon and Siem Reap to France.

29. *Rumtum* is the pseudonym of this Cambodian writer <http://www.topix.com/ forum/th/bangkok/T8QQC10L6JB7CF3JS#comments> (accessed 30 January 2010).

30. Thongchai Winichakul, "Prawatisat Thai Baep Rachachatniyom: Chak Yuk Ananikhonm Amphrang Su Rachachatniyom Mai Ru Latthi Sadet Phor Khorn Kradumphi Thai Nai Patchuban" [Royalist-nationalist history: From the era of crypto-colonialism to the new royalist-nationalism, or the contemporary Thai bourgeois cult of Rama V], *Silapawathanatham* [Arts and culture] 23, no. 1 (2001): 50, quoted in Jory, *Problem in Contemporary Thai Nationalist Historiography*.

31. Sarit Thanarat, "Kham Prasai Khong Phanathan Chomphon Sarit Thanarat, Nayok Rattamontri kieowkap Khadi Prasat Phra Viharn Thang Wittayu Krachaiseang Lae Wittayu Toratat 4 Karakadakhom Song Pan Ha Roi Ha"

[Address by H.E. Field Marshal Sarit Thanarat, Prime Minister, regarding the Phra Viharn Temple case on the national radio and television stations, 4 July 1962], 1962.

32. Nopporn Wong-Anan, "Temple Tantrums Stalk Thai–Cambodia Relations", Reuters, 20 July 2008.

33. Chonticha Sathayawatthana, ed., *Botrian Chak Hedkarn Khwamroonrang Nai Kamphucha* [Lessons from violent incident in Cambodia] (Bangkok: Kanghan, 2003), p. 30.

34. James N. Rosenau defined linkage politics as any recurrent sequence of behaviour that originated in one system and was reacted to in another; it was the interconnection between domestic and international realms. He declared, "Politics everywhere, it would seem, are related to politics everywhere else." See James N. Rosenau, "Introduction: Political Science in a Shrinking World", in *Linkage Politics*, edited by James N. Rosenau (New York: Free Press, 1969), p. 2, quoted in Yale H. Ferguson and Richard W. Mansbach, *Remapping Global Politics: History's Revenge and Future Shock* (Cambridge: Cambridge University Press, 2004), p. 17.

35. See Sunai Phasuk, *Nayobai Tang Prathet Khong Thai: Suksa Krabuankarnkamnod Nayobai Khong Ratthaban Pon-ek Chatichai Choonhavan Tor Panha Kumphucha, Si Singhakom 1988–23 Kumphaphan 1991* [Thai foreign policy: A study of foreign policy making process under the Chatichai Choonhavan government, 4 August 1988–23 February 1991] (Bangkok: Institute of Asian Studies, 1997).

36. Pavin Chachavalpongpun, "Diplomacy Under Siege: Thailand's Political Crisis and the Impact on Foreign Policy", *Contemporary Southeast Asia* 31, no. 3 (December 2009): 448–49.

37. "Thaksin Obtains Cambodian Citizenship in March 2009" <http://ki-media. blogspot.com/2010_01_01_archive.html> (accessed 9 January 2010).

38. Supalak Ganjanakhundee, "Hun Sen Settling Scores but Is It Worth It?", *The Nation*, 7 November 2009.

39. "Sampas Charnvit Kasetsiri: Tonnee Pen Khon Thai Ki Fai Thi Torsukan Kanathi Kamphucha Luayou Faidiew" [Interview Charnvit Kasetsiri: How many factions are now in Thailand fighting among themselves? While Cambodia has only one faction.] *Prachatai*, 8 November 2009 <http://www.prachatai. com/journal/2009/11/26512>.

40. Jory, *Problem in Contemporary Thai Nationalist Historiography*. According to Charnvit, Thais are also not particularly fond of Norodom Sihanouk. For example, a Thai riddle asks, "What colour (*si*) do Thai people hate?" The answer is neither red (*si daeng*) nor black (*si dam*), but "Si-hanouk". See Charnvit, "Thailand–Cambodia: A Love-Hate Relationship".

41. Ministry of Foreign Affairs of Thailand, *Relations between Thailand and Cambodia*, p. 2.

42. "Hun Sen Lets Fly at Abhisit", *Bangkok Post*, 9 February 2010.
43. See <http://www.youtube.com/user/abhisitorg#p/u/33/qIEh2wESFss> (accessed 13 February 2010).
44. "Thaksin Shinawatra Appointed Economics Adviser to Cambodia", Timeonline, 5 November 2009 <http://www.timesonline.co.uk/tol/news/world/asia/article6904000.ece> (accessed 13 February 2010).
45. See <http://cppdailynews.blogspot.com/> (accessed 13 February 2010).
46. "Cambodia Lambast Google Earth for locating Temple in Thai Soil", *The Nation*, 10 February 2010.
47. Puangthong Pawakapan gave this statement during the Mekong Media Forum, held at Chulalongkorn University, Bangkok, Thailand, on 12 December 2009. Puangthong is Assistant Professor at the Department of International relations at Chulalongkorn University.
48. Sampas Charnvit Kasetsiri: Tonnee Pen Khon Thai Ki Fai Thi Torsukan Kanathi Kamphucha Luayou Faidiew" [Interview Charnvit Kasetsiri: How many factions are now in Thailand fighting among themselves? While Cambodia has only one faction].
49. For further discussion, see Charnvit Kasetsiri, *Latthi Chatniyom Thai/Siam Nai Kampucha: Lae Koranee Suksa Khao Prah Viharn* [Siamese/Thai Nationalism and Cambodia: A Case Study of the Preah Vihear Temple] (Bangkok: Toyota Thailand Foundation, the Foundation for the Promotion of Social Science and Humanities, 2009).
50. Jory, *Problem in Contemporary Thai Nationalist Historiography*.
51. Source: Ministry of Foreign Affairs of Thailand <http://www.mfa.go.th/web/2386.php?id=51> (accessed 13 February 2010).
52. "Noppadon Nahcha Thookdah Khaichat Tornahthood Acharn Thammasat Kadkant Amnard Tadsinkhadi Khong San Pokklong" [Noppadon was criticised for selling the country in front of foreign diplomats, Thammasat University's professors object the role of the administrative court], S!News, 30 June 2008 <http://news.sanook.com/politic/politic_281852.php> (accessed 13 February 2010).
53. In, "Preah Vihear for Koh Kong and Natural Oil/Gas" <http://antithaksin.wordpress.com/2008/10/16/preah-vihear-for-koh-kong-and-natuaral-gasoil/> (accessed 29 March 2009).
54. Wassana Nanuam, "Thaksin Set to Invest Big Time in Cambodia", *Bangkok Post*, 19 June 2008.
55. Neth Pheaktra, "Koh Kong to Become Second Hong Kong", *Mekong Times*, 26 May 2008.
56. Wassana Nanuam, "Thaksin Set to Invest Big Time in Cambodia", *Bangkok Post*, 19 June 2008.

57. Yossawadee Hongthong, "Abhisit Calls on Thai MPs to Vote against PM", *The Nation*, 23 June 2008.

58. Noppadon Pattama, *Phom Mai Dai Khai Chart* [I did not sell my country] (Bangkok: Kledthai, 2008), p. 61.

59. On 28 July 2008, Sondhi Limthongkul, leader of the PAD, took to the stage at about 9 p.m. to address the crowd rallying near Government House in Bangkok, and proposed this way out of the crisis <http://www.prachatai.com/english/node/732> (accessed 13 February 2010).

60. See his interview at <http://www.youtube.com /watch?v=_UCi-mgmIDs>.

61. See <http://www.asiafinest.com/forum/index.php?showtopic=198660> (accessed 13 February 2010).

62. "Hun Sen Blasted at Kasit for Allegedly Insulting him by Calling him a Gangster", *The Nation*, 31 March 2009.

63. "Cambodia's PM Hun Sen May Misunderstand Thai FM", *The Nation*, 31 March 2009.

64. You Ay, "Editorial Coverage of Hun Sen is not Fair", *The Nation*, 3 November 2009.

65. Shawn W. Crispin, "Plots Seen in Thaksin's Cambodia Gambit", Asia Times, 12 November 2009 <http://www.atimes.com/atimes/Southeast_Asia/KK12Ae01.html> (accessed 13 February 2010).

66. Veera Prateepchaikul, "Does Hun Sen Want to Play in our Political Sandbox?", *Bangkok Post*, 26 October 2009.

67. "Govt to Consider Revoking MoU with Cambodia", *Bangkok Post*, 6 November 2009.

68. Marwaan Macan-Markar, "Thai–Cambodia Tension Gives Rise to Schools with Bunkers", IPS, 24 November 2009 <http://ipsnews.net/news.asp?idnews=49385> (accessed 13 February 2010).

69. The poll was conducted between 25 October and 5 November 2009 and involved 3,709 people, aged 18 and up, in twenty-one provinces. By region, support for the Abhisit government was 88.2 per cent in the South, 68.9 per cent in Central, 68.8 per cent in Bangkok, 64.6 per cent in the North, and 53.1 per cent in the Northeast. See "Souring Public Support for the Government", *Bangkok Post*, 6 November 2009.

70. "Yet Another Unprovoked Outburst from Hun Sen", *Bangkok Post*, 1 December 2010.

71. Veera Prateepchaikul, "Hun Sen's Latest Antic Unbecoming of a Premier", *Bangkok Post*, 9 February 2010.

72. Paul Busbarat, "Thai–Cambodian Dispute over the Preah Vihear Temple Revisited", Policy Net, 30 August 2008 <http://www.policy-net.org/blogs/thefareast/thaicambod> (accessed 13 February 2010).

7

COMPARING BILATERAL OVERHANGS OR LEGACIES IN EAST AND SOUTHEAST ASIA

N. Ganesan

The five case studies in this book clearly prove the fact that overhangs or legacies are a very real phenomenon in East and Southeast Asian international relations. In this regard it is arguable that history and historical memories have enduring value in foreign policy formulation. And, interestingly enough, many of the case studies point to the fact that important developments deriving from the pre-independence or colonial periods had a formative effect on informing policy output in the post-independence period. It may therefore be hypothesized that historical experiences and grievances in particular have had a continuous impact on elite and mass perceptions. Aspects of such perceptions have been imprinted for posterity. Importantly, it is also abundantly clear that there are specific reference points that have led to the creation of the overhang or legacy, and such critical conjunctures invariably deal with some sense of insult or injustice felt by victimized states. Such states regarded themselves the victims of callous exploitation or conquest and occupation at some point in their history and that memory has been preserved over time. As a result of such preservation there appears to be an ongoing demand to seek some form of apology or conciliatory gesture from the aggressor state. This is certainly the case with regard to the perceptions of both the Koreans and Chinese in relation to the Japanese. In both cases one gets the sense that Japan has been unable or unwilling to placate this feeling, at least as observed by the authors.

The cases that involve Thailand are interesting since they are so dissimilar from the cases involving Japan. The Thai overhangs or legacies with Myanmar and Cambodia appear to suggest that the archetypical Thai national is portrayed in contradistinction to that of those from neighbouring countries. This appears to be the case especially if Thailand had a history of conflicts with the countries and had been dealt severe defeats in the past. There seems to be a need to correct past defeats that are then characterized as injustices that need to be retold differently in order to salvage national pride. The retold narrative disadvantages the other party in terms of a character flaw or deficit that in turn led to the Thai military defeat. However, the retold narrative is then used to stoke nationalist sentiments in characterizing the other party as unreliable and unworthy of proper treatment. Subsequently, the stereotypical other is easily held responsible for frayed bilateral relations and made to bear the brunt of the blame. This situation also allows the military to claim itself as the guardian and restorer of national pride, away from democratic national institutions. The narrative is in turn intertwined with the control of policy output towards neighbouring countries and assists the military in retaining a certain pride of place among national institutions.

Systemic structures, ideology and regime types also appear to have had an impact on bilateral overhangs or legacies. So, for example, during the Cold War when Japan and South Korea were alliance partners with the United States in the fight against communism, shared strategic and ideological interests suppressed bilateral tensions. In any event, such tensions were much less obvious than now. Whereas the reordering of systemic structures away from bipolarity and the collapse of communism share some of the responsibility for the worsened situation, developmental gains made by South Korea are equally important in nudging the issue to a higher plane. After all, for much of the 1960s and 1970s as well as into part of the 1980s, Korea benefitted from Japanese aid that spurred its own economic development and enhanced status. In this regard,

China's overhang or legacy with Japan continued throughout the Cold War, given ideological differences, and has also become more important as the country has gained national prestige on account of its rapid recent development.

The situation between China and Vietnam provides a case where sub-systemic structural rivalry for power and influence in the Asia-Pacific region in the 1970s led to tensions notwithstanding a common ideology in communism. The Sino–Soviet rift in the 1960s and the 1970s contributed to this overhang or legacy, in particular the Soviet attempt to create a third force in Vietnam to deflect the threat of China.[1] In this regard, it may well be argued that structural and strategic considerations have the potential to displace common ideological considerations. Put differently, competitive notions of national interest and power can serve to undermine common ideological considerations. Both these cases do however suggest that better standing in the international system augurs the potential for states that regard themselves as having been mistreated in the past to seek some form of recognition of their previous condition. And such recognition is likely to imply some form of remedial action by the other party as well.

As for regime types, the case studies point in the direction of several interesting conclusions. The first and perhaps most obvious observation is that states with non-democratic regime types have far better control of the domestic citizenry and the foreign policy agenda than democratic states. So, for example, China, Myanmar and Vietnam have far better control over citizen groups and their policy agendas than countries like Japan and Thailand. Such control does not however necessarily imply that overhangs or legacies can be dealt with rationally. After all, such states are equally capable of posturing and stoking domestic sentiments than populist right-wing groups in Thailand and Japan. Rather, what is implied here is that such countries are able to exercise far better control of their own environments and agendas in turn. Democratic societies, on account of their preservation of the fundamental liberties of free speech, writing and association, are sometimes unable to deal with civic groups that abuse such rights and sow hatred. In fact, Japan is home to a number of such groups that regularly try to influence opinion against China and Korea. And Thailand is home to a number of similar groups that spew such hatred towards Cambodia as noted by Pavin. Nonetheless, governments in democratic societies do have the means to restrain such groups should they so choose. Additionally, they need not take such negative sentiments into account when formulating policy.

Regime types that espouse an ideology with distinctive cultural traits or views in stereotypical terms can also present problems. For example, many leaders of the LDP government in Japan, including Koizumi Junichiro, saw nothing wrong in paying a visit to the Yasukuni Shrine as noted by Lam Peng Er. On the other hand, more sensitive leaders from the same party avoided such visits in order not to stoke tensions with China. In the case of Thailand, governments led by the Democrat Party have traditionally had a poor relationship with Myanmar. At least part of this reason is rooted in the ideological belief that a military junta being in power is an unacceptable development. Conversely, governments in Thailand that were led by the military have traditionally had a good bilateral relationship with Myanmar on account of personal familiarity, shared worldviews and business interests. Even the Thaksin government, despite having been popularly elected, had a cosy relationship with the military junta in Myanmar on account of shared business interests. More nationalist governments have articulated Thainess in contradistinction to other nationalities as noted by both Pavin and Aung Myoe. In such a situation, it is not difficult to see why nationalistic rhetoric is meant to glorify one party and put down the other. In a recent book, Pavin argues that Thaksin's highly nationalistic rhetoric was actually at odds with his international diplomacy where he sought a greater role for Thailand in the regional arena.[2] This notion of nationalism in relational terms is clearly an undesirable practice and is likely in turn to generate ill will with neighbouring countries. And governments that lack legitimacy or are easily manipulated by populist constituencies are much more vulnerable to nationalistic rhetoric that endangers bilateral ties.

This discourse on nationalism also highlights the importance of ethnicity in bilateral relations. Whereas it is true that many countries in Southeast Asia are multi-ethnic states, the same is not true of Northeast Asian countries. As a consequence of having relatively homogeneous populations, it is easy to have to think and behave in mutually exclusive terms. Hence, it is clear that in popular Chinese and Korean belief systems, Japanese are regarded as aggressors and capable of hegemonic behaviour when given the opportunity. Similarly, it is not uncommon for the Japanese to regard Chinese and Koreans with a measure of distrust. And even today, right-wing politicians, academics and newspapers regularly disparage the minority communities from the region that reside in Japan. Ethnicity also appears to be a problem in Sino–Vietnamese bilateral relations and is in fact one of the issues that has led to conflict in the past. The same observation can be made of Cambodia under the Khmer Rouge regarding Vietnamese settlers, and Ramses Amer makes this clear in a recent publication.[3] This notion of insiders and outsiders harkens to the older notion of nation as a cultural community rather than just a population resident within the territorial confines of a state. Whatever the case may be, the combination of different ethnicity, hazy notions of contested loyalties and proximity to border areas is a heady brew that invites undue attention at times when comfort levels between states are low.

The evidence from the case studies also seems to indicate that the markers for the discourse on overhangs or legacies have a clear anchor in traditional notions of security. In international relations, the conventional issues pertain to territoriality and sovereignty. In other words, regardless of whether specific individuals or groups are more affected by issues, there is a sense in which the state is involved in the discourse. In the Japanese case, frayed relations with China and Korea clearly involve notions of the infringement of sovereignty and of crimes committed against the inhabitants of these countries. Whilst it is arguable that some of these episodes preceded statehood in the region as we now understand it, the fact remains that there was some notion of a Korean and a Chinese nation in the past. And such transgressions are viewed with anger, although the states themselves may not have been in a position to resist such transgressions in the past. International law was also unavailable then and was certainly not regarded as applicable to these states; the pecking order was strictly determined on the basis of armed might. The bilateral relations involving Thailand also point in the direction of historical conflict over territory.

Importantly, this classical notion of security considerations has continued into present times. In all the cases examined here, there are overlapping territorial claims. And whilst there has been some attempt on the part of states like Vietnam to delimit its overlapping claims, many countries have simply elected to let the issue fester. Consequently, such claims remain an issue that can be invoked in order to justify a particular course of action. And the issue itself remains as an irritant in bilateral relations. Typically, ownership tends to rest with the stronger country or as a result of some post-conflict settlement, as was the case with disputed territories involving Japan on the one hand and Russia and China on the other. In so far as these territories are not developed or their resources extracted, the disagreement is likely to remain relatively dormant. However, any attempt to change the status quo typically leads to heightened tensions. The overlapping claims between China and Vietnam over the Paracel Islands and between China on the one hand and the six other claimants on the other over the Spratly Islands also attest to this practice. Recent Japanese moves to nationalize islands whose sovereignty is disputed with China has led to similarly heightened tensions in East Asia. And if there is an absence of political will by elites on both sides to settle the issue amicably, then it becomes a long-term problem. In fact, in many such cases, there is an absence of the kind of will displayed by Indonesia and Malaysia in 2002 and Malaysia and Singapore in 2008 to have such claims settled through international arbitration. Part of the reason for this may well be the fear that elites will be unable to face nationalist groups and constituencies if they lose out in such a settlement, which is often viewed as a loss of national pride rather than a simple legal settlement of a territorial dispute. And in a worst-case scenario, the country that loses in the settlement can quite simply refuse to honour the outcome of arbitration, as has been the case with Thailand and the Preah Vihear Temple dispute with Cambodia. Worse still, when such issues are not amicably resolved, they remain as powerful condensation symbols to stir the national psyche. Fringe right-wing groups that are unhappy with an incumbent government often seize such opportunities to weaken the administration. Again, the Thai case is instructive since the foreign minister, Noppadon Pattama, was brought down as a politician precisely on the charge of having ceded Thai territory and sovereignty to Cambodia in going along with the Cambodian decision to endorse the Preah Vihear Temple complex as a UNESCO heritage site.

In Northeast Asia, there are similar overlapping territorial claims that are regularly subjected to such nationalistic rantings. Fortunately, since many of the claims are over island shoals and maritime demarcations, they are far less accessible to unscrupulous politicians and fringe groups. In fact, Meredith Weiss has noted how Indonesian public opinion was whipped up when there was an incident in Ambalat when an Indonesian and a Malaysian warship grazed each other while asserting their control over disputed claims and resources. Rabble rousing apparently reached such a high pitch that there were many volunteers prepared to travel to Ambalat in support of Indonesian claims until they found out that the disputed territory was a maritime issue. Afterwards, the idea quite simply dissipated.[4] There are often similar attempts by fringe groups in China, Japan and Korea to plant flags and reiterate overlapping claims. Such groups are typically dissuaded by the authorities from fulfilling their threats or made to turn around before they reach their destination by the relevant navies. States that restrain such right-wing nationalist groups are to be commended for exercising responsible international behaviour rather than inflaming bilateral relations.

Non-traditional issues are indeed part of the mosaic of bilateral overhangs or legacies. Nonetheless, they appear to play a lesser role than traditional security issues. Non-traditional issues are likely to be of much more recent vintage and typically embellish an existing overhang or legacy. So, for example, the contaminated food (*gyoza,* or dumplings) issue strained China–Japan relations in 2008 and served to highlight seemingly lax Chinese food standards as well as Japan's heavy reliance on imported food from China. Whilst the issue led to strained relations between the two countries, as an issue, it did not have sufficient weight to determine the course of bilateral relations in the long run. Simply put, the issue was simply not sufficiently important to alter the template of bilateral relations. Other similar issues, like illegal fishing, that technically do not threaten the territoriality or integrity of the state, fall into the same category. In fact the Japanese Coast Guard routinely detains Chinese and Korean trawlers for fishing in Japanese territorial waters. Consequently, it would be fair to argue that bilateral overhangs or legacies are likely to involve issues that have significantly challenged or undermined the traditional parameters of a state.

As for the question of who stokes the overhangs or legacies and makes them significant in everyday bilateral discourse, there are obviously quite a few contenders. At the highest or most important level, states or state agencies appear quite capable of nourishing an overhang or legacy by utilizing them for political mileage. So, for example, Junichiro Koizumi's visit to the Yasukuni Shrine despite Chinese and Korean protestations was meant to appease the right-wing constituencies as well as demonstrate the position of the ranking political elite in the country. It would be superfluous for politicians to claim that such highly symbolic acts are conducted in their private capacities. Actions of public officials are always subjected to scrutiny and consequently it is incumbent upon politicians to exercise far greater discretion than private citizens in their activities. This is generally understood as a universal principle and indeed one of the demands of holding political office. Distinctions between the public and private realms are blurred in such cases.

Similarly, it is disingenuous for Japanese politicians to "manage" the education of the younger generation by conveniently ignoring the atrocities committed by Japanese occupation troops before and during World War II. The textbook issue looms large in the overhangs or legacies between China and Japan on the one hand and Korea and Japan on the other simply because the perception is that Japan is trying to whitewash its own political past. And in so doing, it opens itself to the charge of not taking responsibility for and coming to terms with its previous actions. Consequently, it is inferred that the country has no intention of lessening the overhang or legacy by atoning for its previous actions. Hence, at least in the Japanese case, it can be argued that the state (read, senior politicians) and state agencies have significantly contributed to the worsening of the overhang or legacy.

The Thai political elite have also made cavalier statements about Cambodia in the past. However, Prime Minister Hun Sen has typically responded with equally venomous statements. And both Pavin's and Aung Myoe's characterization of the Thai elites leaves much to be desired, at least in terms of lessening the burdens of history. Aung Myoe's assertion that the Thai elites have always maintained a buffer policy of supporting anti-government forces from immediately adjacent states is certainly far from a good-neighbour policy. In other words, the Thai elites — especially those from the military — hope to secure peace and strength by ensuring that neighbouring states are kept weak and divided. The government of Myanmar has consistently maintained that the Thai army has provided moral and material support to the Shan United Revolutionary Army (SURA) and the Karen National Union (KNU). And recent evidence clearly indicates that the Thai military is also attempting to chart the country's foreign policy towards Cambodia. The confusing signals with regard to the use of banned cluster bombs during the 2011 conflict with Cambodia over the Preah Vihear Temple complex and the Thai army's attempts to block the stationing of Indonesian monitors in the disputed border areas has certainly been frustrating for ASEAN and for Indonesia, that was trying to broker a truce between the two parties. The Thai military's position was that the Indonesian input would simply complicate the situation and that the conflict would be best dealt with by the involved parties alone, through existing mechanisms like the Joint Boundary Committee (JBC) and the Joint Border Meetings (JBM). Yet, the agreement reached in the UN was for Indonesia to assist the two countries through ASEAN to bring about a lasting end to the conflict.

The intransigence of the Thai military should come as no surprise to observers of the regional political situation. After all, the Thai military is a very powerful actor in domestic politics and has traditionally sought a strategic alignment with the monarchy and the bureaucracy. During the height of the Cold War, when the country had a strategic alliance with the United States, the military also received external support and added legitimacy. Although some of that legitimacy began to erode in the 1990s with the country's changed political economy that displaced the military from its pride of place in domestic politics, more recently and especially after the September 2006 coup against the Thaksin government, it has gradually clawed back its power. With a weak Democrat-led minority government that required the support of the traditional pillars of the country like the monarchy and the military, new opportunities for the appropriation of power emerged and the military has been quick to capitalize on the new-found space. Constitutional changes have also allowed for many retired members of the military to obtain seats in the country's senate. More recently, the newly appointed National Legislative Assembly, that was sworn into power by royal decree in August 2014 after the coup against the Yingluck government, has more than half the cohort drawn from serving and retired military officers. And the institution that links the military and the monarchy is the Privy Council, whose president and leading members are all drawn from the military as well. Under the circumstances it is arguable whether the Thai military is likely to remain powerful for much longer. And the political party system has been severely compromised by politically motivated judicial decisions against opposition political parties linked to Thaksin Shinawatra.[5] Consequently, some of the structural restraints that obtained in the 1990s when Thailand was undergoing meaningful democratization have been reversed.

The literature in political science and social science in general has traditionally favoured civilian rule over that of the military. And the reasons for this preference are numerous. Chief among them is that the military, with its legitimate claim to the use of force, has a disproportionate advantage over civilian contenders for power. It also has the general tendency to evolve a corporate culture that benefits its own immediate interests rather than those of the citizens; hence, the assertion among academics and policymakers that the military's role should be confined to external defence rather than issues of public safety such as law and order. It is also for this reason that structural representation of military interests within government is frowned upon. Accordingly, the preference is for what is generally described as civilian supremacy over the military. In other words, the military should be subjected to a civilian chain of command and, barring emergencies, should be kept confined to the barracks.

The involvement of state agencies in the replication of overhangs or legacies is a dangerous precedent. And the Thai and Japanese cases suggest that the state or elites representing them are quite capable of direct involvement in the dissemination of an overhang or legacy. State agencies like educational institutions and military training academies seem equally capable of such actions. Consequently, it comes as no surprise that fringe right-wing constituencies are capable of similar activities. After all, if the state that is supposed to behave rationally and soothe the negative impact of overhangs or legacies deliberately engages in provocative activities, then it has little by way of moral legitimacy to bring its weight to bear on groups that worsen bilateral overhangs or legacies. Interestingly, the states that are accused of worsening bilateral overhangs or legacies are the seemingly hegemonic actors within the bilateral relationship. Japan was the expansionist state in relation to China and Korea, and Thailand has been the hegemon with regard to Cambodia in the post-independence period. Burma, owing to its self-imposed isolation under Ne Win from 1962 to 1988, did not have regular relations with Thailand, and it is seemingly the ignominy of having been defeated in the past that inspires the latter's continued affirmation of the overhang or legacy and the buffer policy of supporting minority ethnic insurgent groups, much to the chagrin of the government in Myanmar.

The case studies also reveal the powerful impact of condensation symbols on bilateral overhangs or legacies. Monuments that are meant to celebrate or honour the victors of ancient battles or those that pay homage or enshrine the remains of those thought to be unjustly persecuted and killed serve as potent symbols of the past. And there are clearly numerous examples of such artefacts in the countries studied. Prime examples of such symbols of the Thai–Myanmar overhang or legacy are the King Naresuan and Queen Suriyothai Monuments in Ayutthaya, the statue of Suphankalaya in Phitsanulok and a second statue of King Naresuan in Mae Sai, on the Thai side of the border. And on the Myanmar side of the border, there are statues of King Bayint Naung in Tachilek and similar statues at the two ends of the Thai–Myanmar border along Kawthaung. Similarly, the Yasukuni Shrine is regarded as representative of all the evil deeds associated with Japanese aggression during World War II, since it contains the remains of Class A war criminals. Consequently, the Chinese and the Koreans view visits to the shrine as a celebration of past atrocities and the glorification of wanton military aggression. Similarly, the Nose Shrine in Japan serves as a powerful symbol of Japanese aggression against Koreans as well. Whereas some of these shrines are fairly old and have existed for quite some time, the statues erected on the Thai and Myanmar side of the borders are of relatively recent vintage. They are meant both to give visual form to the overhang or legacy as well as serve as tit-for-tat gestures in how the past is retold. Monuments of more recent vintage are clearly meant to be a source of provocation rather than an act of pacification. In this regard the Thai–Myanmar bilateral overhang or legacy has witnessed a proliferation of such symbols. It can only be hoped that the Thai–Cambodian situation will not deteriorate to such a point.

In international relations there exists a debate on the impact of structural factors versus elite preferences in foreign policy output that is often referred to as agency considerations.[6] Whereas structural factors are generally thought to have a disproportionate impact on the policy output of medium and smaller states, large states are thought to have greater latitude in the articulation of policy. Consequently, it is generally thought that the elite of larger states are able to exercise their personal preferences much more than smaller states. Yet, the case studies that we have examined reveal that bilateral overhangs or legacies and the relations that they inform maintain a certain independence from larger structural opportunities and constraints. A good measure of the reason for this is that the overhangs or legacies generally do not impinge on the interests of other states, and the issues are reasonably well contained within the countries that are directly involved in the relationship. Consequently, even elites from small and medium countries are able to exercise leverage in relation to overhangs or legacies. Since these are deeply embedded within the psyche of the states and their elites, antagonistic policy output by one of the parties in the relationship is often reciprocated by the other. And the evidence on this score is clear in reference to the output of Cambodia in relation to Thailand, or Vietnam in relation to China. Naturally, if the bilateral relationship drifts in the direction of conflict with the potential for regional destabilization, then other countries or regional organizations are likely to become involved to avoid a worst-case scenario. In this regard there appear to be certain limits that overhangs or legacies and their use are subjected to. Other constraints are likely to be the disruption of trade and economic ties that tend to be dense between geographically proximate states. And these observations are clearly borne out in the bilateral relationships that have been examined in this book.

When the Sino–Japanese relationship deteriorated over the tainted food incident in 2008, vital linkages between Chinese producers of foodstuffs and Japanese distributors and consumers of the same were at risk of disruption. Consequently, whereas there was a need to enforce greater vigilance over food safety standards in China, it was equally important that the relationship was brought to an even keel as soon as possible. And every time relations between Thailand and Myanmar are frayed, the private sector is the first to complain loudly. The typical Myanmar reaction of closing down border crossings has an immediate and deleterious impact on the many Thai industries across the border that rely on cheap labour from Myanmar. Similarly, during the recent Thai–Cambodian frictions over the Preah Vihear Temple complex, ASEAN, through Indonesian leadership, attempted to break the impasse after Cambodian appeals for international involvement. Not only did the situation set a bad precedent for regional relations and reflect badly on ASEAN — since both Thailand and Cambodia are members of the association — more importantly, both countries are signatories to the Treaty of Amity and Cooperation (TAC). As an ASEAN-inspired treaty that has been lodged with the United Nations and with ASEAN attempts to get external powers to accede to the terms of the treaty that outlaws the use of force to settle disputes, the actions of Thailand and Cambodia detracted from the spirit of the TAC. Importantly, it is also an affront to the newly signed ASEAN Charter that is meant to promote the emergence of a security community among its members. Hence, it is arguable that structural restraints exist even in the face of adventurous foreign policy output by elites. The Thai case is however complicated by the fact that decision-making power is diffuse, as explained earlier, and the military appears keen to retain a measure of control over foreign policy decision-making towards neighbouring countries. In this regard, the Thai situation needs greater and more rational political development compared to many other countries in the region.

To come full circle and return to the discussion on international relations theory at the start of the book, it is clear that overhangs or legacies are motivated by archetypical realist security considerations that have involved territoriality and sovereignty. Although old cultural nations did not have the kind of territorially bounded states that we are familiar with now, it is arguable that there was a strong conception of a cultural community that included aspects of territorial control and ownership. To the extent that notions of territoriality and sovereignty were involved from the outset, the realist school has an indelible imprint on the concept of overhangs or legacies in international relations. After all, both of them are traditional markers of state security and they were essentially construed in competitive zero-sum terms. Similarly, the structural restraints, if they derive from sub-systemic structures like ASEAN as in the Thai–Cambodian and Thai–Myanmar cases, also point in the direction of realist theory. The three levels of analysis that realism subscribes to captures this dynamic at the second tier between the global system and the individual states. The restraints that states exercise on the basis of the loss of economic opportunities tend in the direction of liberalism, where the overarching concern is with mutual gain rather than mutual fear. Transnational cooperation with economic gains is clearly well within, and preferred in, the liberal tradition. The motivations of the elites from the countries in a poor bilateral relationship and the involvement of external parties will help to determine if actions are essentially motivated by realist or liberal conceptions of gains and losses.

So what is the place of constructivism in bilateral overhangs or legacies? Its place lies in the manner in which historians, politicians and activists have chosen to portray the other. Since overhangs or legacies involve a mental conception of the other, it tends to be framed within specific cultural contexts. Within the confines of the story of the virtuous self lies the description of the stereotypical other that is framed in terms that are regarded as unacceptable and unscrupulous behaviour. These mental images are most clearly reflected in the Thai image of Cambodia and Myanmar, and are clearly meant to portray the other party in unflattering terms and as untrustworthy. And when the story is re-invoked time and again, it becomes an established frame of reference that is meant to inspire negative sentiments and anger. Such emotions can then be channelled into whatever activities are deemed an appropriate response to the situation at hand. Notwithstanding the utility of overhangs or legacies to create and sustain negative images, they are not in the interest of diplomacy and proper conduct of states. The simple reason for this is that their use automatically positions the other party on the defensive, and is more than likely to invite a similar negative response as a tit-for-tat action, which is common in diplomatic circles.

Constructivism is also useful in its identification of ideas and ideational norms in the creation of a cultural construct. Inter-subjective relationships and value-laden judgements attributed to individuals or organizations also inform us why elites behave in a certain manner or why their ascension to power unsettles others. Japanese Prime Minister Abe Shinzo is clearly a case in point. He is viewed by both China and Korea as fundamentally unrepentant for the country's past military aggression. His right-wing decisions on constitutional amendments and changes in the terms for the use of force and the export of arms in 2014 are clearly viewed with unease and alarm in Northeast Asia.

The final question to consider is, what is the shelf life of overhangs or legacies, and how can their impact be minimized? Ideally, negative images of neighbouring states should not be played up by a state as part of responsible international behaviour. It is certainly no way to accrue goodwill and soft power in the international arena. Consequently, the state and its agencies should refrain from utilizing overhangs or legacies in their foreign policy output. Importantly, such efforts among its own citizens and fringe groups trying to gain political mileage should be opposed. In order to preserve cordial ties with proximate neighbours, countries should act against groups that incite hatred and violence. Even in liberal democracies, such behaviour would be regarded as unacceptable and subject to criminal proceedings. Such restraint by the state and enforcement of similar norms in the public domain can certainly help to alleviate the negative impact of overhangs or legacies on bilateral relations in East and Southeast Asia. Importantly, such behaviour will also lead to a visibly more just and moralistic structural order that is favoured by theorists from all the different schools of thought.

Notes

1. The classic study of the Sino–Soviet conflict is Donald Zagoria, *The Sino–Soviet Conflict, 1956–1961* (New Jersey: Princeton University Press, 1962).
2. See Pavin Chachavalpongpun, *Reinventing Thailand: Thaksin and his Foreign Policy* (Singapore: Institute of Southeast Asian Studies, 2010), chap. 6; and N. Ganesan, "Thaksin and the Politics of Domestic and Regional Political Consolidation in Thailand", *Contemporary Southeast Asia* 26, no. 1 (2004): 26–44.
3. Ramses Amer, "Cambodia and Vietnam: A Troubled Relationship", in *International Relations in Southeast Asia: Between Bilateralism and Multilateralism*, edited by N. Ganesan and Ramses Amer (Singapore: Institute of Southeast Asian Studies, 2010), pp. 92–116.
4. Meredith Weiss, "Malaysia–Indonesia Bilateral Relations: Sibling Rivals in a Fraught Family", in *International Relations in Southeast Asia: Between Bilateralism and Multilateralism*, edited by N. Ganesan and Ramses Amer (Singapore: Institute of Southeast Asian Studies, 2010), pp. 17189.
5. N. Ganesan, "Worsening Schisms in Thai Domestic Politics", *Japanese Journal of Political Science* 11, no. 1 (2010): 125–47. On the linkages between the military and the monarchy, see Duncan McCargo, "Network Monarchy and Legitimacy Crises in Thailand", *Pacific Review* 18, no. 4 (2005): 499–519.
6. See, for example, Walter Carlsnaes, "The Agency-Structure Problem in Foreign Policy Analysis" *International Studies Quarterly* 36, no. 3 (1992): 245–70.

BIBLIOGRAPHY

Acharya, Amitav. *Whose Ideas Matter?: Agency and Power in Asian Regionalism*. Singapore: Institute of Southeast Asian Studies, 2010.
———. *The Quest for Identity: International Relations of Southeast Asia*. Singapore: Oxford University Press, 2000.
Amer, Ramses. *The Ethnic Chinese in Vietnam and Sino–Vietnamese Relations*. Kuala Lumpur: Forum, 1991.
———. "Sino–Vietnamese Normalization in the Light of the Crisis of the Late 1970s", *Pacific Affairs* 67, no. 3 (1994): 357–83.
———. "Sino–Vietnamese Relations: Past, Present and Future". In *Vietnamese Foreign Policy in Transition*, edited by Carlyle A. Thayer and Ramses Amer. Singapore: Institute for Southeast Asian Studies; New York: St Martin's Press, 1999.
———. *The Sino–Vietnamese Approach to Managing Boundary Disputes*, Maritime Briefing 3, no. 5. Durham: International Boundaries Research Unit, University of Durham, 2002.
———. "Sino–Vietnamese Wars". In *Southeast Asia: A Historical Encyclopedia, From Angkor Wat to East Timor, Vol. III: R-Z*, edited by Ooi Keat Gin. Santa Barbara, CA: ABC-CLIO, 2004.
———. "Assessing Sino–Vietnamese Relations through the Management of Contentious Issues". *Contemporary Southeast Asia* 26, no. 2 (2004): 320–45.
———. "Explaining the Resolution of the China–Vietnam Conflict: How Relevant is Zartman's "Ripeness Theory?" *Asian Journal of Political Science* 12, no. 2 (2004): 109–25.
———. "Indochina–China Relations". In *Berkshire Encyclopedia of China Vol. 3 Huai River to Old Prose Movement*, edited by Karen Christensen and Linsun Cheng. Great Barrington, MA: Berkshire, 2009.
———. "Vietnam–China Relations". In *Berkshire Encyclopedia of China Vol. 5 Tangshan Earthquake, Great to ZUO Zongtan*, edited by Karen Christensen and Linsun Cheng. Great Barrington, MA: Berkshire, 2009.
———. "The Sino–Vietnamese Approach to Managing Border Disputes — Lessons,

Relevance and Implications for the South China Sea Situation". In *The South China Sea: Cooperation For Regional Security and Developments, Proceedings of the International Workshop*, co-organized by the Diplomatic Academy of Vietnam and the Vietnam Lawyers' Association, 26–27 November 2009, Hanoi, Vietnam, edited by Tran Truong Thuy. Hanoi: The Gioi Publishers and Diplomatic Academy of Vietnam, 2010.

———. "Cambodia and Vietnam: A Troubled Relationship". In *International Relations in Southeast Asia: Between Bilateralism and Multilateralism*, edited by N. Ganesan and Ramses Amer. Singapore: Institute of Southeast Asian Studies, 2010.

———. "Vietnam in 2009 — Facing the Global Recession". *Asian Survey* 50, no. 1 (2010): 211–17.

———. "Vietnam in 2010 — Regional Leadership", *Asian Survey* 51, no. 1 (2011): 196–201.

———. "Dispute Settlement and Conflict Management in the South China Sea — Assessing Progress and Challenges". In *The South China Sea: Towards a Region of Peace, Security and Cooperation*, edited by Tran Truong Thuy. Hanoi: The Gioi Publishers and Diplomatic Academy of Vietnam, 2011.

———. "Sino–Vietnamese Border Disputes". In *Beijing's Power and China's Borders: Twenty Neighbors in Asia*, edited by Bruce Elleman, Stephen Kotkin and Clive Schofield. Armonk, NY; London: Sharpe, 2012.

———. "China, Vietnam and the South China Sea — Disputes and Dispute Management", *Ocean Development & International Law* 45, no. 1 (2014): 17–40.

———. "China–Vietnam Drilling Rig Incident: Reflections and Implications", Policy Brief no. 158 (2014). Nacka: Institute for Security and Development Policy.

Amer, Ramses and Hong Thao Nguyen. "The Management of Vietnam's Border Disputes: What Impact on Its Sovereignty and Regional Integration?" *Contemporary Southeast Asia* 27, no. 3 (2005): 429–52.

———. "Vietnam's Border Disputes — Assessing the Impact on Its Regional Integration". In *Vietnam's New Order: International Perspectives on the State and Reform in Vietnam*, edited by Stéphanie Balme and Mark Sidel. Houndmills, Basingstoke, Hampshire: Palgrave Macmillan, 2007.

———. "Vietnam's Border Disputes: Legal and Conflict Management Dimensions". In *The Asian Yearbook of International Law* 12 (2005–2006), edited by B.S. Chimni, Miyoshi Masahiro and Thio Li-ann. Leiden and Boston: Nijhoff, 2007.

Amer, Ramses and Jianwei Li. "Recent Developments in the South China Sea — An Assessment of the Core Bilateral Relationship between China and Vietnam". In *Maritime Security Issues in the South China Sea and the Arctic: Sharpened Competition or Collaboration?*, edited by Gordon Houlden and Nong Hong. Beijing: China Democracy and Legal System Publishing House, 2012.

An Asia Watch Report. *Khmer Rouge Abuses along the Thai–Cambodian Border*. Washington: Asia Watch Committee, 1989.

Asahi Shimbun. "Kim Took a Realistic Approach; Now It's Japan's Turn", 12 October 1998.

Aung, Sithu. "Internal Insurgency and Outside interference". *Working People's Daily*, 8 March 1991.

Ay, You. "Editorial Coverage of Hun Sen is not Fair", *The Nation*, 3 November 2009.

Baker, Chris. "Ayutthaya Rising: From Land or Sea?" *Journal of Southeast Asian Studies* 34, no. 1 (2003): 41–62.

Baldwin, David A. "Neorealism, Neoliberalism and World Politics". In *Neorealism and Neoliberalism: The Contemporary Debate,* edited by David A. Baldwin. New York: Columbia University Press, 1993.

Bangkok Post. "Govt to Consider Revoking MoU with Cambodia", 6 November 2009.

————. "Souring Public Support for the Government", 6 November 2009.

————. "Hun Sen Lets Fly at Abhisit", 9 February 2010.

————. "Yet Another Unprovoked Outburst from Hun Sen", 1 December 2010.

Barmé, Scot. *Luang Wichit Wathakan and the Creation of a Thai Identity.* Singapore: Institute of Southeast Asian Studies, 1993.

Bix, Herbert P. *Hirohito and the Making of Modern Japan.* New York: Harper Collins, 2000.

Boonma-klee, Venika. *Burma: Thai Foreign Policy under Chatichai Chunhavan's Government.* Bangkok: Thailand Research Fund, 1997.

Boudet, Paul. "La conquête de la Cochinchine par les Nguyên et le rôle des émigrés chinois" [The conquest of Cochinchine by the Nguyens and the role of the Chinese migrants]. *Bulletin de l'École Française d'Extrême-Orient* Tome 42 (1942): 115–32.

Breslauer, George W. and Philip E. Tetlock, eds., *Learning in U.S. and Soviet Foreign Policy.* Boulder, CO: Westview, 1991.

British Broadcasting Corporation Summary of World Broadcasts Part Three Far East/3363 G/1 (21 October 1998) and 3364 G/1 (22 October 1998).

Bull, Hedley. *The Anarchical Society: A Study of Order in World Politics.* New York: Columbia University Press, 1977.

Busbarat, Paul. "Thai–Cambodian Dispute over the Preah Vihear Temple Revisited". *Policy Net,* 30 August 2008 <http://www.policy-net.org/blogs/thefareast/thaicambod>.

Buttinger, Joseph. *A Dragon Defiant: A Short Story of Vietnam.* Newton Abbot, Devon: David & Charles, 1972.

Buzan, Barry. *People, States and Fear,* 2nd ed. New York: Harvester-Wheatsheaf, 1991.

Carlsnaes, Walter. "The Agency-Structure Problem in Foreign Policy Analysis". *International Studies Quarterly* 36, no. 3 (1992): 245–70.

Cha, Victor D. *Alignment Despite Antagonism: The United States–Korea–Japan Security Triangle.* Stanford, CA: Stanford University Press, 1999.

Chachavalpongpun, Pavin. *A Plastic Nation: The Curse of Thainess in Thai–Burmese Relations*. Lanham, MA: University Press of America, 2005.

———. "Diplomacy Under Siege: Thailand's Political Crisis and the Impact on Foreign Policy". *Contemporary Southeast Asia* 31, no. 3 (2009): 447–67.

———. "The Temple of Doom: Hysteria about the Preah Vihear Temple in the Thai Nationalist Discourse". *Legitimacy Crisis and Conflict in Thailand*, edited by Marc Askew. Chiang Mai: Silkworm Books, 2010.

———. *Reinventing Thailand: Thaksin and His Foreign Policy*. Singapore: Institute of Southeast Asian Studies, 2010.

———. "Embedding Embittered History: Unending Conflicts in Thai–Cambodian Relations". *Asian Affairs* 43, no. 1 (2012): 81–102.

Chanda, Nayan. *Brother Enemy: The War after the War: A History of Indochina since the Fall of Saigon*. Orlando: Harcourt Brace Jovanovich, 1986.

Chandler, David P. *A History of Cambodia*, 4th ed. Boulder, CO: Westview, 2007.

Chein, Tun Aung. "Translation of the Yodaya Yazawun" (draft manuscript).

Chen, Jian. "China, the Vietnam War, and the Sino-American rapprochement, 1968–1973". In *The Third Indochina War: Conflict between China, Vietnam and Cambodia, 1972–79*, edited by Odd Arne Westad and Sophie Quinn-Judge. London: Routledge, 2006.

Chen, King C. *China's War with Vietnam, 1979: Issues, Decisions, and Implication*. Stanford: Stanford University, Hoover Institution Press, 1987.

Cheong, Sung-Hwa. *The Politics of Anti-Japanese Sentiment in Korea: Japanese–South Korean Relations under American Occupation, 1945–1952*. New York: Greenwood Press, 1991.

China Daily, "Fukuda Leads Japan PM Race, Won't Visit Yasukuni", 16 September 2007.

Chutintaranond, Sunait. "The Image of the Burmese Enemy in Thai Perceptions and Historical Writings". In *On Both Sides of the Tenasserim Range: History of Siamese–Burmese Relations*, edited by Sunait Chutintaranond and Than Tun. Bangkok: Chulalongkorn University, 1995.

———. *Suriyothai in the Context of Thai–Myanmar History and Historical Perspective*, vol. 1, *Views and Vision*. Yangon: Universities Historical Research Centre, 2001.

Claude, Inis L. *Power and International Relations*. New York: Random House, 1962.

Copeland, Matthew Phillip. *Contested Nationalism and the 1932 Overthrow of the Absolute Monarchy in Siam*. PhD Dissertation. The Australian National University, 1993.

Crawford, Neta C. "The Passion of World Politics: Propositions on Emotion and Emotional Relationships", *International Security* 24, no. 4 (2000): 116–56.

Crispin, Shawn W. "Plots Seen in Thaksin's Cambodia Gambit", Asia Times,

12 November 2009 <http://www.atimes.com/atimes/Southeast_Asia/KK12Ae01.html>.

Cumings, Bruce. *Korea's Place in the Sun: A Modern History*. New York: Norton, 1997.

Curtis, Gerald L. *The Japanese Way of Politics*. New York: Columbia University Press, 1988.

Dent, Christopher. "The New Economic Bilateralism in Southeast Asia: Region-Convergent or Region-Divergent?" *International Relations of the Asia-Pacific 6*, no. 1 (2006): 81–111.

Devéria, Gabriel. *Histoire des relations de la Chine avec L'Annam — Vietnam du XVI au XIX siècle* [History of the relations of China with Annam — Vietnam from the 16th to the 19th centuries]. Paris: Ernest Leroux éditeur, 1880.

Dower, John W. *Japan in War and Peace: Selected Essays*. New York: New Press, 1993.

Dudden, Alexis. *Troubled Apologies and Japan, Korea and the United States*. New York: Columbia University Press, 2008.

Duiker, William J. *China and Vietnam: The Roots of Conflict*. Indochina Research Monograph, no. 1. Berkeley: Institute of East Asian Studies, University of California, 1986.

Edelman, Murray. *The Symbolic Uses of Politics*. Urbana: University of Illinois Press, 1964.

Edwards, Penny. *Cambodge: The Cultivation of a Nation, 1860–1945*. Honolulu: University of Hawai'i Press, 2007.

Elliot, David W.P., ed. *The Third Indochina Conflict*. Boulder, CO: Westview, 1982.

Elster, Jon. "Rationality and Emotions", *Economic Journal* 106, no. 438 (1996): 1386–97.

———. *Alchemies of the Mind: Rationality and the Emotions*. Cambridge University Press, 1999.

Evans, Grant and Kelvin Rowley. *Red Brotherhood at War: Indochina Since the Fall of Saigon*. London: Verso Editions, 1984.

Fairbank, John K., Edwin O. Reischauer, and Albert M. Craig. *East Asia: Traditions and Transformation*, rev. ed. Boston: Houghton Mifflin, 1989.

Fearon, James D. "Counterfactuals and Hypothesis Testing in Political Science". *World Politics* 43, no. 2 (1991): 169–95.

Ferguson, Yale H. and Richard W. Mansbach. *Remapping Global Politics: History's Revenge and Future Shock*. Cambridge: Cambridge University Press, 2004.

Frost, Mervyn. *Ethics in International Relations: A Constitutive Theory*. Cambridge: Cambridge University Press, 1996.

Fujiwara, Riichirio. "Vietnamese Dynasties' Policies toward Chinese Immigrants". *Acta Asiatica*, no. 18 (March 1970): 43–69.

Funnell, Victor C. "Vietnam and the Sino-Soviet Conflict 1965–1976". *Studies in Comparative Communism* 11, nos. 1–2 (1978): 42–169.

Gaiko ni kansuru yoron chosa [Public opinion survey on international relations], Naikakufu daijin kanbo seifu hokoku shitsu, October 2009.

Ganesan, N. "Thaksin and the Politics of Domestic and Regional Political Consolidation in Thailand". *Contemporary Southeast Asia* 26, no. 1 (2004): 26–44.

———. "Worsening Schisms in Thai Domestic Politics". *Japanese Journal of Political Science* 11, no. 1 (2010): 125–47.

Ganesan, N., and Ramses Amer. eds., *International Relations in Southeast Asia: Between Bilateralism and Multilateralism*. Singapore: Institute of Southeast Asian Studies, 2010.

Ganjanakhundee, Supalak. "Hun Sen Settling Scores but is it Worth it?" *The Nation*, 7 November 2009.

Gaspardone, Émile. "Un chinois des mers du sud. Le fondateur de Hà-tiên" [A Chinese from the South Seas. The founder of Hatien]. *Journal Asiatique* [Asiatic journal] 240 (1952): 363–385.

General Statistics Office of Vietnam. "Exports of Goods by Group, by Country and Territory" <http://www.gso.gov.vn/default_en.aspx?tabid=472&idmid =3&ItemID=9134>.

———. "Foreign Direct Investment Projects Licensed from 1988 to 2008 by Main Counterparts" <http://www.gso.gov.vn/default_en.aspx?tabid=471&idmid =3&ItemID=8708>.

———. "Imports of Goods by Country Group, by Country and Territory" <http:// www.gso.gov.vn/default_en.aspx?tabid=472&idmid=3&ItemID=9130>.

Gilks, Anne. *The Breakdown of the Sino–Vietnamese Alliance, 1970–1979*, China Research Monograph, no. 39. Berkeley: Institute of East Asian Studies, University of California, 1982.

Hack, Karl. "The Long March to Peace of the Malayan Communist Party in Southern Thailand". In *Thai South and Malay North: Ethnic Interactions on the Plural Peninsula*, edited by Michael J. Montesano and Patrick Jory. Singapore: NUS Press, 2008.

Hane, Mikiso. *Modern Japan: A Historical Survey*, 2nd ed. Boulder, CO: Westview, 1992.

Harris, Ian. *Cambodian Buddhism: History and Practice*. Honolulu: University of Hawai'i Press, 2005.

Harris, Sheldon H. *Factories of Death: Japanese Biological Warfare, 1932–45, and the American Cover-Up*. London: Routledge, 1994.

Hatada, Takashi. *Han-Il kwan'gye wa yôksahak* [Japanese–Korean relations and historiography]. Seoul: Yôksa yôn'guhoe, 1992.

———. *Han-Il kwan'gyesa ûi chaejomyông* [Refocusing on history of Korea–Japan relations]. Seoul: Yôksa yôn'guhoe, 1992.

He, Yinan. "National Mythmaking and the Problems of History in Sino–Japanese Relations". In *Japan's Relations with China: Facing a Rising Power*, edited by P.E. Lam. London: Routledge, 2006.

Heazle, Michael and Nick Knight, eds., *China–Japan Relations in the Twenty-first Century: Creating a Future Past?* Cheltenham, England: 2007.

Hensengerth, Oliver. *Regionalism in China–Vietnam Relations. Institution-building in the Greater Mekong Subregion.* London: Routledge, 2009.

Holmgren, Jennifer. *Chinese Colonisation of Northern Vietnam: Administrative Geography and Political Development in the Tonking Delta First to Sixth Centuries A.D.* Oriental Monograph Series, no. 27, Faculty of Asian Studies. Canberra ACT: Australian National University, 1980.

Holsti, K.J. *International Politics: A Framework for Analysis*, 5th ed. New Jersey: Prentice-Hall, 1988.

Hongthong, Yossawadee. "Abhisit Calls on Thai MPs to Vote against PM". *The Nation*, 23 June 2008.

Hood, Steven J. *Dragons Entangled: Indochina and the China–Vietnam War.* Armonk: East Gate Books, 1992.

International Studies: Southeast Asia, no. 55. Athens: Centre for International Studies, Ohio University, 1980.

Japan External Trade Organization. "Analysis of Japan–China Trade in 2013 and Outlook for 2014", 28 February 2014 <http://www.jetro.go.jp/en/news/releases/20140228009–news>.

Jervis, Robert. "Hypotheses on Misperception". *World Politics* 20, no. 3 (1968): 454–79.

———. *Perception and Misperception in International Politics* (Princeton, NJ: Princeton University Press, 1976.

———. "Cooperation under the Security Dilemma". *World Politics* 30, no. 2 (1978): 194–99.

———. "Morality and International Strategy". In *The Meaning of the Nuclear Revolution: Statecraft and the Prospects of Armageddon*. Ithaca, NY: Cornell University Press, 1989.

———. "The Future of World Politics: Will It Resemble the Past?" *International Security* 16, no. 3 (1991/92): 39–73.

Jervis, Robert and Jack Snyder, eds. *Dominoes and Bandwagons: Strategic Beliefs and Great Power Competition in the Eurasian Rimland*. New York: Oxford University Press, 1991.

Jory, Patrick. "Problem in Contemporary Thai Nationalist Historiography". *Kyoto Review of Southeast Asia* 2 (March 2003) <http://kyotoreview.cseas.kyoto-u.ac.jp/issue/issue2/article_251.html>.

Joyaux, François. *La China et le règlement du premier conflict d'Indochine* [China and the settlement of the First Indochina Conflict]. Série internationale – 9,

Université de Paris-I Panthéon-Sorbonne, Institut d'histoire des relations internationals contemporaines (IHRIC). Geneva 1954; repr., Paris: Publication de la Sorbonne, 1979.

Jumsai, M. L Manich. *Popular History of Thailand*. Bangkok: Chalermnit, 1976.

K.I Media. "Thaksin Obtains Cambodian Citizenship in March 2009", 1 February 2010 <http://ki-media.blogspot.com/2010_01_01_archive.html>.

Kagawa, Toyohiko. "Appeal to President Syngman Rhee", *Mainichi Shimbun*, 13 December 1955.

Kang, Man-Gil. "The Nature and Process of the Korean National Liberation Movement during the Japanese Colonial Period". *Korea Journal* 36, no. 1 (1996): 5–19.

Kasetsiri, Charnvit. "Thailand-Cambodia: A Love-Hate Relationship". *Kyoto Review of Southeast Asia* 3 (March 2003) <http://www.charnvitkasetsiri.com/PDF/Thailand-Cambodia.pdf>.

———. *Latthi Chatniyom Thai/Siam Nai Kampucha: Lae Koranee Suksa Khao Prah Viharn* [Siamese/Thai nationalism and Cambodia: A case study of the Preah Vihear Temple]. Bangkok: Toyota Thailand Foundation, the Foundation for the Promotion of Social Science and Humanities, 2009.

Kaung, Kappiya Kan. "Latest Cheap Jokes of Sukhumbhand". *Kyemon* (newspaper), 19 May 2000.

———. "Latest Cheap Jokes of Sukhumbhand". *New Light of Myanmar*, 21 May 2000.

Keohane, Robert O. "Liliputian's Dilemmas: Small States in International Politics". *International Organization* 23, no. 1 (1969): 291–310.

———. *Neorealism and its Critics*. New York: Columbia University Press, 1986.

———. "International Institutions: Two Approaches". In *International Institutions and State Power: Essays in International Relations Theory*. Boulder, CO: Westview, 1989.

Kim, Gilho. "Mimisuka wiryongje/미미쓰카 위령제" [Memorial service at Mimisuka]. *Jeju Today*, 20 August 2001 <http://www.ijejutoday.com/news/articleView.html?idxno=110119>.

Kim, Kwang Bong. *The Korea–Japan Treaty Crisis and the Instability of the Korean Political System*. New York: Praeger, 1971.

Kim, Tae-Hyo and Brad Glosserman, eds. *The Future of U.S.–Korea–Japan Relations: Balancing Values and Interests*. Washington, DC: CSIS Press, 2004.

Kim, Wonik. "Rethinking Colonialism and the Origins of the Developmental State in East Asia". *Journal of Contemporary Asia* 39, no. 3 (2009): 382–99.

Kim, Yong-Sik. *Saebyôk ûi yaksok: Kim Yong-Sik oegyo 33–nyôn* [Promise at the dawn: Thirty-three-year diplomacy of Kim Yong-Sik]. Seoul: Kimy ngsa, 1993.

Krairiksh, Benchapa. *Nao Khmer* [Being in Cambodia]. Bangkok: Matichon Books, 2004.

Krasner, Stephen D. ed., *International Regimes*. Ithaca, NY: Cornell University Press, 1983.

Kristof, Nicholas D. "Korean Leader, in Japan, Urges Healing of Old Wounds". *New York Times*, 8 October 1998.

Lam, Peng Er. "Japan's Differing Approaches on the Apology Issue to China and South Korea". *American Asian Review* (US) 20, no. 3 (2002): 31–54.

———. "Japan's Deteriorating Ties with China: The Koizumi Factor". *China: An International Journal* 3, no. 2 (2005): 275–91.

———. *Japan's Relations With China: Facing a Rising Power*. London: Routledge, 2006.

———. "Koizumi Junichiro: The Iconoclast Who Remade Japanese Politics". In *Dissident Democrats in Asia*, edited by Haig Patapan, John Kane and Benjamin Wong. New York: Palgrave, 2008.

Lee, Soon-Won. "Korean–Japanese Discord, 1945–1965: A Case Study of International Conflict". PhD dissertation, Rutgers University, 1967.

Lind, Jennifer. *Sorry States: Apologies in International Politics*. Cornell: Cornell University Press, 2008.

Ma, Tin Win. "How Did Opium Arrive at the Golden Triangle Region?" *New Light of Myanmar*, 17 May 2001.

———. "How Did Opium Arrive at the Golden Triangle Region?" *Kyemon*, 17 May 2001.

———. "Phra Narit Did Not Amount to Much". *Kyemon*, 28 May 2001.

———. "Phra Narit Did Not Amount to Much". *New Light of Myanmar*, 28 May 2001.

———. "Will Tell All That is True, Barring None". *Kyemon*, 30 May 2001.

———. "Will Tell All That is True, Barring None". *New Light of Myanmar*, 30 May 2001.

———. "A New Tune from Ayutthaya". In *So Bold the Courage as Blood Red*, edited by Ma Tin Win. Yangon: News and Periodical Enterprises, 2002.

Macan-Markar, Marwaan. "Thai–Cambodia Tension Gives Rise to Schools with Bunkers", IPS, 24 November 2009 <http://ipsnews.net/news.asp?idnews=49385>.

Macdonald, Donald Stone. *U.S.–Korean Relations from Liberation to Self-Reliance: The Twenty-Year Record: An Interpretative Summary of the Archives of the U.S. Department of State for the Period of 1945–1965*. Boulder, CO: Westview, 1992.

Mainichi Shimbun. "Ties That Tempt Fate: Koizumi and Yasukuni Shrine", 13 August 2001.

Maung, U Nyein. *Shaehaung Myanmar Kyauksar Myar* [Ancient Myanmar stone inscriptions]. Yangon: Department of Archaeology, 1972.

McCargo, Duncan. "Network Monarchy and Legitimacy Crises in Thailand". *Pacific Review* 18, no. 4 (2005): 499–519.

McCoy, Alfred W. *The Politics of Heroin in Southeast Asia*. Singapore: Harper & Row, 1972.

Mendel, Jr., Douglas H. *The Japanese People and Foreign Policy: A Study of Public Opinion in Post-Treaty Japan*. Westport, CT: Greenwood, 1961.

Ming, Wan. "Koizumi's Visits to the Yasukuni Shrine". In *Sino-Japanese relations: Interaction, Logic and Transformation*, edited by Ming Wan. Stanford: Stanford University Press, 2006.

Ministry of Foreign Affairs and Trade (MOFAT – Republic of Korea). *2009 Diplomatic White Paper*.

Ministry of Foreign Affairs of Thailand. *Relations between Thailand and Cambodia*. Bangkok: Prachandra, 1959.

Ministry of Foreign Affairs of the People's Republic of China. "China–Vietnam Issues a Joint Communiqué" <http://www.fmprc.gov.cn/eng/wjb/zzjg/yzs/gjlb/2792/2793/t163759.htm>.

———. "China–Vietnam, Land Boundary Survey Work Completed 2008/12/31" <http://www.fmprc.gov.cn/eng/zxxx/t530192.htm>.

Ministry of Foreign Affairs, Socialist Republic of Vietnam. "Joint Statement: On the Completion of the Demarcation and Markers Placement on the Entire Land Border Line between Vietnam and China" <http://www.mofa.gov.vn/en/cn_vakv/ca_tbd/nr040818094447/ns090106100042/newsitem_print_preview>.

———. "PM asks Yunnan to Cooperate in Using River Water" <http://www.mofa.gov.vn/en/nr040807104143/nr040807105001/ns071030081930/newsitem_print_preview>.

———. "PM Urges Cooperation between Border Provinces and Yunnan" <http://www.mofa.gov.vn/en/nr040807104143/nr040807105001/ns070405094302/newsitem_print_preview>.

———. "Viet Nam, China Hold Government-level Border Negotiations" <http://www.mofa.gov.vn/en/nr040807104143/nr040807105001/ns070122102447/newsitem_print_preview>.

———. "Vietnam and China Issue Joint Statement" <http://www.mofa.gov.vn/en/nr040807104143/nr040807105001/ns050726144049/newsitem_print_preview>.

———. "Vietnam, China Reach Awareness to Enrich Partnership" <http://www.mofa.gov.vn/en/nr040807104143/nr040807105001/ns081027154132/newsitem_print_preview>.

———. "Vietnam–China Economic Ties Continue Growth" <http://www.mofa.gov.vn/en/nr040807104143/nr040807105001/ns080602095212/newsitem_print_preview>.

———. "Viet Nam, China Issue Joint Statement" <http://www.mofa.gov.vn/en/nr040807104143/nr040807105001/ns130624152141/newsitem_print_preview>.

———. "VN, China Issue Joint Statement" <http://www.mofa.gov.vn/en/nr040807104143/nr040807105001/ns131016041515/newsitem_print_preview>.

————. "VN–China Basic Principles on Settlement of Sea Issues" <http://www.mofa.gov.vn/en/nr040807104143/nr040807105001/ns131016150351/newsitem_print_preview>.

————. "President Hails Stronger Ties with Yunnan" <http://www.mofa.gov.vn/en/nr040807104143/nr040807105001/ns120404145555/newsitem_print_preview>.

————. *The Truth about Viet Nam–China Relations over the Last 30 Years*. Hanoi: Ministry of Foreign Affairs, Socialist Republic of Vietnam, 1979.

Mitsui, Hideko. "The Resignification of the 'Comfort Women' through NGO Trials". In *Rethinking Historical Injustice and Reconciliation in Northeast Asia: The Korean Experience*, edited by Gi-Wook Shin, Soon-won Park, and Daqing Yang. Oxford: Routledge, 2008.

Moon, Chung-In. "International Quasi-Crisis: Theory and a Case of Japan–South Korean Bilateral Friction". *Asian Perspective* 15, no. 2 (1991): 99–123.

Morgenthau, Hans J. *Politics among Nations*, 6th ed. New York: Knopf, 1976.

Nanuam, Wassana. "Thaksin Set to Invest Big Time in Cambodia". *Bangkok Post*, 19 June 2008.

The Nation. "Hun Sen Blasted at Kasit for Allegedly Insulting Him by Calling Him a Gangster", 31 March 2009.

————. "Cambodia's PM Hun Sen May Misunderstand Thai FM", 31 March 2009.

————. "Cambodia Lambast Google Earth for Locating Temple in Thai Soil", 10 February 2010.

New York Times. "House Wants Japan Apology on Sex Slaves", 31 July 2007.

Nguyen, Lien-Hang T. "The Sino–Vietnamese Split and the Indochina War, 1968–1975". In *The Third Indochina War: Conflict between China, Vietnam and Cambodia, 1972–79*, edited by Odd Arne Westad and Sophie Quinn-Judge. London: Routledge, 2006.

Nguyen, Phu Trong. "Vietnam–China Joint Statement", Communist Party of Vietnam Online Newspaper, 11–15 October, 2011 <http://www.cpv.org.vn/cpv/Modules/News/NewsDetail.aspx?co_id=30107&cn_id=48489>.

Nhan Dan. "Vietnam and China Fulfil Land Border Demarcation" <http://www.nhandan.com.vn/english/news/life/010109/life_biengioi.htm>.

————. "Vietnam and China Issue Joint Press Communiqué" <http://www.nhandan.com.vn/english/news/190507/domestic_pr.htm>.

————. "Vietnam and China Issue Joint Statement" <http://www.nhandan.com.vn/english/news/020608/domestic_vn.htm>.

————. "Vietnam and China Show Goodwill on Sea Issues" <http://www.nhandan.com.vn/english/news/130706/domestic_vn.htm>.

————. "Vietnam–China Joint Communiqué" <http://www.nhandan.com.vn/english/news/250806/domestic_commu.htm>.

————. "Vietnam–China Joint Statement" <http://www.nhandan.com.vn/english/news/171106/domestic_vnchi.htm>.

Noriko, Kamachi. "Japanese Writings on Post-1945 Japan–China Relations". In *Japan's Relations with China: Facing a Rising Power*, edited by P.E. Lam. London: Routledge, 2006.

Nye, Joseph and Robert O. Keohane. *Power and Interdependence: World Politics in Transition*. Boston: Little Brown, 1977.

Nye, Jr., Joseph S. "Nuclear Learning and U.S.–Soviet Security Regimes". *International Organization* 41, no. 3 (1987): 371–402.

————. *Soft Power: The Means to Success in World Politics*. New York: Public Affairs, 2004.

Nyo, Nga Khin. "Ayaekyone Thetlone kaunghma" [Only the stamina is essential in time of emergency]. *Kyemon*, 2–3 March 2001.

O'Dowd, Edward C. *Chinese Military Strategy in the Third Indochina War: The Last Maoist War*. London: Routledge, 2007.

Olson, Lawrence. *Japan in Postwar Asia*. New York: Praeger, 1970.

Paepanawan, Anucha. *Exclusive: Kanmuang Ruang Khao Phra Viharn* [Exclusive: The political case of Khao Phra Viharn]. Bangkok: Kleung Aksorn, 2008.

Pak, Sil. *Han'guk oegyo pisa* [A hidden history of Korean diplomacy]. Seoul: Kirinwôn, 1980.

Park, Soon-Won. "The Politics of Remembrance: The Case of Korean Forced Laborers in the Second World War". In *Rethinking Historical Injustice and Reconciliation in Northeast Asia: The Korean Experience*, edited by Gi-Wook Shin, Soon-won Park, and Daqing Yang. Oxford: Routledge, 2008.

Pattama, Noppadon. *Phom Mai Dai Khai Chart* [I did not sell my country]. Bangkok: Kledthai, 2008.

Pempel, T.J. "Challenges to Bilateralism: Changing Foes, Capital Flows, and Complex Forums". In *Beyond Bilateralism: U.S.–Japan Relations in the New Asia Pacific*, edited by Ellis Krauss and T.J. Pempel. Stanford: Stanford University Press, 2004.

People's Daily and Xinhua News Agency Commentators. *On the Vietnamese Foreign Ministry's White Book Concerning Viet Nam–China Relations*. Beijing: Foreign Languages Press, 1979.

Phasuk, Sunai. *Nayobai Tang Prathet Khong Thai: Suksa Krabuankarnkamnod Nayobai Khong Ratthaban Pon-ek Chatichai Choonhavan Tor Panha Kumphucha, Si Singhakom 1988–23 Kumphaphan 1991* [Thai foreign policy: A study of foreign policy making process under the Chatichai Choonhavan government, 4 August 1988–23 February 1991]. Bangkok: Institute of Asian Studies, 1997.

Pheaktra, Neth. "Koh Kong to Become Second Hong Kong". *Mekong Times*, 26 May 2008.

Phongpaichit, Pasuk, Sungsidh Piriyarangsan, and Nualnoi Treerat. *Guns, Gambling,*

Ganja: Thailand's Illegal Economy and Public Policy. Bangkok: Silkworm Books, 1998.

Prachathai, "Sampas Charnvit Kasetsiri: Tonnee Pen Khon Thai Ki Fai Thi Torsukan Kanathi Kamphucha Luayou Faidiew" [Interview Charnvit Kasetsiri: How Many Factions Are Now in Thailand Fighting among Themselves? While Cambodia Has Only One Faction], 8 November 2009 <http://www.prachatai.com/journal/2009/11/26512>.

Prateepchaikul, Veera. "Does Hun Sen Want to Play in our Political Sandbox?" *Bangkok Post*, 26 October 2009.

———. "Hun Sen's Latest Antic Unbecoming of a Premier". *Bangkok Post*, 9 February 2010.

Prince Chakrabongse, Chula. *Lords of Life: A History of the Kings of Thailand*, 3rd ed. Bangkok: DD Books, 1982.

Reischauer, Edwin O. *The Japanese Today: Change and Continuity*. Cambridge, MA: Belknap Press of Harvard University Press, 1988. First published 1977.

Rosenau, James N. *Domestic Sources of Foreign Policy*. Glencoe: Free Press, 1967.

———. "Introduction: Political Science in a Shrinking World". In *Linkage Politics*, edited by James Rosenau. New York: Free Press, 1969.

———. *Linkage Politics*. Glencoe: Free Press, 1969.

Ross, Robert R. *The Indochina Tangle: China's Vietnam Policy 1975–1979*. New York: East Asian Institute, Columbia University, Columbia University Press, 1988.

Russell, Gregory T. "(Review on) Order and Justice in International Relations". *Ethics & International Affairs* 18, no. 1 (2004): 107, 109.

Ryosei, Kokubun. "The Shifting Nature of Japan–China Relations after the Cold War". In *Japan's Relations with China: Facing a Rising Power*, edited by P.E. Lam. London: Routledge, 2006.

S!News. "Noppadon Nahcha Thookdah Khaichat Tornahthood Acharn Thammasat Kadkant Amnard Tadsinkhadi Khong San Pokklong" [Noppadon was criticised for selling the country in front of foreign diplomats, Thammasat University's professors object the role of the administrative court], 30 June 2008 <http://news.sanook.com/politic/politic_281852.php>.

Sansom, George. *A History of Japan to 1334*. Stanford, CA: Stanford University Press, 1958.

Sathayawatthana, Chonticha. ed., *Botrian Chak Hedkarn Khwamroonrang Nai Kamphucha* [Lessons from violent incident in Cambodia]. Bangkok: Kanghan, 2003.

Satoshi, Amako, ed., *Chukoku wa kyoi ka* [Is China a threat?]. Tokyo: Keiso shoten, 1997.

Scherer, Klaus. "Emotions Can Be Rational". *Social Science Information* 24, no. 2 (1985): 331–35.

Sharp, Bruce. *Counting Hell: The Death Toll of the Khmer Rouge Regime in Cambodia*, 1 April 2005 <http://www.mekong.net/cambodia/deaths.htm>.

Shibuichi, Daiki. "Japan's History Textbook Controversy: Social Movements and Governments". *Electronic Journal of Contemporary Japanese Studies*, 4 March 2008 <http://www.japanesestudies.org.uk/discussionpapers/2008/Shibuichi.html>.

Shin, Gi-Wook, Soon-won Park, and Daqing Yang. *Rethinking Historical Injustice and Reconciliation in Northeast Asia: The Korean Experience*. Oxford: Routledge, 2008.

Singer, J. David. "The Levels-of-Analysis Problem in International Relations". *World Politics* 14, no. 1 (1961): 77–92.

Smyser, W.R. *The Independent Vietnamese: Vietnamese Communism between Russia and China 1956–1969*, Papers in International Studies, Southeast Asia, no. 55. Athens: Centre for International Studies, Ohio University, 1980.

Snyder, Glenn H. "The Security Dilemma in Alliance Politics". *World Politics* 36, no. 4 (1984): 461–95.

———. *Alliance Politics*. Ithaca, NY: Cornell University Press, 1997.

Soe, Myint (Natala). *"Lu Meik Hnar Yan Mashipa"* [No henchmen available for hire]. *Kyemon*, 9 March 2001.

Soh, Chunghee Sarah. "The Korean 'Comfort Women' Tragedy as Structural Violence". In *Rethinking Historical Injustice and Reconciliation in Northeast Asia: The Korean Experience*, edited by Gi-Wook Shin, Soon-won Park, and Daqing Yang. Oxford: Routledge, 2008.

Solingen, Etel. "Multilateralism, Regionalism, and Bilateralism: Conceptual Overview from International Relations Theory". In *International Relations in Southeast Asia*, edited by N. Ganesan and Ramses Amer. Singapore: Institute of Southeast Asian Studies, 2010.

Suwannathat-Pian, Kobkua. "Thai Wartime Leadership Reconsidered: Phibun and Pridi". *Journal of Southeast Asian Studies* 27, no. 1 (1996): 166–78.

Tanaka, Yuki. *Hidden Horrors: Japanese War Crimes in World War II*. Boulder, CO: Westview, 1998.

Tetlock, Philip E. and Aaron Belkin, eds., *Counterfactual Thoughts Experiments in World Politics: Logical, Methodological, and Psychological Perspectives*. Princeton, NJ: Princeton University Press, 1996.

Thanarat, Sarit. Kham Prasai Khong Phanathan Chomphon Sarit Thanarat, Nayok Rattamontri kieowkap Khadi Prasat Phra Viharn Thang Wittayu Krachaiseang Lae Wittayu Toratat 4 Karakadakhom Song Pan Ha Roi Ha [Address by H.E. Field Marshal Sarit Thanarat, Prime Minister, Regarding the Phra Viharn Temple Case on the National Radio and Television Stations, 4 July 1962], 1962.

Thayer, Carlyle A. "4 Reasons China Removed Oil Rig HYSY-981 Sooner Than

Planned", *The Diplomat*, 22 July 2014 <http://thediplomat.com/2014/07/4–reasons-china-removed-oil-rig-hysy-981–sooner-than-planned>.

———. "Vietnam, China and the Oil Rig Crisis: Who Blinked?", *The Diplomat*, 4 August 2014 <http://thediplomat.com/2014/08/vietnam-china-and-the-oil-rig-crisis-who-blinked/.

Thet Shey, Thadinhtauk. "Hma Tapa Achar Mashi" [No other things]. *Myanma Alin* (newspaper), 2 April 2001.

Thompson, William R. "The Regional Subsystem: A Conceptual Explication and a Propositional Inventory". *International Studies Quarterly* 17, no. 1 (1973): 89–117.

Tienchan, Bunruam, Praphat Chaleimak, and Saranya Wichatham. *Khrai Dai Khrai Sia Khwam Khat Yaeng Thi Ban Plai: Prasad Khao Phra Viharn* [Who won who lost, The uncontrollable conflict: Khao Phra Viharn]. Bangkok: Animate Group, 2008.

Timeonline. "Thaksin Shinawatra Appointed Economics Adviser to Cambodia", 5 November 2009 <http://www.timesonline.co.uk/tol/news/world/asia/article6904000.ece>.

Toe, Hla. *Bayint Naung Mintaragyi Bawa Atwe Akhaw Yonekyichet Hnit Saung Ywethmu Myar* [Philosophy of life and activities of King Bayint Naung]. Naypyitaw: Department of Historical Research, 2010.

Ukala, *Maha Yazawungyi* [Great chronicle], vol. 2. Yangon: Yarpyae, 2006.

———. *Maha Yazawungyi* [Great chronicle], vol. 3. Yangon: Yarpyae, 2006.

United Nations High Commissioner for Refugees (UNHCR). "2013 UNHCR Regional Operations Profile – East Asia and the Pacific. China. Statistical Snapshot" <http://www.unhcr.org/cgi-bin/texis/vtx/page?page=49e487cd6&submit=GO>.

Vachon, Michelle. "Building History: Researchers Surprised by Battambang Finds". *Cambodian Daily*, 16 August 2003.

Vella, Walter F. *Siam under Rama III 1824–1851*. New York: Association for Asian Studies, 1957.

———. *Chaiyo! King Vajiravudh and the Development of Thai Nationalism*. Honolulu: University Press of Hawai'i, 1978.

Viet Nam News. "PM Khai Orders an All-out War against Smugglers", 18 October 1997.

———. "Smuggling, Fraud Still Rampant in 1997", 18 October 1997.

———. "Ministry to Intensify Smuggling Fight", 13 November 1997.

Vital, David. *The Inequality of States*. Clarendon: Oxford University Press, 1967.

Vogel, Ezra, Yuan Ming, and Akihiko Tanaka, Eds. *The Golden Age of the U.S.–China–Japan Triangle: 1972–1989*. Cambridge: Harvard University Asia Center, 2002.

Walt, Stephen M. *The Origins of Alliances*. Ithaca, NY: Cornell University Press, 1987.

———. "Alliance Formation in Southwest Asia: Balancing and Bandwagoning in Cold War Competition". In *Dominoes and Bandwagons: Strategic Beliefs and Great Power Competition in the Eurasian Rimland*, edited by Robert Jervis and Jack Snyder. New York: Oxford University Press, 1991.

Waltz, Kenneth. *Man, the State and War*. New York: Columbia University Press, 1954.

———. *Theory of International Politics*. Reading, MA: Addison-Wesley, 1979.

Webster's Encyclopedic Unabridged Dictionary of the English Language. New York: Gramercy Books, 1996.

Weinstein, Franklin B. and Fuji Kamiya, eds. *The Security of Korea: U.S. and Japanese Perspectives on the 1980s*. Boulder, CO: Westview, 1980.

Weiss, Meredith. "Malaysia–Indonesia Bilateral Relations: Sibling Rivals in a Fraught Family". In *International Relations in Southeast Asia: Between Bilateralism and Multilateralism*, edited by N. Ganesan and Ramses Amer. Singapore: Institute of Southeast Asian Studies, 2010.

Welfield, John. *An Empire in Eclipse: Japan in the Postwar American Alliance System: A Study in the Interaction of Domestic Politics and Foreign Policy*. London: Athlone, 1988.

Wendt, Alexander. *Social Theory of International Politics*. Cambridge: Cambridge University Press, 1999.

———. "Anarchy is What States Make of It: The Social Construction of Power Politics". *International Organization* 46, no. 2 (1992): 391–425.

Westad, Odd Arne and Sophie Quinn-Judge, eds. *The Third Indochina War: Conflict between China, Vietnam and Cambodia, 1972–79*. London: Routledge, 2006.

Wickberg, Edgar, comp. *Historical Interaction of China and Vietnam: Institutional and Cultural Themes*. East Asian Series Research Publication, no. 4. Center for East Asian Studies, University of Kansas, 1969.

Winichakul, Thongchai. *Siam Mapped: A History of the Geo-Body of a Nation*. Honolulu: University of Hawai'i Press, 1994.

———. "Prawatisat Thai Baep Rachachatniyom: Chak Yuk Ananikhonm Amphrang Su Rachachatniyom Mai Ru Latthi Sadet Phor Khorn Kradumphi Thai Nai Patchuban" [Royalist-nationalist history: From the era of crypto-colonialism to the new royalist-nationalism, or the contemporary Thai bourgeois cult of Rama V], *Silapawathanatham* [Arts and culture] 23, no. 1 (2001).

———. "Preah Vihear Could be a Time Bomb", *The Nation*, 30 June 2008.

Womack, Brantley. *China and Vietnam: The Politics of Asymmetry*. New York: Cambridge University Press, 2006.

Wong-Anan, Nopporn. "Temple Tantrums Stalk Thai–Cambodia Relations", Reuters, 20 July 2008.

Woodside, Alexander Barton. *Vietnam and the Chinese Model: A comparative Study of the Nguyên and Ch'ing Civil Government in the First Half of the Nineteenth Century*. Cambridge, MA: Harvard University Press, 1971.

Wright, Michael. "Khao Phra Viharn: Some Historical Background". Matichon
    Online, 31 July 2008 <http://www.matichon.co.th/news_detail.php?newsid
    =43665&grpid=04&catid=01>.
Yang, Jonghoe. "Colonial Legacy and Modern Economic Growth in Korea:
    A Critical Examination of Their Relationships". *Development and Society* 33,
    no. 1 (2004): 1–24
Yi, Tong-Wŏn, *Taet'ongryŏng ŭl kŭrimyô* [I miss President Park]. Seoul: Koryŏwŏn,
    1992.
Yoon, Tae-Ryong. "Searching for a New Paradigm for Korea–Japan Relations".
    IRI Review 12, no. 2. Ilmin International Relations Institute, Korea University,
    Fall 2007.
————. "Learning to Cooperate Not to Cooperate: Bargaining for the 1965 Korea–
    Japan Normalization". *Asian Perspective* 32, no. 2 (2008): 59–91.
Yoshibumi, Wakamiya and Watanake Tsuneo. "Yomiuri and Asahi Editors Call for
    a National Memorial to Replace Yasukuni". *Ronza*, 9 February 2006.
Zagoria, Donald. *The Sino–Soviet Conflict, 1956–1961.* Princeton, NJ: Princeton
    University Press, 1962.

Index

www.ingramcontent.com/pod-product-compliance
Lightning Source LLC
Chambersburg PA
CBHW072123020426
42334CB00018B/1695